Whitewashed

Whitewashed

*America's Invisible
Middle Eastern Minority*

John Tehranian

NEW YORK UNIVERSITY PRESS
New York and London

NEW YORK UNIVERSITY PRESS
New York and London
www.nyupress.org

Library of Congress Cataloging-in-Publication Data
Tehranian, John.
Whitewashed : America's invisible Middle Eastern minority /
John Tehranian.
p. cm. — (Critical America)
Includes bibliographical references and index.
ISBN-13: 978-0-8147-8306-1 (cloth : alk. paper)
ISBN-10: 0-8147-8306-6 (cloth : alk. paper)
1. Arab Americans—Social conditions. 2. Iranian Americans—
Social conditions. 3. Turkish Americans—Social conditions. 4. Arab
Americans—Legal status, laws, etc. 5. Iranian Americans—Legal
status, laws, etc. 6. Turkish Americans—Legal status, laws, etc.
7. Whites—Race identity—United States. 8. Racism—United States.
9. Race discrimination—United States. 10. United States—Race
relations. I. Title.
E184.A65T45   2008
 305.89'4073—dc22   2008027819

New York University Press books are printed on acid-free paper,
and their binding materials are chosen for strength and durability.
We strive to use environmentally responsible suppliers and materials
to the greatest extent possible in publishing our books.

Manufactured in the United States of America

10 9 8 7 6 5 4 3 2 1

For Katie and Majid

Contents

Acknowledgments

I would like to extend my deepest appreciation to my students, colleagues, friends, and family, especially Peter Afrasiabi, Tony Anghie, Chris Arledge, Mark Bartholomew, Ruba Batnaji, Steven Burt, Tim Canova, Zev Eigen, Martha Ertman, Leslie Francis, Tracey Harrach, Mat Higbee, Lauren Hood, Erika George, Daniel Greenwood, Jed Gushman, Ernesto Hernandez, Corey Johanningmeier, Laura Kessler, Brett Kia-Keating, Maryam Kia-Keating, Terry Kogan, Mitchel Lasser, Erik Luna, Tom Lund, Kaiponanea Matsumura, Daniel Medwed, Natalie Morris, Chad Pekron, Bethany Rabe, Geoffrey Rapp, Rita Reusch, Anne Rimoin, Alice Ristroph, Daniel Rosenthal, James Scott, Mona Shahabian, Ken Stahl, Holmes Stoner, Joseph Su, Debora Threedy, Manuel Utset, Maral Vahdani, Todd Winter, and Jeremy Wooden, for their encouragement, assistance, and constructive criticism. I also owe a profound debt of gratitude to Richard Delgado, Deborah Gershenowitz, and Jean Stefancic. Without their interest in my work and their unflagging support, this project would never have reached fruition.

Introduction

The Price of the Ticket

While on the academic job market several years ago, I received an invitation to interview for a tenure-track law professorship. Having made the school's short list, I visited the campus for a pleasant day of meetings with the faculty and received strong indications of support for my candidacy. I strove, however, to keep my expectations in check. As the son of two professors, I had been repeatedly regaled with horror stories about the whimsical and pernicious nature of department politics around hiring time. The moral to these tales was always the same: Never become a professor.

Having brazenly ignored my parents' advice on career choice, I proceeded to downplay their admonitions about the vagaries of the academic hiring process, and I remained cautiously optimistic. But, it turns out, my confidence was misplaced.

The day of decision arrived, and I did not get the job. It seemed that a small minority of professors cast their ballots, in block, against my candidacy. Under department rules, full-time tenure-track positions required an affirmative vote of 75 percent of the faculty. I ended up one vote shy of the needed supermajority.

The following day, one of the faculty members called me to relay the results of the vote. The tenor of our discussion was unremarkable until he dropped a rather curious line. "You shouldn't take any of this personally," he said cryptically. "The group that voted against you thought you'd be a great colleague and a wonderful addition to the law school. It was just a race issue."

A race issue? I asked him to repeat himself. I had heard him correctly. Nonplussed, I remember muttering in a robotic voice, "Well, it's sad to think that there might still be discrimination against minorities."

"No, no, John," he said, sounding surprised. "They objected to the fact that you're white."

I was stunned.

"White?" I said.

"Yeah. They insisted that we hire a minority candidate. They simply won't accept another white male hire."

Though the dissenters to my candidacy were apparently a group of progressive liberals concerned about minority representation on the faculty, they appeared blind to the irony that the full-time faculty lacked a single professor of Middle Eastern descent—a fact made more pronounced by the school's presence in a community with a large Middle Eastern population and student body. More concerned with diversity de jure than de facto, the school counted statistical appearances over reality. Still in shock, I responded, "They do know that I'm Middle Eastern, don't they?"

"Yes, of course," he said, "so they consider you white."

I was flabbergasted. I had suspected that I would come face-to-face with discrimination at some point in my professional life, but I had never thought that it would be so unabashed and that it would stem from being considered white. At wit's end, I said the only thing that came to mind: "White, huh? That's not what they call me at the airport."

Several days later, I received another phone call. This time, it was the dean of the law school on the line. He was calling to present me with a formal offer to join the faculty. I asked him what circuitous chain of events had led to this reversal. Apparently, the more level-headed faculty members vigorously protested the decision on my candidacy. After consulting with the president and general counsel of the university, the dean had determined that the law school's actions had violated numerous federal and state antidiscrimination laws.

"They all agreed that they would love to have you on the faculty. The sole objection to your candidacy was your ethnic background—a small block of our faculty objected to the fact that you were white. They wanted the position to go to a minority candidate." The university had overruled the hiring decision but had not reconsidered its underlying premise: my whiteness.

Utterly perplexed, I contemplated the offer . . . and politely declined. Yet the experience was not without merit. It served as a remarkable introduction to the bizarre realities of academic hiring, especially for law faculties. The fiasco also highlighted the degeneration of the politics of race in the workplace. Most significantly, the incident forced me to confront and consider a profound but inadequately contemplated issue: the ambiguous racial status of Middle Eastern individuals and their treatment in our legal system. This book is the result of these topical, timely, and personal contemplations.

The Middle Eastern question lies at the heart of the most pressing issues of our time—the ongoing conflicts in the region and the war on terror(ism), the delicate balancing act between preserving our national security interests and protecting our constitutional rights and civil liberties, and the debate over immigration, assimilation, and our national identity. Yet paradoxically enough, little attention is focused on our domestic Middle Eastern population and its place in American society. Unlike many other racial minorities in our country, Middle Eastern Americans have faced rising, rather than diminishing, degrees of discrimination over time—a fact highlighted by recent targeted immigration policies, racial profiling, a war on terrorism with a decided racialist bent, and growing rates of job discrimination and hate crime. Strangely, however, Middle Eastern Americans are not even considered a minority in official government data, and despite extensive participation in the economic life of our country, they have remained socially and politically marginalized. Simply put, the modern civil rights movement has not done enough to advance the freedoms of those of Middle Eastern descent. Moreover, a complex web of legal, political, and social dynamics has rendered Middle Eastern Americans relatively invisible as a collective force.

The dualistic and contested ontology of the Middle Eastern racial condition therefore creates an unusual paradox. Reified as the other, Americans of Middle Eastern descent do not enjoy the benefits of white privilege. Yet, as white under the law, they are denied the fruits of remedial action. As Anita Famili has eloquently noted,

> Middle Eastern Americans remain an invisible group. They are both interpolated into the category of Caucasian while simultaneously racialized as an "other." . . . Middle Eastern Americans do not appropriately fit into the prevailing categories of race. Rather, their ethnic/racial identity is constantly contested.[1]

This book examines the antinomy of Middle Eastern racial classification and assesses the broad legal, political, and social implications of this dualistic identity. To this effect, the book interweaves personal experiences and anecdotes with jurisprudence, academic theory, and popular culture. My aim is not only to identify and assess the systemic issues facing Middle

Eastern Americans but also to launch a dialogue, both inside the academy and with the public at large, that addresses the particular civil rights issues facing our Middle Eastern population. In short, this book seeks to lift the veil shrouding America's invisible Middle Eastern minority.

In the process, this study finds itself at the intersection of three broad areas of scholarship. First, more than a quarter century has passed since the publication of Edward Said's landmark book *Orientalism*,[2] which deconstructed the colonial ideology afflicting scholarly and popular thinking in the West about the East, particularly the Islamic and/or Arab world. The dramatic events of the past few decades have shed new light on Said's theories. Moreover, there has been little attempt to examine the mediation of law, race, and Middle Eastern descent. This study aims to address this shortcoming.

Second, this study builds on the growing body of more general literature that examines the social construction of race and the critical role of the law in the process of mediating identity. Specifically, *Whitewashed* joins several important works on the recursive impact of stereotyping in defining legal and social relationships and rights for groups. The works of Steven Bender and Robert Chang represent two notable examples. In *Greasers and Gringos*,[3] Bender examines the ways in which media-driven stereotypes about Latinos have contributed to their unfair treatment in the American legal system, as demeaning constructions have influenced and legitimated discriminatory conduct. Similarly, in *Disoriented*,[4] Chang construes the reification of Asian American identification and its impact on the legal rights of individuals of Asian descent in the United States. By applying the insights of Bender, Chang, and others to the Middle Eastern community, I endeavor to assess the ways in which stereotyping has resulted in the community's disparate treatment before the law. This study also documents how stereotyping has triggered a vicious circle of paranoia, distrust, and shame within the Middle Eastern community and has led to the community's willful invisibility in the body politic. The study also builds on a growing body of literature examining the interplay among immigration policy, civil rights, and race.

Finally, this work adds to a growing body of literature that aims to diversify the voice of legal scholarship. In a salient moment two decades ago, Richard Delgado, one of the founders of critical race theory, famously critiqued existing tomes on civil rights as the product of an inner sanctum of a dozen white male academics.[5] In the intervening years, scholars have responded to Delgado's critique, advancing the African American, Latino, Native American, and Asian American voices within the legal system, especially in the academy. This study seeks to add to this body of literature by bringing a Middle Eastern American voice to the discourse on race and law at an especially critical juncture. It also seeks to advance the movement beyond the historical black/white paradigm. Like most Americans, academics have historically focused on the dichotomy between black and white and not on the broader racial issues in our nation. Although the black/white paradigm has played a profound role in our nation's history, it does not address the myriad issues related to individuals caught in blurry and gray portions of the divide.

With these goals in mind, chapter 1 begins by assessing the meaning of whiteness and its historical and continuing relevance to the exercise of social, economic, political, and legal rights in our society. Besides documenting the constructed nature of race and the concept of whiteness, I emphasize the important role of performance in the race-making process. To this effect, I focus on a series of cases from the late nineteenth and early twentieth centuries in which immigrants seeking naturalization eligibility litigated their racial status before the courts. In my exegesis of these cases, I examine the impact of law in shaping white identity and linking it to the privileges of citizenship and full participation in the Republic. As I argue, besides playing an intricate role in constructing the notion of race, the law advanced a strict assimilationist directive, especially to Middle Eastern immigrants who found themselves straddling the white/ nonwhite divide. Drawing on recent identity theories, I argue that courts determined whiteness through performance. The potential for immigrants to assimilate within mainstream Anglo-American culture was put on trial. Successful litigants demonstrated evidence of whiteness in their character, religious practices and beliefs, class orientation, language, ability to intermarry, and a host of other traits that had nothing to do with intrinsic racial grouping. Thus, a dramaturgy of whiteness emerged—courts played an instrumental role in limiting naturalization to those new immigrant groups that judges saw as most fit to carry on the values and traditions of our Republic. The courts thereby sent a clear message to immigrants: the rights enjoyed by white males could be obtained only through assimilatory behavior. White privilege became a quid pro quo for white performance, especially for Middle Eastern immigrants, who faced the greatest debate over their racial classification.

Chapter 2 documents the fate of Middle Easterners in these early race trials and highlights how these cases set the tone for the Middle Eastern experience in the United States—a process of incomplete assimilation that has resulted in the relative invisibility of Middle Easterners from critical political and social institutions in our society. In making this argument, I trace the relationship of individuals of Middle Eastern descent to the construction of whiteness, while also examining the mechanisms through which a separate Middle Eastern identity began to take shape. Drawing on the history of early Middle Eastern immigration to the United States and the impact of the naturalization/whiteness cases, I chart one of the most curious aspects of Middle Eastern identity—the antinomy of Middle Eastern legal and racial classification and its attendant consequences. Middle Eastern Americans are caught in a Catch-22. Through a bizarre fiction, the state has adopted the uniform and mandatory classification of all individuals of Middle Eastern descent as white. On paper, therefore, they appear no different than a blue-eyed, blond-haired individual of Northern European descent. Yet reality does not mesh with this bureaucratic position. On the street, Middle Eastern Americans suffer from the types of discrimination and racial animus endured by recognized minority groups. The dualistic and contested ontology of the Middle Eastern racial condition therefore creates an unusual paradox. Reified as the other, Americans of Middle Eastern descent do not enjoy the benefits of white privilege. Yet, as white under the law, they are denied the fruits of remedial action.

Chapter 3 assesses the notable consequences of the dualist ontology of Middle Eastern racial classification. After examining the origins and development of the terms *Middle East* and *Middle Eastern,* I identify two salient mechanisms driven by the contested nature of Middle Eastern racial identification: a process that I dub *selective racialization* and a series of practices identified by Kenji Yoshino as *covering.*[6] First, society selectively racializes Americans of Middle Eastern descent. When they conform to social norms or achieve success in American society, they are perceived as nothing more than white. When they transgress, they are racialized as Middle Eastern. As such, selective racialization helps to perpetuate and ossify stereotypes and provides a powerful panopticonian tool that encourages assimilatory activities. All the while, Middle Easterners themselves rationally adapt to discrimination and hostility by exploiting their position at the precipice of the white/nonwhite divide through strategic covering. For example, many Middle Eastern Americans Anglicize their names so as not to draw attention to themselves; those of Muslim faith refrain from prayer or the donning of head scarves; men avoid wearing facial hair; and many Middle Eastern Americans adopt alternative narratives about their family history to avoid the contagion of association with the Middle East.

Despite their short-term benefits, however, such tactics are not without profound costs and consequences, as they have exacerbated the relative invisibility of the Middle Eastern population in the body politic and in civil society and frustrated any semblance of a civil rights movement for the group. At the same time, covering and selective racialization have fueled a stereotyping feedback loop that, in combination with geopolitical conditions, has tainted public perceptions of Middle Easterners.

Building on the issue of prejudice, chapter 4 turns its attention to the role of the media in both reflecting and, more recursively, encouraging invidious stereotyping of Middle Easterners. On both the big and small screens, and in novels and advertising alike, recent years have witnessed a mostly one-sided portrayal of Middle Easterners in the mass media: the image of the Middle Easterner as a bloodthirsty terrorist, rabid religious fundamentalist, or misogynistic heathen. Chapter 4 documents this disturbing trend and then, with a particular focus on racial profiling, assesses its impact on public policy and its psychological toll on the Middle Eastern community.

Chapter 5 examines the broad assault on the civil rights of individuals of Middle Eastern descent by paying specific attention to the war on terror(ism) and its taut mediation of the relationship between Middle Easterners and American government and society. As I argue, recent years have witnessed the chilling reproblematization of the Middle Eastern population from friendly foreigner to enemy alien, from enemy alien to enemy race—a trend accelerated by the events of 9/11. This chapter includes an analysis of the numerous policies that have led to this attack on the civil rights of individuals of Middle Eastern descent, including the promulgation of immigration regulations such as Special Registration, the passage of legislation such as the USA Patriot Act, the widespread use of racial profiling, and the indefinite detention of nonenemy combatants at Guantánamo Bay. In particular, I critique the judiciary's continuing immunization of such practices from constitutional scrutiny and discuss the ongoing threat to the civil rights of Middle Easterners in the broader context of international events.

Finally, chapter 6 focuses on concrete reforms that can address the growing assault on the civil rights of Middle Eastern Americans. As I argue, the state's bizarre racial fiction of Middle Eastern whiteness has fostered an invisibility that paradoxically enables the perpetuation and even expansion of discriminatory conduct, both privately and by the state, against individuals of Middle Eastern descent. Specifically, the refusal to keep statistics about Americans of Middle Eastern descent—as distinct from those of European descent—has forestalled analysis and resolution of the specific issues facing Arab, Iranian, and Turkish Americans, problems that have grown more exigent in the post-9/11 world order. Such a tack has also shielded from public scrutiny the persistent, and rising, discrimination against Middle Eastern Americans.

Among other things, therefore, I emphasize the need to reform media portrayals of the Middle East and of Middle Easterners, foster greater political action in the Middle Eastern community via grassroots initiatives, tackle the airline industry's problematic treatment of Middle Easterners, reevaluate immigration law's plenary powers doctrine and the practice of profiling, increase enforcement efforts against both public and private discrimination against Middle Eastern Americans, raise public consciousness about the Middle Eastern American community in order to dismantle stereotypes and, finally, achieve government recognition of Middle Eastern descent as a distinct racial category. The development of the category for Middle Eastern racial status will limit the pernicious process of selective racialization and will enable Middle Eastern Americans to take control of a category already being imposed on them from without. A simple, yet crucial, observation supports this proposal: in a bureaucratic age, the only thing worse than being reduced to a statistic is not being reduced to one. I advocate this proposal cognizant of its risk in essentializing race as fact, rather than as construct. Yet, in the immediate term, such a step makes sense as the best approach to addressing the unique issues facing Middle Eastern Americans. To this end, I also emphasize the critical need to expand the Middle Eastern presence in elite American legal circles, including the academy, judiciary, and upper echelons of private practice, as a vehicle to advance recognition of issues related to the Middle Eastern population.

Upon hearing about this book project, one of my oldest childhood friends (with whom I attended high school, college, and law school) responded with a degree of uneasy bemusement: "As a Persian-Armenian-Irish Catholic-Quaker from Hawaii who lives in Utah and California," he quipped, "you are the perfect person to comment on the plight of Middle Eastern Muslims!" He then doled out some gratuitous marketing advice: "The book would probably sell more if you pulled an Alcindor and changed your first name to Haditha or something." For a second, I felt as if he were right (about my qualifications, not about the book's prospects). I do not purport (nor do I want) to represent the Middle East or Middle Eastern

Americans. In many ways, I am hardly representative of the Middle Eastern population. But upon further reflection, it became clear to me that, if anything, my life experience and personal background could not have done a better job of preparing me to write this book.

The category *Middle Eastern* immediately conjures up two ethnic and religious coordinates on a Cartesian identity graph: Arab and Muslim. I am neither Arab nor Muslim, but both of these identities are frequently imposed on me when am I am perceived as being Middle Eastern. This study's embrace of a Middle Eastern identity is not meant to advance the all-too-common vision of a homogeneous or monolithic Middle Easterner—a task that our society has already performed all too well. Indeed, the goal for the organization of a Middle Eastern identity—and of its embrace by Americans of Middle Eastern descent—is to take control of the category currently being imposed from without on Middle Easterners, many of whom are, like me, neither Arab nor Muslim. The category would serve as a vehicle to highlight the shared experiences of members of the group as the Other and to provide a more unified voice to address the particular set of challenges facing the Middle Eastern population. Importantly, the category would have an opportunity to be deconstructed from within and, in an ideal world, would ultimately fade away, leaving individuals free to construct their own identities.

In my regular life, I am an entertainment and intellectual-property attorney and law professor. I handle copyright, trademark, patent, and licensing-related litigation for Hollywood studios, screenwriters, authors, artists, architects, and musicians and for publishing, new media, and high-tech companies. I teach, lecture, and write about these topics. I would prefer to be doing scholarship about the copyright's fair-use doctrine and its impact on expressive rights, the challenges facing international harmonization of innovation policy, and the effect of digital technology on the future of intellectual-property rights. But, as much as I would like to concentrate solely on intellectual-property matters, I simply cannot. As writer James Baldwin once noted, racial consciousness may be the "price of the ticket" we pay to be an American.[7] Without exaggeration, and despite my greatest hopes, the issue of race affects me on a daily basis. In this regard, I am reminded of the words of legal scholar Robert Chang:

> I have been told that engaging in nontraditional legal scholarship may hurt my job prospects, that I should write a piece on intellectual property, where my training as a molecular biologist will lend me credibility.

I try to follow this advice, but my mind wanders. I think about the American border guard who stopped me when I tried to return to the United States after a brief visit to Canada. My valid Ohio driver's license was not good enough to let me return to my country. . . .

. . . These are the thoughts that intrude when I think about intellectual property. I try to push them away; I try to silence them. But I am tired of silence.

And so, I raise my voice.[8]

Richard Delgado has recounted a similar dilemma. "When I began teaching law in the mid-1970's," he recounts, "I was told by a number of well-meaning senior colleagues to 'play things straight' in my scholarship—to establish a reputation as a scholar in some mainstream legal area and not get too caught up in civil rights or other 'ethnic' subject."[9]

Thankfully, my own academic colleagues have been nothing but supportive of my now not-so-tangential venture into race and the law, despite my own personal reluctance: as much I want to focus on other matters, reality gets in the way. Besides the personal impact of race on my quotidian existence, there is a stunning dearth of scholarship about Middle Eastern Americans. For example, during the preliminary stages of researching this book, I posed a few questions to a psychology professor of Middle Eastern descent. Contemplating the psychic anxiety wrought by the in-betweenness of Middle Eastern racial identity and reflecting on the high rates of depression and drug abuse that I had personally witnessed in the Iranian American community, I asked her to point me in the right direction within the psychological literature, especially to empirical studies, on the subject. There was a thoughtful pause before she informed me that I was unlikely to find anything. She was right. In my own field, the annals of the law-review literature are similarly lacking. But for the occasional article about Islamic law and some recent analyses of the war on terrorism, Middle Easterners are all too invisible in legal research, even in the leading critical race theory tracts. The persistent invisibility of Middle Eastern Americans damages their social, political, and legal rights and has compelled me to write this book. And I do so with hope.

As novelist Richard Bausch has argued, writing "is always an inherently optimistic act because it stems from the belief that there will be civilized others whose sensibilities you may affect if you are lucky and good enough and faithful to the task at hand."[10] No country has ever been more open and welcoming to immigrants than the United States, and no country has ever demonstrated a greater respect for civil rights and the protection of minorities. We have risen to the challenges posed by the past, and I am confident that we can do so again. However, with respect to the Middle Eastern question, there is significant work to be done. Ideally, this book represents an important first step.

1

Constructing Caucasians
A Brief History of Whiteness

Though in many natural objects, whiteness refiningly enhances beauty, as if imparting some special virtue of its own, as in marbles, japonicas, and pearls; and though various nations have in some way recognised a certain royal pre-eminence in this hue; even the barbaric, grand old kings of Pegu placing the title "Lord of the White Elephant" above all their other magniloquent descriptions of dominion; and the modern kings of Siam unfurling the same snow-white quadruped in the royal standard; and the Hanoverian flag bearing the one figure of a snow-white charger; and the great Austrian Empire, Caesarian heir to the overlording Rome, having for the imperial color the same imperial hue; and though this pre-eminence in it applies to the human race itself, giving the white man ideal mastership over every dusky tribe; and though, besides all this, whiteness has been even made significant of gladness, for among the Romans a white stone marked a joyful day; and though in other mortal sympathies and symbolisings, this same hue is made the emblem of many touching, noble things— the innocence of brides, the benignity of age; though among the Red Men of America the giving of the white belt of wampum was the deepest pledge of honor; though in many climes, whiteness typifies the majesty of Justice in the ermine of the Judge, and contributes to the daily state of kings and queens drawn by milk-white steeds; though even in the higher mysteries of the most august religions it has been made the symbol of the divine spotlessness and power; by the Persian fire-worshippers, the white forked flame being held the holiest on the altar; and in the Greek mythologies, Great Jove himself being made incarnate in a snow-white bull; and though to the noble Iroquois, the mid-winter sacrifice of the sacred White Dog was by far the holiest festival of their theology, that spotless, faithful creature being held the purest envoy they could send to the Great Spirit with the annual tithings of their own fidelity; and though directly from the Latin word for white, all Christian priests derive the name of one part of their sacred vesture, the alb or tunic, worn beneath the cassock; and though among the holy pomps of the Romish faith, white is specially employed in the celebration of the Passion of our Lord; though in the Vision of St. John, white robes are given to the redeemed, and the four-and-twenty elders stand clothed in white before the great white throne, and the Holy One that sitteth there white like wool; *yet for all these accumulated associations, with whatever is sweet, and honorable, and sublime, there yet lurks an elusive something in the innermost idea of this hue, which strikes more of panic to the soul than that redness which affrights in blood.*

—Herman Melville, *Moby-Dick*[1]

The Wages of Whiteness: Why Whiteness Matters

The antinomy of whiteness has haunted our nation since its founding. For much of American history, the concept of whiteness has embodied an ostensibly august and pure tradition while simultaneously enforcing a regime of fear and oppression. Herman Melville's 459-word sentence from *Moby-Dick* unmasks the color white in all its contradictory honor and terror. Captain Ahab's mad search for the great white whale matches the American Republic's fruitless search for a concept of race around which it could organize itself.[2] Even today, the concept and boundaries of race remain vital to understanding our society. To almost all Americans, the word *white* has transcended its chromatic meaning, instead weaving itself into the fabric of social, political, and economic life through connotations of race. Yet despite the importance of racial definitions to individual identities and social structures, whiteness has remained an elusive, abstract, and even absurd concept with immense power.

Throughout American history, racial classifications have wielded exceptional influence. Until 1952, federal law provided naturalization rights only to individuals who were white or black, but nothing "in-between." The American legal system was forced to confront the task of defining what or who constituted the white race for the purposes of naturalization when, during the late nineteenth and early twentieth centuries, a wave of new immigration from non-Anglo-Saxon countries arrived on our shores.

Litigation over the concept of whiteness resulted, yielding life-altering consequences. While the trials often grew senseless, with judges delving into the depths of antiquity, reconstructing history, and spouting rigid ideologies in order to justify their rulings, the reification of whiteness had a profound impact on shaping the immigrant experience in the United States.

Specifically, the naturalization trials transformed whiteness into a material concept imbued with rights and privileges. Citizenship, of course, meant the franchise; whiteness therefore had important ramifications for the exercise of fundamental political rights. Only at the turn of the century did the inextricable nexus between citizenship and voting rights come into being. Although most of us conflate the term *citizen* with *voter,* the two concepts are not necessarily synonymous.[3] The Constitution itself does not prevent the enfranchisement of noncitizens in any election, be it federal, state, or local. Contrary to the dominant practice today, during the nation's infancy many states routinely granted noncitizens the right to vote. As late as the nineteenth century, twenty-two states and territories extended the franchise to noncitizens.[4] With the outpouring of xenophobic fervor at the turn of the century and jingoistic sentiments during World War I, however, alien voting rights quickly disappeared.

The changing composition of the immigration pool, from northern and western Europeans to southern and eastern Europeans, precipitated a crisis of whiteness that challenged our national identity. Responding to increased anti-immigrant sentiments, Congress instituted a series of racially grounded quotas meant to curtail the flow into the Republic of these groups with dubious whiteness.[5] Not to be outdone, state legislatures responded by revoking the right of these aliens to vote. Whiteness begat naturalization. And naturalization begat voting rights. Thus, whiteness became a virtual prerequisite for the franchise. In 1926, Arkansas became the final state to abandon alien suffrage.[6] Today, only a handful of localities—such as Takoma Park, Maryland, and Cambridge, Massachusetts—still grant noncitizens the franchise.[7]

At the same time, whiteness affected social and economic rights. As Cheryl Harris argues, "in the early years of the country, it was not the concept of race alone that operated to oppress Blacks and Indians; rather, it was the *interaction* between conceptions of race and property that played a critical role in establishing and maintaining racial and economic subordination."[8] Similarly, for immigrants of the late nineteenth and early twentieth centuries, the critical interaction between racial classifications (through the whiteness requirement for naturalization) and property played an instrumental part in the creation of socioeconomic hierarchies. In California, whiteness determined the limitations imposed on an immigrant's participation in the economy. The Alien Land Law,[9] passed in 1920 and upheld as constitutional by the Supreme Court,[10] prevented many noncitizens from owning property in the state. Furthermore, other regulations restrained nonnaturalized immigrants from exercising certain economic rights such as obtaining fishing[11] or law[12] licenses. All told, the social, political, and economic rights of new immigrants were intricately tied to racial definitions. Specifically, notions of whiteness affected who would be treated as property, who could own property, and who would wield the social standing and power that is inextricably linked to property.

At first blush, a seemingly vestigial discussion about the relationship between whiteness and the exercise of rights may seem to lack contemporary relevance. To be sure, our reformed immigration laws no longer draw facial distinctions based on race, and the past half century has witnessed the end of many pernicious race-based practices, including segregation. Even in our more "enlightened" era, however, the concept of whiteness, and even *relative* whiteness, continues to carry tremendous weight, despite the rhetoric of race blindness that permeates public discourse.

To illustrate this point, I am reminded of several mock election spots from an episode of *Saturday Night Live* during the 1988 presidential race between George H. W. Bush and Michael Dukakis. In one scene, a map featuring Europe, North Africa, and the Middle East appears on the screen. At the top left corner, above the northern European countries, the heads of several presidents hover. The announcer—the omniscient voice of authority—informs us, "Franklin Delano Roosevelt was of white northern European heritage. Thomas Jefferson was of white northern European heritage. John F. Kennedy was of white northern European heritage. George Herbert Walker Bush is of white northern European heritage."[13] Then, with more than a hint of disdain, the announcer asks, "But Michael Dukakis?"[14] Dukakis's head then materializes just above the Mediterranean Sea. "Bush," concludes the spot, "he's whiter."[15] A second spot on the broadcast put another twist on the same theme by presenting a police lineup featuring various presidents: "John F. Kennedy was six-foot-one. Abraham Lincoln was six-foot-five. Franklin Delano Roosevelt was six-foot-one. George Bush is six-foot-two."[16] Then, after a pregnant pause, the announcer remarks in horror, "But Michael Dukakis is five-foot-five-and-a-half."[17] The conclusion is inevitable: "Bush. He's taller."[18]

With their wicked sarcasm, the fake advertisements highlighted a latent motif that was, in fact, embedded throughout the election campaign: our notion of what the commander in chief should look like and the racial subtext underlying that notion. Indeed, two pivotal moments—both imbued with the specter of racial politics—cost Dukakis the election.[19] Commentators have focused extensively on the racial dimensions of the first moment—the infamous Willie Horton attack advertisement. Under a program supported by Dukakis while he served as Massachusetts governor, Horton, a convicted African American serving a life sentence without the possibility of parole for murder, enjoyed a weekend furlough during which he committed armed robbery and raped a woman. The advertisement, featuring Horton's dark visage, prominent Afro, and unkempt beard, seized on Horton's menacing image—described by the advertisement's producer as "every suburban mother's greatest fear"[20]—to dramatically turn the electoral tide.

The second pivotal moment was more subtle in its racial undertones, but no less important. During a visit to the General Dynamics plant in Michigan, Dukakis took part in a photo opportunity to bolster his image on national security issues. The resulting image, which featured Dukakis atop an M1 Abrams tank donning a military helmet, resulted in an unmitigated public relations disaster and appeared to cement concerns about the fitness of Dukakis (who, ironically, was a U.S. Army veteran) to serve as the commander in chief. In many ways, the photographs were no less opportunistic or ridiculous than any other piece of contrived election propaganda commonly disseminated in the age of mass media. Nevertheless, something about Dukakis's image on the tank resonated with attacks on his ability to serve as our country's military leader. One cannot help but wonder whether the concerns ultimately had root in the presence of a diminutive, pileous, and swarthy Mediterranean atop a military vehicle, instead of our accepted Anglo-Saxon image of leadership and might. In the end, the campaign raised serious questions about Dukakis's Americanness, patriotism (exacerbated by his Greek roots and his gubernatorial veto of a bill mandating the Pledge of Allegiance in public schools), toughness, and capacity to adequately project our self-image to the world. And these concerns ultimately translated into a landslide victory for the elder Bush.[21]

Besides these anecdotal tales, recent empirical evidence supports the profound and continuing salience of whiteness in our society. Quite simply, despite Panglossian assertions of its unimportance, color still matters and plays an ongoing and critical role in the ability of individuals to succeed in the United States. In a groundbreaking study of the relationship between pigmentation and socioeconomic achievement among legal immigrants to the United States, Joni Hersch, a law and economics professor at Vanderbilt University, found that the average "light"-skinned immigrant outearned her "dark"-skinned equivalent by approximately 10 percent, even when controlling for race, country of origin, English ability, education, and occupation.[22] Perhaps most disturbingly of all, Hersch found that the detriment of a dark complexion was so significant that it sometimes wiped out any benefits accrued from educational attainment. As Hersch noted, "I thought that once we controlled for race and nationality, I expected the difference to go away, but even with people from the same country, the same race—skin color really matters."[23] The study added to a body of literature documenting the adverse impact of darker skin tone on earning rates and the continued importance of whiteness in the marketplace. For example, a 2006 study published in the *American Economic Review* found that, even among blacks, skin color had a substantial impact on wages. With all things being equal, lighter-skinned black men significantly outearned their medium- and darker-skinned counterparts.[24]

A more recent study found profound race-based judgments taking place on a subconscious level. Vetting a vast, thirteen-year data pool capturing split-second decisions, a study of whistle-blowing in the National Basketball Association found that white referees called fouls at a greater rate against black players than against white players. The study also found that, although black officials called fouls more frequently against white, rather than black, players, the overall effect of this bias was less pronounced. All told, however, the unconscious factoring of race by referees was significant enough for the authors of the study to conclude that "the probability of a team winning is noticeably affected by the racial composition of the refereeing crew."[25]

One of the clearer examples of the psychic importance of whiteness to our society came in September 2002, when panicked headlines around the world proclaimed that the white race was headed toward extinction.[26] Citing a recently released report misattributed to the World Health Organization, the media announced that low rates of reproduction in European countries and increasing rates of intermarriage had led experts to predict that the last true blond would be born in 2022 in Finland. Blonds were, in the words of the BBC, "an endangered species."[27]

To the chagrin of the media, the study turned out to be a hoax.[28] Reports of whiteness's death were exaggerated, and the disappearance of the blond gene had no proper scientific basis. Although social trends may eventually render the category of whiteness meaningless, the widespread circulation of the false WHO findings and their almost alarmist resonance with the public highlight a continuing fact: the power of whiteness still pervades our social, economic, and political lives. All the while, however, the definition of whiteness remains as elusive as ever.

Of Skulls, Citizenship, and Assimilation: The Negotiation of Whiteness

An examination of the tortuous history of whiteness is instructive in what it reveals about the socially constructed nature of the category and its resulting ambiguity and fluidity. From the ancient world to colonial America, the concept of whiteness had no broad racial significance. In his hagiography of Sparta's King Agesilaus, ancient Greek historian Xenophon uses the term *white* to refer simply to the light skin color of the Persians and to the way it contrasted with the tanned tone of the Greeks. Ironically, if Xenophon attaches any meaning to a pale skin color, it is one of weakness: "The soldiers who saw the white skins of these folk, unused to strip for toil, soft and sleek and lazy-looking, as of people who could only stir abroad in carriages, concluded that a war with women would scarcely be more formidable."[29] Two millennia later, in the early days of colonial settlement in the Americas, whiteness still had only literal chromatic meaning. Historian Theodore Allen's exhaustive survey of archival materials from the Virginia colony reveals no instances of the word *white* being used as a designator of racial or social status until an antimiscegenation statute in 1691.[30] Quips Allen, "When the first Africans arrived in Virginia in 1619, there were no white people there," since, quite simply, the concept did not exist.[31] Even the first colonial reference to *white*—found in the 1691 statute referenced by Allen—leaves the scope of the term indeterminate, referring only in passing to "English, and other white women."[32] At the time, the concept still had little import beyond its application to individuals of Anglo-Saxon stock. Thus, in the seventeenth and eighteenth centuries, the term *whiteness* remained blithely nebulous, in large part due to the binary nature of the settler population in the colonies, which consisted mostly of individuals of either English or African descent.

By the eighteenth century, however, whiteness began to take on a racial ontology in popular colloquy. We shall explore the reasons for this epistemological transformation in a moment. At the same time, the concept of being *Caucasian*—a notion initially distinct from whiteness—leaped into existence in scientific circles. The word initially emerged from the annals of anthropology, when ethnologists began to study the origins and development of human society. In the process, anthropologists separated individuals into three distinct racial categories: the Caucasoid, the Mongoloid, and the Negroid. This tripartite division, first promulgated in the late eighteenth century, rapidly gained popular currency and has colored understandings of racial belonging ever since.

The term *Caucasian* initially entered public discourse through the work of German scholar Johann Friedrich Blumenbach. In his 1775 treatise, *On the Natural Variety of Mankind*, Blumenbach employed the moniker to refer to the inhabitants of Europe, the Middle East (or Asia Minor/ Southwest Asia, as it was known at the time), and North Africa.[33] His use of the sobriquet was entirely accidental—the skull of a Georgian woman happened to be his favorite in his collection. As Thomas Henry Huxley, a prominent nineteenth-century British evolutionary biologist, explained, "Of all the odd myths that have arisen in the scientific world, the 'Caucasian mystery' invented quite innocently by Blumenbach is the oddest. A Georgian woman's skull was the handsomest in his collection. Hence it became his model exemplar of human skulls, from which all others might be regarded as deviations; and out of this, by some strange intellectual hocus-pocus, grew up the notion that the Caucasian man is the prototypic 'Adamic' man."[34] Ultimately, Blumenbach classified humans into five groups (Caucasian, Mongolian, Ethiopian, Malay, and American). His categorizations became known throughout the Western world upon his tome's translation into English in 1807, thereby firmly establishing the "Caucasian" typology as scientific fact.

Although ethnologists drew on Blumenbach's work over the subsequent generations, questions arose about the "correct" number of human races. There was extensive debate and disagreement, with subsequent leading ethnologists reducing the tally to three (Caucasian, Mongolian, and Ethiopian) or four (adding either Malay/Australian/Polynesian or Amer-Indians as separate categories).[35] As sociologist Brewton Berry later observed, the vast disagreement among scientists attempting to divide humanity by race only served to reflect the arbitrary and constructed nature of the categories in the first place: "Hardly two [scientists] agree as to the number and composition of the races. Thus one scholar makes an elaborate classification of twenty-nine races; another tells us there are six; Huxley gives us four; Kroeber, three; Goldenweiser, five; and Boas inclines to two, while his colleague, Linton, says there are twelve or fifteen. Even my dullest students sometimes note this apparent contradiction."[36] Nevertheless, the Caucasian category enjoyed uniform adoption in the major scientific treatises of the nineteenth and early twentieth centuries.[37]

The terms *Caucasian* and *white* were soon used interchangeably, and the reasons for this etymological confluence are particularly revealing. Internationally, the concept of whiteness emerged as Europeans—particularly the English—began to distinguish themselves from other populations, especially those subjected to imperial designs or slavery.[38] It is not surprising, therefore, that the work of ethnologists, cast with a veneer of scientific infallibility, became instrumental in this project. The theories of race provided a basis for division, a means to explain who deserved rights protected by the state and who did not. *Caucasian* became conflated with *white* and the concept of whiteness became a tool of imperialism, used to scientifically rationalize and legitimate the distinction between the conqueror and the conquered, the colonist and the subject, the center and the periphery.

In the United States, the construction of whiteness played an integral role in the nation-building process. As Matthew Frye Jacobson has argued, starting with the Irish Famine of 1840, the United States experienced several waves of immigration that precipitated a "crisis of whiteness."[39] Until 1840, individuals freely entering the United States descended almost exclusively from Anglo-Saxon stock.[40] The Founding Fathers, for example, either came from the British Isles or possessed northwestern European ancestry. The original thirteen colonies were almost entirely populated by individuals of similar descent. Starting with a wave of immigration triggered by the Irish Potato Famine, however, the ethnic composition of émigrés to the United States changed dramatically. Suddenly, individuals from Ireland, Greece, Germany, Italy, and Russia sought refuge in the United States. To the surprise of modern observers, the racial status of these new immigrants was far from certain and their whiteness far from assured.[41] Many individuals of European descent had difficulty integrating into mainstream American society. If anything, they sometimes found themselves on the "dark" side of the white/black divide. Yet their identities were subject to negotiation. And the process and outcome of these negotiations illuminates the race-making process and provides potent evidence of the constructed nature of the enterprise.[42]

As a powerful social tool, the concept of whiteness has had to remain pliable and responsive to the needs and goals of the society it serves. A simple examination of the remarkable transformation in the term's meaning over the past two centuries demonstrates this malleability. The designation, which initially referred only to individuals of Anglo-Saxon descent, has over time taken on an entirely different meaning, expanding to encompass Germans, Irish, and, later, Slavs, Italians, and Greeks, among others. As legal scholar Kevin Johnson instructively posits, "Classifying European immigrants as nonwhite becomes understandable only with the realization that race is a social and legal creation. The slow social assimilation, or 'whitening,' of various immigrant groups, such as the Irish and Jews, evidences how concepts of races are figments of our collective imagination, albeit with real-life consequences."[43]

Bearing the designation "the blacks of Europe," the Irish faced a lengthy struggle to establish their white bona fides.[44] Noel Ignatiev's study, *How the Irish Became White*, provides a thorough historical account of the arduous battle. The Irish suffered pervasive discrimination upon arrival in the United States. In Boston, employers frequently refused to hire individuals of Irish descent. "HELP WANTED—IRISH NEED NOT APPLY HERE TO WORK," their signs read.[45] The circumstances surrounding a notorious 1906 Texas murder also reflected the prevalent attitudes toward the Irish at the time.[46] In the matter, H. L. Mays, a black male, stood accused of murdering a "white boy" in his late teens. It is not the crime but, rather, its instigating circumstances that powerfully capture the prevailing prejudices of the period. While working in the yards of the Southern Pacific Railroad Company, the victim had apparently taunted Mays by calling him "Irish." Despite Mays's repeated objections, the victim continued to insult Mays with the ethnic epithet. Ultimately, Mays drew a pistol and shot and killed his ridiculer. Of course, this is not to say that the Irish were somehow beneath blacks in the social hierarchy of early-nineteenth-century Texas. Nevertheless, the fact that the term *Irish* was viewed as an insult to a black man at the time demonstrates just how much prejudice existed against the Irish—a state of affairs rather unfamiliar to most modern observers.[47] Indeed, sufficiently removed from historical memory, these harsh realities have now become the stuff of safe, mainstream ethnic humor. For example, in the popular movie *The Commitments*, released in 1991, the main character, an Irish musician named Jimmy, drolly remarks that "[t]he Irish are the blacks of Europe. Dubliners are the blacks of Ireland. North Dubliners are the blacks of Dublin."[48]

Even the Germans and Scandinavians faced questions about their whiteness. No less than Benjamin Franklin once asked, "Why should Pennsylvania, founded by the English, become a Colony of Aliens, who will shortly be so numerous as to Germanize us instead of our Anglifying them, and will never adopt our Language or Customs, any more than they acquire our Complexion?" He went on to note that the Germans ("the Saxons only excepted"), along with the Swedes (!), "are generally of what we call a swarthy Complexion. . . . The English[] make the principal Body of White People of the Face of the Earth."[49] Even two centuries later, German Americans still had to fight all the way to the Supreme Court to reverse convictions against them for illegally teaching German at parochial schools in contravention of laws in Nebraska, Iowa, and Ohio.[50]

In later years, other immigrant groups faced the same lengthy inquiries into their whiteness. Italians, for example, often found themselves on the "wrong" side of the white/black divide. In the South, Italian children were sometimes forcibly segregated with blacks.[51] Officials pointed to their darker skin and facial features as possible evidence of black ancestry. *Rollins v. State*, a 1922 case from Alabama, reflects the prevailing view of Italian racial status at the time. Jim Rollins, a black male, had married Edith Labue, a woman of Sicilian descent. In response, the State of Alabama prosecuted him for the crime of miscegenation. The government had procured a confession after a city detective had pushed the muzzle of a loaded revolver against Jim Rollins's head and threatened to kill him if he did not sign an admission of guilt to the charge of miscegenation. In a surprising move for the time, the Alabama Court of Appeals reversed his conviction. Unfortunately, the court's ruling had little to do with an aversion to discrimination or Jim Crow; rather, Ms. Labue's racial status functioned as the case's fulcrum.

Acknowledging Labue's Sicilian origins, the court found that "[t]here was no competent evidence to show that the woman in question, Edith Labue, was a white woman, or that she did not have negro blood in her veins and was not the descendant of a negro."[52] The whiteness of a Sicilian was therefore far from legally assured. Indeed, drawing on the one-drop rule, one observer has argued that Alabama's definition of race "effectively labeled as 'Negro' every Mediterranean native from Athens to Gibraltar since ancient times."[53] Apparently, a sexual relationship between a black person and an Italian was far less transgressive than one between a black person and an Anglo.

Although in the unusual case of Labue, racial ambiguity played to the benefit of an Italian, in most instances it did not. As late as the 1940s, segregation efforts at times included Italians. In California, Italians were occasionally designated as Latinos. A notable 1944 federal lawsuit involved the segregation of a public swimming pool in San Bernardino. The pool barred entry to all Latinos, a classification it defined as "people from the score or more Latin American Republics and from *Italy*, Spain and Portugal."[54] As historians Leonard Dinnerstein and David Reimers note, "Italians . . . were one of the most despised groups [in America]. Old-stock Americans called them wops, dagos and guineas and referred to them as the 'Chinese of Europe' and 'just as bad as the Negroes.'"[55] *Guinea* is the European name for a portion of the African West Coast, and in the early nineteenth century, it served as a general reference to blacks.[56] As such, its use as a derogatory term for someone of Italian stock created an implicit link to African heritage. Strikingly, just as blacks were frequently portrayed as being incapable of "civilized" behavior, so were the Italians. In a piece written in 1875, the venerable *New York Times* thought it "perhaps hopeless to think of civilizing [Italians], or keeping them in order, except by the arm of the law."[57] Just like African Americans, Italian Americans also suffered from the time-honored Southern tradition of lynching.[58]

Other notable groups, including the Greeks and Slavs, also found themselves initially excluded from the category of white.[59] In Nebraska, a tide of Greek immigration at the turn of the century resulted in escalating tensions between traditional American whites and the newcomers. By 1909, an outright race riot had broken out, pitting the whites against the Greek "Other." Following the death of a police officer trying to arrest a Greek man, an angry mob of more than one thousand men gathered in South Omaha and raided "Greek Town," destroying businesses, burning buildings, and physically assaulting every Greek individual they encountered. All the while, the authorities stood down, refusing to intervene. In the aftermath of the riot, much of the Greek population in Omaha moved out of state. As the *Omaha Daily News* wrote at the time, "Their quarters have been unsanitary; they have insulted women. . . . Herded together in lodging houses and living cheaply, Greeks are a menace to the American laboring man—just as the Japs, Italians, and other similar laborers are."[60] Even a generation later, the view of Greeks had barely changed. They were still, in the popular imagination, not white. For example, in a notorious criminal case that made it to the Nebraska Supreme Court, a group of Anglos waylaid a Greek man named Pappas. Before brutally robbing, beating, and forcibly sodomizing him, one of the perpetrators revealed the underlying racial animus goading the attack, declaring, "You * * * Greeks ain't going to run this town, the white people are going to run this town."[61]

The hostility experienced by Greeks in Nebraska was not merely an isolated incident. In Idaho, the Greeks found themselves run out of the town of Mountain View. In Birmingham, Alabama, during a heated 1920 political campaign, one candidate for office epitomized the zeitgeist of the time when he handed out handbills declaring, "They have disqualified the negro, an American citizen, from voting in the white primary. The Greek and Syrian should also be disqualified. I DON'T WANT THEIR VOTE. If I can't be elected by white men, I don't want the office."[62] A 1930 miscegenation case in Alabama even questioned the whiteness of Greeks explicitly. The judge—coincidentally, the same member of the bench who presided over *Rollins v. State*—questioned the Greek woman's white bona fides, referring to her as "Alexander Markos, a Greek woman, alleged to be a white person."[63] The whiteness of Greeks was far from assured.

Slavs were treated little better.[64] "The Slavs," argued one turn-of-the-century physician, "are immune to certain kinds of dirt. They can stand what would kill a *white man*."[65] This statement typifies the attitude toward Slavs at the time. The etymological link between *Slav* and *slave*—a link that removed Slavs from the concept of whiteness and its concomitant virtue of freedom, thereby relegating them to the realm of blackness and its natural consequence of servitude—also symbolizes the subordinate standing of persons of Slavic descent.[66]

Thus, without detracting from the unique historical role of the United States in opening its doors to immigrants from around the world, it is critical to acknowledge the profound suspicion facing new groups entering the country around the turn of the century. A 1907 debate on immigration reform in Congress captures the anti-immigrant zeitgeist of the time. Congressman John Burnett of Alabama, a member of the House of Representatives Committee on Immigration and Naturalization, exemplified the rampant hostility toward these new immigrants when he proclaimed, "I regard the Syrian and peoples from other parts of Asia Minor as the most undesirable, and the South Italians, Poles and Russians next."[67] As he emphatically concluded, these new immigrant groups were, unequivocally, not white.[68] Another prominent politician, Senator F. M. Simmons of North Carolina, referred to new immigrants as "nothing more than the degenerate progeny of the Asiatic hoards [*sic*] which, long centuries ago, overran the shores of the Mediterranean . . . the spawn of the Phoenician curse."[69]

Ultimately, assimilatory forces prevailed. The post-1840 immigrant groups, previously referred to as the Celtic, Nordic, Alpine, and

Mediterranean races, were gradually absorbed into the allegedly homogeneous and mythic "white" race. The concept of whiteness was then beatified with the scientific term *Caucasian,* which granted it new legitimacy and virility.[70] In forging a sense of nationhood among its heterogeneous population, the United States unified itself around this new scientific concept of race. Today, we unquestionably define any individual of Irish, Italian, Slavic, or Greek descent as white.

Dramaturgy and Racial Identification

Whiteness has been, and continues to be, intricately related to privilege. Yet, as the historical examples of the Irish, Italians, Slavs, and Greeks demonstrate, the concept of whiteness has always been riddled with ambiguity and fluidity. There is nothing intrinsic, factual, or natural about racial categories. Instead, as our analysis reveals, race is a social construct, guided in large part by performance. In a vivid example of Kurt Vonnegut's admonition that "We are what we pretend to be,"[71] race is often dictated by dramaturgy: time and time again, the privileges of whiteness have been doled out to those who best perform whiteness.

This ideology can readily been seen in the world of sports. Recently, Major League Baseball put together a list of the top Latino players in baseball history. The list appeared to define Latino eligibility on the basis of blood/ethnicity instead of country of origin, as evidenced by the fact that several notable American-born players of Latin heritage, including Alex Rodriguez, made the list. However, the list omitted one significant name: Ted Williams. Though not a widely publicized fact, Williams's mother was Mexican.

As one of the greatest baseball players of all time (and the holder of the second-highest career OPS[72] in baseball history), Williams had certainly earned a spot on the list based on his outstanding career numbers. But the issue facing Major League Baseball was whether he was, in fact, Latino. According to Major League Baseball's upper brass, the answer was a resounding no. Williams's race was not categorized by any innate sense of biology or blood; instead, it was wholly determined by performance and perception. What mattered to Major League Baseball was that the world had always perceived Ted Williams as a white baseball player.

Williams himself contributed to this perception, saying little, if anything, publicly about his Mexican heritage, an attitude aided by his stronger resemblance to his Welsh/English father, Sam, than his mother, May.

"He never made a point of letting it be known," said Williams's nephew. "He didn't promote it. He was very friendly with our Mexican relatives on a private basis, but sometimes he shunned them in public because he didn't want it to be known."[73] Given the stakes at risk, who could blame him? After all, he started playing professional baseball in the era before Jackie Robinson, and he spent his entire career with the Boston Red Sox—the last team in Major League Baseball to desegregate its clubhouse. Williams's whitewashing was not without its psychic consequences, however. He once ominously remarked to a family member that the fans in Boston were good to him but that he feared they "don't know who [he] really was."[74]

Undoubtedly, Major League Baseball's economic and promotional interests affected the decision to exclude Williams from their Latino Legends list. After all, the motivating purpose behind the widely publicized list was to advance Major League Baseball's link to the Hispanic community, which has never embraced Williams as Latino. As a result, Williams's presence on the list would, if anything, have actively undermined the project's distinctly utilitarian bent. The Williams issue poignantly demonstrates how performance and perception can trump biological condition in the categorization heuristic. In addition to his lighter features and Anglo-Saxon surname, Williams was not Latin because he did not perform and was not perceived as such. As an individual caught in the middle of a racial dividing point, he had the ability to become white. In life, it inured vastly to his benefit. In death, it has served to his detriment.

A more farcical reminder of the resonance of dramaturgy comes from Den Fujita, an eccentric billionaire who franchised the most American of institutions—McDonald's—in Japan. In the 1970s, Fujita told his fellow Japanese that the raison d'être behind his vigorous embrace of the American fast-food chain was simple: "If we eat McDonald's hamburgers and potatoes for a thousand years, we will become taller, our skin will become white, and our hair will be blonde."[75] He later added, "And when we become blonde we can conquer the world."[76] Whether or not Fujita actually believed these statements is not important—perhaps they reflected his sincere convictions, or possibly nothing more than salesmanship. What is important, however, is that he thought others would believe him. The proclamation represents a remarkable moment in the macabre ideology of whiteness, a bizarre and twisted reinterpretation of the Lemarckian fallacy.

Fujita's syllogism encapsulates a common trope in the annals of racial praxis: the mediation of the relationship between race and privilege
through the performative lens. Quite simply, Fujita equated white performance with the reward of white privilege. In the imagination of Japan's
hamburger czar, the calculus meant that eating like the whites would
transform the Japanese into whites and subsequently endow them with
the powers of whiteness. The results, in the case of Fujita's vision, are
comical—an entire race growing blonder with each bite of the Big Mac.
But, in less whimsical scenarios, the impact of this dramaturgical quid
pro quo is profound.

As off-kilter as Fujita's remarks appear upon cursory examination, they
reflect a critical trend. Throughout the course of American history, white
performance has played an instrumental role in determining the scope of
social, political, and economic freedoms by, inter alia, rationalizing conditions of servitude, guiding Native American property rights, determining
wartime internment policies, delimiting the scope of segregation, and al-
lotting naturalization rights.

The origins of the black/white color dichotomy illustrate how American notions of race have long grounded themselves in performative,
rather than in scientific or naturalistic, criteria. Contrary to the assumptions of some primordialist scholars, who have posited the relative rigidity
of color lines over time,[77] black and white were not fixed or "natural" categories when the first Africans arrived on American shores. The Africans
who were brought to the American colonies were initially distinguished
from Europeans primarily on the basis of religion, not color. Instead of a
bifurcation between white and black to define the Self and the Other,[78] the
English called themselves "Christians" while referring to the Others—the
Africans—as "heathens."[79] Indeed, blacks and non-English servants of European descent were often vested with a similar legal status, the key line
of demarcation being one of religion, not race or color.[80]

The report from the first race case in the Americas, *Re Davis*,[81] illustrates this point. In the 1630 Virginia decision, the defendant received
punishment for engaging in sexual relations with a nameless individual of
African descent. The complete report reads, "Hugh Davis is to be soundly
whipt before an assembly of negroes & others for abusing himself to the
dishonor of God and shame of Christianity by defiling his body in lying
with a negro which fault he is to actk Next sabbath day."[82] As the language
of the report demonstrates, Davis's crime was grounded in its betrayal of
his religion, not necessarily his race. This view is consistent with statutes

of the time, which condemned sexual relations between "any Christian" and a "Negro man or woman."[83]

The division of society based on religious, rather than chromatic, grounds meshes with the view—largely abandoned but still extant in some fundamentalist Christian sects—that people of darker skin can become lighter by becoming faithful Christians. This belief is based on the biblical account of the "curse" placed on Cain by God for murdering his brother. Under one interpretation of this account, dark-skinned people are Cain's progeny, and they can rid themselves of the "curse" of dark skin by re-penting and converting to Christianity. One twist on this parable comes from the Church of Jesus Christ of Latter-Day Saints. Until Mormon lead-ers declared that they had received a revelation from God in 1978 repudi-ating the practice of race discrimination, the Church formally denied the priesthood to blacks. The theology underlying the practice stemmed from the curse placed on the Canaanites and was bolstered by passages from the Book of Mormon regarding a race of people known as the Lamanites, whose black skin represented their spiritual blindness and constituted the mark of the curse.[84] Significantly, the Lamanites were not irretriev-ably condemned to damnation: through conversation, "their skin became white" and "their curse was taken from them."[85] More broadly, the link between righteousness and skin tone, grounded in the biblical Hamitic myth, has played an instrumental role in the public discourse legitimating Western colonialism, and even slavery, throughout the centuries.[86]

Thus, Western society initially rationalized the division between the free and the enslaved on religious rather than racial grounds. Only after 1680, when the first major slave codes went into effect in the American colonies,[87] did the new white/black dichotomy emerge. Two factors ac-count for the emergence of a divide based on skin color rather than on religion. First, some blacks had converted to Christianity in an attempt to use baptism as a means to escape bondage. Second, as slavery grew increasingly national in scope, society needed a more legible and easily ascertainable basis than religious affiliation to effect differentiation. As Michel Foucault and James C. Scott have argued, to render subjects vis-ible to their gaze, hegemons frequently ground their power/knowledge systems in identity signifiers, such as a person's race or appellation.[88] The effectiveness of such signifiers as a tool for legibility naturally depends on their immutable quality. When such signifiers turn out to be fluid, socially constructed, and malleable through time and space, the carefully constructed edifice surrounding such signifiers loses its value. The most effective stigma, therefore, is a visible and immutable one, argues sociolo-gist Erving Goffman, as it prevents individuals from averting discrimina-tion and differentiation by exercising control over identifying informa-tion.[89] The facile perception of skin tone provided the ideal foil for such individual end-runs on the prevailing social strati. Social anthropologist F. G. Bailey has suggested in his studies on organizational structures in India that color provides a powerful tool of legibility to enforce hierar-chies over a large territory.[90] As a result, in the American Colonies, the principal criterion for distinguishing the English from the Africans trans-formed from mutable religious affiliations to immutable differences in skin tone.

Statutory reform in a number of states cemented this change by pre-venting blacks from escaping slavery through conversion to Christian-ity. In 1667, one such state, Virginia, passed a statute providing that "[w]hereas some doubts have arisen whether children that are slaves by birth, and by the charity and pity of their owners made partakers of the blessed sacrament of baptism, should by virtue of their baptism be made free, it is enacted that *baptism does not alter the condition of the person as to his bondage or freedom.*"[91] South Carolina followed suit in 1690, when it closed the conversion "loophole" by dictating that "no slave shall be free by becoming a [C]hristian."[92] Thus, the law limited subversion of the racial hierarchy by constraining the social mobility of blacks.[93] The care-ful patrolling of the black/white divide then became integral to the for-mation of national identity. As Benedict Anderson reminds us, a "nation is imagined as limited because even the largest of them, encompassing perhaps a billion living human beings has finite, if elastic, boundaries, beyond which lie other nations. No nation imagines itself coterminous with mankind."[94] Likewise, with racial identification inextricably tied to notions of American nationhood and the rights of citizenship (whether an individual was a person or nonperson in the eyes of the state), the concept of whiteness was inherently limited since it had no value without the existence of an Other. Skin tone became the immutable stigma and identifier of the Other.

Since conversion was no longer an option for manumission, many mulattoes resorted to litigation over their ancestry in order to escape the shackles of slavery. Obliged to hear their cases,[95] the legal system was forced to ascertain race, and in so doing, performance, rather than actual skin color, became the dispositive evidentiary standard. The racial-deter-mination cases of the antebellum South often turned on the ability of a petitioner to establish whiteness through the embrace of Southern notions of virtue and honor[96]—concepts fundamentally imbued with performative strains and deeply embedded in the region's Christian code of conduct.

In yet another example of the power of performance, our nation's most famous jurist, John Marshall, made assimilability a clear criterion for the extension of fundamental property rights. In *Johnson v. M'Intosh*,[97] the Marshall-led Supreme Court heard an appeal involving competing title claims to a parcel of land in Illinois. Thomas Johnson had purchased land from the Piankeshaw tribe in 1773 and 1775. At a later date, another individual, William M'Intosh, obtained title to the same parcel through a land-grant patent from the U.S. government. To resolve the issue of title, the Court had to determine the natural-law rights of Native Americans to the properties they occupied in the New World prior to the arrival of the Europeans.

In a tortuous opinion in which he laid out his historical interpretation of European land acquisition in the New World, Chief Justice Marshall, writing for a unanimous Court, held that M'Intosh and his heirs were the rightful owners. As Marshall argued, although Native Americans had the right of occupancy to the lands constituting the New World, they never actually owned the land, as title belonged to the Europeans who "discovered" the lands. "Discovery," he reasoned, "is the foundation of title, in European nations, and this overlooks all proprietary rights in the natives."[98] Thus, the Piankeshaw had no title to convey to Thomas Johnson, and, as such, M'Intosh was the rightful owner of the Illinois parcel.

The logic of Marshall's decision is of particular salience. He legitimized the result of the case—which effectively deprived Native Americans of an ability to claim title to their ancestral lands—on assimilatory grounds. Even in the act of conquest, began Marshall, a conqueror should ordinarily respect the property rights of the conquered:

> as a general rule, . . . the conquered shall not be wantonly oppressed, and . . . their condition shall remain as eligible as is compatible with the objects of the conquest. Most usually, they are incorporated with the victorious nation, and become subjects or citizens of the government with which they are connected. The new and old members of the society mingle with each other; the distinction between them is gradually lost, and they make one people. Where this incorporation is practicable, humanity demands, and a wise policy requires, that *the rights of the conquered to property should remain unimpaired.*[99]

But, reasoned Marshall, the Native American situation warranted a sharp deviation from this default rule since "the tribes of Indians inhabiting this country were fierce savages, whose occupation was war."[100] More specifically, they were a "people with whom it was impossible to mix."[101] The conclusion, to Marshall, was irrepressible: since the Native Americans would not readily assimilate into white society, they were not entitled to the right of property. The Supreme Court's message was therefore clear: integrate into white society by conforming to white norms of civilized behavior, or your rights will be jeopardized. White privilege required white performance.

Marshall's attitude toward the original settlers of the continent was far from unique in the New World. Around the same time in the Southern Hemisphere, Columbian liberal Pedro Fermin de Vargas promulgated his own version of the performance quid pro quo, positing that "to expand our agriculture it would be necessary to Hispanicize our Indians. Their idleness, stupidity, and indifference towards normal endeavours causes one to think that they come from a degenerate race which deteriorates in proportion to the distance from its origin. . . . it would be very desirable that the Indians be extinguished, by miscegenation with the whites, declaring them free of tribute or other charges, and giving them private property in land."[102] Both the Anglo policy of separation, epitomized in Marshall's opinion, and the Spanish policy of miscegenation, exemplified in de Vargas's statement, were governed by performative criteria that begat the possibility of redemption. Private property and the other rights of citizenship simply followed.

More than a century later, assimilationist criteria guided the executive and judiciary in determining the scope of civil rights during wartime. During World War II, President Roosevelt responded to military concerns about national security by signing Executive Order 9066, which authorized the forcible internment of approximately 120,000 Japanese and Japanese Americans residing on the West Coast. Fred Korematsu, an American citizen of Japanese ancestry affected by the internment policy, challenged the government's actions, arguing that they violated his fundamental constitutional rights. Ultimately, the Supreme Court upheld the legality of the internment by appealing to performative norms to legitimize the roundups. As Justice Murphy's dissent in *Korematsu* observed, outright racism and the failure of Japanese immigrants to assimilate themselves into the White Republic played a vital role in the military's decision to single out Japanese, as opposed to Germans and Italians, for internment.[103] As Murphy argued, justification for the internment rested "mainly upon questionable racial and sociological grounds not ordinary within the realm of expert military judgment."[104] Indeed, the nexus between race and performance was explicit, as "[i]ndividuals of Japanese ancestry are condemned because they are said to be 'a large, unassimilated, tightly knit racial group, bound to an enemy nation by strong ties of race, culture, custom and religion.'"[105] Among other things, the government pointed to the allegedly widespread practice of holding "emperor worshipping ceremonies" as evidence of the decidedly un-American activities of Japanese Americans and their potential for disloyalty.[106] Accordingly, white performance by both German and Italian Americans was rewarded with protection from internment, and the failure of Japanese Americans to assimilate was punished. Ironically, in a rarely mentioned fact about the case, it was Fred Korematsu's refusal to be separated from his Italian American girlfriend that instigated his challenge to the internment policy.

Even the practice of segregation was mediated by performative gauges. While blacks faced segregation in the South, Latinos endured a similar struggle against institutionalized segregation—a plight that is only recently getting the popular and scholarly attention that it deserves.[107] For example, it was not until the Ninth Circuit's decision in *Westminster School Dist. of Orange County v. Mendez* in 1947 that segregation in Orange County, California was struck down by court order (though not deemed unconstitutional). Even then, the victory was only partial. In a move partly dictated by the need to distinguish the then-binding "separate but equal" doctrine from *Plessy v. Ferguson*, the Ninth Circuit found that, whereas the California legislature could segregate by legislation, local administrative bodies could not. Similarly, it was not until 1954, with the *Hernandez v. Texas*[108] decision announced just two weeks before *Brown v. Board of Education,* that the Supreme Court struck down the effective exclusion of Latinos from juries in Jackson County, Texas. For the first time, the Court applied the Equal Protection Clause to a case "not directed solely against discrimination . . . between whites and Negroes" and found the policy unconstitutional.[109]

The treatment of Latinos varied, even in California, where their place in our racial epistemology remained riddled with ambiguity. As a result, segregation was sometimes practiced on a performative model. In Oxnard, California, the school board followed a general policy of Anglo-Mexican segregation, but with one significant exception: Mexican children who most closely performed whiteness. Secret minutes from school board meetings in 1938, first discovered and authenticated during the course of segregation litigation some thirty-six years later, revealed a policy to integrate only the "brightest" and "cleanest" Mexican children into the white classrooms.[110] Once again, white performance was rewarded with white privilege.

Of course, these examples are not meant to suggest that performance is the sole factor in determining racial categorization. But in determining the concept of servitude, the creation of property rights, the imposition of wartime security measures, the institution of segregation, and the allotment of naturalization rights, performance has, time and time again, played a critical role in mediating the relationship between race and privilege. Nowhere is this observation clearer than in the subject of the next chapter—the naturalization trials that took place in the late nineteenth and early twentieth centuries. These cases begin our specific focus on the racialization of individuals of Middle Eastern descent.

2

Performing Whiteness
Law, Dramaturgy, and the Paradox of
Middle Eastern Racial Classification

Whitewashing Aunt Polly's Fence

As a response to the country's heterogeneous immigrant roots, the American nation-building project has historically organized itself around a conception of whiteness that has determined the metes and bounds of group and individual rights and rationalized the prevailing social hierarchy. In what is perhaps the quintessential American bildungsroman, *The Adventures of Tom Sawyer*, Mark Twain provides a powerful metaphor for the execution of this collective enterprise. In a key scene that captures the insouciant charm and cunning of the novel's protagonist, Tom Sawyer is charged with the daunting task of whitewashing the long picket fence at Aunt Polly's home. But it is a beautiful Saturday morning, and Tom would rather be gallivanting about Cardiff Hill instead. Denied the right to spend the day as he pleases, Tom finds himself overcome with grief. In Twain's deliciously melodramatic characterization, "All gladness left [Tom] and a deep melancholy settled down upon his spirit. . . . Life to him seemed hollow, and existence but a burden."[1] But not all hope is lost. Before taking his first brush stroke, Tom notices Jim walking by, heading to the town pump to gather water. Tom wonders how Jim keeps his good attitude while doing such "hateful work," and he concludes that it is because "[t]here was company at the pump. White, mulatto, and Negro boys and girls were always there waiting their turns, resting, trading playthings, quarreling, fighting, skylarking."[2] Tom then hatches a plot to relieve himself of the work and spend the day at play.

In a ploy to lure his friends to his aid, Tom feigns thorough enchantment with the whitewashing task, refusing invitations from passersby to play. His exaggerated enthusiasm over the work at hand soon draws the curiosity of his friends, who quickly grow envious and start pleading with Tom to let them participate. Before long, Tom is auctioning off the right to paint the fence. In the end, he acquires a veritable treasure-trove of goodies (including a dead rat, a key that "wouldn't unlock anything," and a kitten with only one eye) from his friends in exchange for the privilege of whitewashing the fence. He then enjoys a day of leisure and company while his friends complete *his* chores: "He had had a nice, good, idle time all the while—plenty of company—and the fence had three coats of white-wash on it. If he hadn't run out of whitewash, he would have bankrupted every boy in the village."[3]

Symbolically, the whitewashing of the fence—a task joined by "white, mulatto, and Negro boys and girls" alike—becomes a group enterprise of an assimilationist nation seeking to maintain social cohesion and develop a collective identity. The Republic rallies around the concept of whiteness, which forms the dividing line, or fence, between citizen and noncitizen, rights holder and guest worker, and leisure class and working class.

As the analysis in chapter 1 demonstrated, whiteness matters, and its power is often mediated by performative criteria—or, put another way, by how well one whitewashes the fence. Yet the process of performance and identity formation is wrought with ambiguity and subtlety, often degenerating into a fruitless search for a key that ultimately "wouldn't unlock anything." Nowhere is this antinomy of whiteness better epito-mized than at the margins of the category—or atop the fence—where the Middle Eastern question lies. Americans of Middle Eastern descent are caught in a bizarre Catch-22. They are branded white by law but simultaneously reified as the Other. They enjoy neither the fruits of re-medial action nor the benefits of white privilege. To understand how this paradoxical situation came about, it is first necessary to examine critically the racialization of Middle Easterners.

To this end, several naturalization disputes from the turn of the twen-tieth century forced courts to address the categorization of Middle East-erners, providing modern observers with remarkable insight into the race-making process. Despite issuing conflicting rulings on the question of Middle Eastern whiteness and often lapsing into absurd historical nar-ratives, the naturalization cases reflected similar techniques in reifying racial constructs around an intricate symptomatology wholly unrelated to biology. An exegesis of these decisions reveals a complex racial landscape both fraught with uncertainty and characterized by the denial of many of the hallmarks of white privilege to Middle Easterners.[4] At the same time, these cases fostered a dramaturgy of whiteness and intricate negotiations of racial belonging that have produced the paradox of Middle Eastern racial heuristics: the classification of Middle Easterners as white before the law but not on the street. The fence, it seems, is white on one side, but not on the other.

The Racial Identification of Middle Eastern Americans in Historical Perspective

The official government position on racial categorization is deceptively clear and uncomplicated. The federal government's Equal Employment Opportunity Commission (EEOC) currently divides racial identification into six seemingly simple categories: "White; Black or African American; Hispanic or Latino; American Indian or Alaska Native; Asian; and Native Hawaiian or Other Pacific Islander."[5] According to this rubric, the EEOC classifies Arabs and other individuals from the Middle East, including Turks, Kurds, and Persians, as "white."[6] Similarly, the Code of Federal Regulations defines someone who is "White, not of Hispanic Origin" as a "person having origins in any of the original people of Europe, North Africa, or the Middle East."[7] The U.S. Census Bureau and the Office of Management and Budget standards are in accord.[8] As a result, federal affirmative-action programs, such as the one supported by the Department of Defense, extend to "[a]ll persons classified as black (not of Hispanic origin), Hispanic, Asian or Pacific Islander, and American Indian or Alaskan Native."[9] Thus, individuals from the Middle East are not considered minorities at the federal level. State guidelines are typically in accord.[10] In California, for example, public universities consider faculty applicants Caucasian if they come from Middle Eastern or North African descent.[11] According to Uncle Sam, a Middle Easterner is as white as a blond-haired, blue-eyed Scandinavian.

Ostensibly, the government formally maintains that such classifications reflect "a social definition of race recognized in this country. They do not conform to any biological, anthropological or genetic criteria."[12] The placement of North African and Middle Eastern individuals in the white category, however, appears to belie this claim.

The only recorded attempt to have Middle Easterners included in affirmative-action considerations was squarely rejected. The National

Association of Iranian Americans petitioned for eligibility for the Small Business Administration's (SBA) minority-procurement affirmative-action program.[13] The petition was firmly denied. The program was limited to "socially disadvantaged groups." Set out by Congress in the Small Business Act,[14] these groups have presumptively "been subjected to racial or ethnic prejudice or cultural bias within American society because of their identities as members of groups and without regard to their individual qualities."[15] Although individuals who trace their ancestry back to such diverse places as Brunei, Palau, Pakistan, Korea, Kiribati, Belize, and Argentina find themselves on the list, Middle Eastern Americans do not.

The assumption that Americans of Middle Eastern descent have not suffered systemic racial prejudice in American society is disingenuous. Indeed, quotidian realities quickly reveal the problematic government categorization of Middle Easterners as white. As any Arab, Turkish, or Iranian American will tell you, Middle Easterners are infrequently treated as white people in their daily lives—certainly not when they deal with the Transportation Security Administration at an airport, when they confront law-enforcement officials at a border check, or when they encounter the police at an otherwise routine traffic stop.

In some instances, the policy renders white by law individuals who would otherwise be considered black by mainstream American society. Take, for example, the case of Mostafa Hefny, an Egyptian immigrant to the United States. To the average American, Mr. Hefny, with his dark skin and tightly curled hair, appears black. By government mandate, however, he must check the white box. This peculiar situation led Hefny to file suit in 1997 to be declared black, rather than white, by law. As he argued, the government's racial classification deprived him of vital opportunities: "I would've had more opportunity for advancement and even for hiring had I been considered black. . . . I was prevented from applying and requesting positions and other benefits for minority person[s] because . . . I was legally white."[16]

Despite the formal classification of Middle Easterners as white, the sinuous and tortured racial status of Middle Easterners is not only ambiguous but a conundrum subject to the vicissitudes of time. A closer examination of the history of Middle Eastern racial classification is thereby warranted. The starting point for this analysis is a series of trials in the late nineteenth and early twentieth centuries that put the race of new immigrants on trial.

Performing Whiteness: The Naturalization Trials

Shortly after the ratification of the Constitution, Congress limited naturalization to "any alien, being a free white person, who shall have resided within the limits and under the jurisdiction of the United States for the term of two years."[17] Following the Civil War, Reconstructionists responded to the *Dred Scott*[18] decision by extending the right of naturalization to "aliens of African nativity and to persons of African descent."[19] So the law remained until 1952: only individuals of white or African ancestry—but no "in-between" ancestries—could become naturalized citizens.[20] During the early years of the Republic, no litigation resulted from these naturalization requirements. At that time, the country's ethnic composition lent itself to a strict division between white and black. As a new wave of immigrants arrived on our shores in the latter half of the nineteenth century, the law was forced to deal with an influx of individuals who did not fit so neatly into the constructed racial categories of the time. The flurry of litigation that ensued strained the concept of whiteness, stretching it to its outer limits. Even the Supreme Court entered the fray, denying petitions by both Takao Ozawa, a resident alien of Japanese descent,[21] and Bhagat Sing Thind, a resident alien of Indian descent,[22] to be declared white and therefore eligible for naturalization. All told, fifty-two cases were reported between 1878 and 1952. In all but one of these cases, an individual sued to be declared white after being refused naturalization by immigration authorities on the grounds of racial ineligibility.[23]

These cases provide one of the clearest examples of the performance/privilege quid pro quo. Moreover, they provide a critical starting point for examining the issue of Middle Eastern racial categorization and bear closer analysis. First, the cases highlight the particular ambiguities facing the hermeneutics of whiteness. Second, they represent the federal government's first systematic confrontation with individuals of Middle Eastern descent. Third, this jurisprudence provides a remarkable blueprint of the race-making process, especially at a time when changing immigration patterns precipitated a crisis of whiteness. Finally, the jurisprudence helps to explain how we arrived at the peculiar categorization by law of Middle Easterners as white.

Taken together, the racial-prerequisite cases highlight the centrality of performative criteria in the race-making process. In making this argument, I depart from the work of Ian F. Haney López, who, in his study entitled *White by Law: The Legal Construction of Race*,[24] analyzes some of the racial-prerequisite cases. According to Haney López, the nineteenth- and early-twentieth-century naturalization jurisprudence featured an ostensible struggle between two competing theories of racial determination: the common-knowledge test and the scientific-evidence inquiry.[25] The common-knowledge test determined race by appealing to the common understanding of the average American—"popular, widely held conceptions of race and racial divisions" often grounded in the interpolation of physical appearance.[26] The scientific-evidence inquiry premised whiteness on the anthropological and ethnological categories of the era—"supposedly objective, technical and specialized knowledge for racial determination."[27] Ultimately, Haney López argues that the Supreme Court's decisions in the *Ozawa* (1922) and *Thind* (1923) cases marked the triumph of the common-knowledge test.[28] The Court acknowledged the failure of the scientific model of racial determination and acceded to an explicitly constructed notion of race. Thus, Haney López posits that "[l]aw constructs race":[29] race is not a scientific reality but a social construct, and the law emerges as one of the most potent forces in this process of construction.[30]

A close textual reading of *Ozawa*, *Thind*, and their progeny, however, reveals that the dominant criterion for determining whiteness was not a scientific standard—explicitly abandoned by the Supreme Court—or a strict common-knowledge test based on the petitioner's physical appearance as interpreted through the eyes of an average American. Instead, whiteness was determined through a performative lens. The potential for immigrants to assimilate within mainstream Anglo-American culture was put on trial. Successful litigants demonstrated evidence of whiteness: through their character, religious practices and beliefs, class orientation, language, ability to intermarry, and a host of other traits that had nothing to do with intrinsic racial grouping or even appearance. Thus, a dramaturgy of whiteness emerged, responsive to the interests of society as defined by the class in power—an "evolutionary functionalism"[31] whereby courts played an instrumental role in limiting naturalization to those new immigrant groups that judges found most fit to carry on the tradition of the "White Republic."[32] The courts thereby sent a clear message to immigrants: the rights enjoyed by white males could be obtained only through assimilatory behavior. White privilege became a quid pro quo for white performance.

The Supreme Court Speaks:
Ozawa, *Thind*, and the Quest for Racial Determination

METHODOLOGIES OF WHITENESS

In 1922, Takao Ozawa's petition for naturalization came before the Supreme Court. The Court ruled that Ozawa, an individual of Japanese ancestry, was not a white person and therefore was ineligible for naturalization.[33] In so ruling, the Court held that membership in the Caucasian race was a necessary (though not sufficient) condition for meeting the common-knowledge definition of "white person."[34] Since Ozawa was not Caucasian, he did not qualify for naturalization.

The following year, *Thind* forced the Supreme Court to clarify which Caucasians constituted "white persons."[35] Bhagat Singh Thind, an immigrant of Asian Indian heritage, petitioned the Court for naturalization rights. Arguing that Indians were classified by anthropologists as Caucasians, Thind claimed to be white and eligible for citizenship. The Supreme Court rejected his petition and elucidated the position they had taken in *Ozawa*. The Court ruled that scientific evidence would no longer be relevant to the racial-determination inquiry.[36] Although a scientific standard was consistent with the ruling in *Ozawa* (by mandating Japanese exclusion from the concept of whiteness), such a test threatened to produce a dangerous result in the *Thind* case, as scientific evidence suggested that individuals with brown or even black skin color who were anthropologically Caucasian would count as whites.[37] Such an outcome would have undermined and delegitimated the carefully constructed system of racial hierarchy that dictated social relations in the United States. Thus, the *Thind* Court abandoned the scientific-inquiry test by ruling that Indians were not white. As the Court concluded, "It may be true that the blond Scandinavian and the brown Hindu have a common ancestor in the dim reaches of antiquity, but the average man knows perfectly well that there are unmistakable and profound differences between them."[38]

Based on this language, scholars such as Haney López and Donald Braman have concluded that *Ozawa* and *Thind* marked the victory of the common-knowledge standard.[39] Braman, for example, argues that *Ozawa* and *Thind* "provide extended examples of the Court's taking note of the scientific community's failure to arrive at a practicable system of racial classification, and turning to a reliance on the statutory meanings developed through the political process. The terms produced were popular and not scientific, indicating and naturalizing an understanding of social groups, not biological ones."[40] Viewed in isolation, the cases appear to vindicate common knowledge. But when applied as precedent, they laid the groundwork for something much more complex—a system of racial determination based not on scientific evidence or even on the common knowledge of an ordinary American but on white performance interpreted through the eyes of the law.[41]

This was nothing new. Legal historian Ariela Gross has examined a series of racial-determination trials that took place in the antebellum South. In these cases, enslaved petitioners sought manumission, claiming that they were white. As Gross has documented, courts often drew racial conclusions using performative criteria—reputation, association, reception in society, and embrace of traditional notions of white manhood and womanhood.[42] For these litigants, their very freedom depended on their ability to perform whiteness. Only a few decades later, white performance facilitated the broader goals of American immigration policy by making citizenship a function of assimilation.

As the foregoing analysis of the racial-prerequisite cases demonstrates, performance of whiteness was evidenced in two ways. A petitioner could point to his own adoption of white values and personal dramaturgy of whiteness as evidence of his appropriate racial categorization. Alternatively, a petitioner could point to the assimilation of his ethnic group into the core Western European, Christian tradition as evidence of his whiteness. Both methods ultimately conditioned citizenship on what constitutional scholar Kenneth Karst has dubbed "Anglo conformity,"[43] in the form of educational attainment, occupational dispersal, language choice, residential location, and intercultural marriage.[44] Thus, *Ozawa* and *Thind* enabled judges to try the ability of individuals to adopt white values and of ethnic groups to assimilate themselves into the White Republic, a tack that has repeated itself in the construction of our immigration laws and policies.[45]

Meanwhile, though the Court rhetorically claimed that its assimilationist criteria bore no value judgment on racial worth, it doth protest too much. "It is very far from our thought to suggest the slightest question of racial superiority or inferiority,"[46] opined the *Thind* Court disingenuously. "What we suggest is merely racial difference, and it is of such character and extent that the great body of our people instinctively recognize it and reject the thought of assimilation."[47] The word choice alone in these sentences—from "very far" to "slightest" and "merely"—betrays the Court's tacit assumptions and motivations.

NOT-SO-COMMON KNOWLEDGE

To begin with, the common-knowledge standard enunciated in *Ozawa* and *Thind* was quite difficult to apply, as the courts did not give clear guidance on what constituted evidence of common knowledge. Both Supreme Court cases suggest that it is necessary to hark back to what the authors of the 1790 naturalization statute intended when they used the term "white person." In *Ozawa*, the Court sought to ascertain how the statute's framers would have ruled had the racial-determination issue been presented to them.[48] Similarly, the *Thind* Court held that "the words of the [naturalization] statute are to be interpreted in accordance with the understanding of the common man from whose vocabulary they were taken."[49] Thus, the Court read the statute as "written in the words of common speech, for common understanding, by unscientific men."[50] This attempt to uncover the intentions of the framers of the 1790 Naturalization Act had a lasting impact. Even in one of the final racial-prerequisite cases, *In re Hassan*, a Michigan federal district judge asserted that courts must determine

> whether the members of the group as a whole are white persons as Congress understood the term in 1790 when it first enacted the statute. In deciding this latter question, the test is not how the group in question would be classified by ethnologists who have made a study of racial origins, but, rather, what groups of peoples then living in 1790 with characteristics then existing were intended by Congress to be classified as "white persons."[51]

In this form, the common-knowledge test led to absurd results and flew in the face of reality, leading a number of judges to demonstrate a selective historical consciousness. For example, the *Thind* Court admitted that, in 1790,

> [t]he immigration of that day was almost exclusively from the British Isles and Northwestern Europe, whence they and their forebears had come. When they extended the privilege of American citizenship to "any alien, being a free white person," it was these immigrants . . . and their kind whom they must have had affirmatively in mind.[52]

Nevertheless, the Court took a conveniently inclusive view of racial categories by contending that Americans at the turn of the nineteenth century considered southern Europeans to be white on an equal footing with those of Anglo-Saxon descent. As Justice Sutherland argued for the Court,

> The succeeding years brought immigrants from Eastern, Southern and Middle Europe, among them the Slavs and the dark-eyed, swarthy people of Alpine and Mediterranean stock, and these were received as *unquestionably* akin to those already here and readily amalgamated with them. It was the descendants of these, and other immigrants of like origin, who constituted the white population of the country when § 2169 [of the U.S. Code], reenacting the naturalization test of 1790, was adopted [in 1802]; and there is no reason to doubt, with like intent and meaning.[53]

Justice Sutherland's revisionist contention that southern Europeans were readily welcomed to the white race revealed a poor sense of historical awareness. A true return to the intent of the 1790 or 1802 authors of the naturalization statute would have required a denial of citizenship rights to immigrants of Slavic, Mediterranean, and even Irish descent. As an earlier court had argued in another racial-prerequisite case, *United States v. Balsara*,[54] any attempt to apply the naturalization law through the intent of the 1790 framers of the statute was farcical:

> The government contends that the words must be construed to mean what the Congress which passed the first naturalization act in 1790 understood them to mean, and, no immigration being then known except from England, Ireland, Scotland, Wales, Germany, Sweden, France, and Holland, Congress must be taken to have intended aliens coming from those countries only. The consequence of this argument, viz., that Russians, Poles, Italians, Greeks, and others, who had not theretofore immigrated, are to be excluded, is . . . absurd.[55]

Even a modified version of the common-knowledge test using the standards of the average person on the street would not perform adequately. A typical American would use skin color and physical features in order to determine a stranger's racial identity. However, *Ozawa*[56] and *Thind*[57] rejected this methodology.[58] Clearly, a skin-color test would not do as a standard for racial determination of whiteness. The United States had already granted white status and naturalization rights to individuals with olive skin tones, such as Italians, Spaniards, and Slavs.

Despite the popular tendency to view race as a direct function of fixed input—skin color—a dispassionate examination suggests otherwise. Consider the following Gedanken experiment: Imagine an alien coming to our planet who is asked to divide humanity into several major groups. Even starting with our own prejudice to perceive and partition by skin color, one would not obtain the racial divisions we have currently framed in our society. A categorization by skin color might well put Dravidian Indians and sub-Saharan Africans in the same category of "black," the Japanese and northern Europeans in the same category of "white," and Mediterraneans and Middle Easterners in the same category of "olive." The arbitrariness of racial classifications becomes readily apparent: despite their chromatic appellations, our racial categories have surprisingly little to do with actual skin color.

Similarly, the *Ozawa* Court maintained that color alone could not be determinative of whiteness. As the Court acknowledged, a skin-color test "is impracticable as that differs greatly among persons of the same race, even among Anglo-Saxons, ranging by imperceptible gradations from the fair blond to the swarthy brunette, the latter being darker than many of the lighter hued persons of the brown or yellow races."[59] Despite the allegedly widespread embrace of the common-knowledge test in jurisprudence leading up to and including *Ozawa* and *Thind*, the common-knowledge test never really triumphed. In fact, *United States v. Dolla*[60] is notable for being the only racial-prerequisite case of the time to actually use inspection of skin color as the primary criterion in rationalizing whiteness.[61]

Performance as a Doctrinal Alternative: White Is as White Does

On one hand, *Thind* had explicitly rejected any further application of the scientific-evidence inquiry. On the other hand, neither *Ozawa* nor *Thind* had provided a workable common-knowledge heuristic for the determination of whiteness. This study proposes an alternative understanding of the jurisprudence of *Ozawa*, *Thind*, and their progeny based on a dramaturgy of whiteness. According to Theodore Allen, "By considering the notion of 'racial oppression' in terms of the substantive, the operative element, namely 'oppression,' it is possible to avoid the contradictions and howling absurdities that result from attempts to splice genetics and sociology [and to learn] the peculiar function of the 'white race.'"[62] Behind the veil of genetics—analyzed through the scientific-evidence inquiry—and the façade of sociology—rationalized through the common-knowledge test—there was a performance standard laid out in *Ozawa* and *Thind* that came to dominate racial-determination jurisprudence. Ultimately, racial determination required more than science or popular understanding (whether in 1790 or 1920). The process served to incentivize an individual dramaturgy of whiteness and assimilatory group behavior. Performance thus became the measure of racial identity, particularly as a tie-breaker in situations in which racial boundaries remained fluid and blurry.

The Supreme Court's jurisprudence in both *Ozawa* and *Thind* contained strong shades of individual performance, despite the Court's rejection of both plaintiffs' petitions. Before examining the performative aspects present in both cases, it is instructive to lay out the theoretical basis for the analysis. Racial categories are largely the constructs of society; they are situationally malleable, rigid at times, flexible at others. As such, racial determination has often been accomplished through the lens of performance.[63] This argument closely parallels the work of theorist Judith Butler on gender. As Butler asserts, we are what we pretend to be: male is as male does, and female is as female does.[64] Gender is therefore a social construct promulgated through public drama. By pointing to the gender performances of drag queens and cross-dressers, Butler subverts the notion of gender as a natural or fixed trait, demonstrating instead that gender is performative, based on a collection of acts representing a mythic ideal. As Butler argues, "gender is always a doing, though not a doing by a subject who might be said to preexist the deed. . . . There is no gender identity behind the expressions of gender; that identity is performatively constituted by the very 'expressions' that are said to be its result."[65] To Butler, public embrace of gender roles is, at its core, nothing more than a drag show. More broadly, aspects of one's identity are formulated through four dramaturgical steps: (1) differentiation of oneself from others; (2) pointing to paragons of one's chosen identity; (3) development of practices to affirm one's chosen identity; and (4) repeated engagement in these practices.[66]

Butler's theory of identity performance is powerfully echoed in both *Ozawa* and *Thind*.[67] For example, the Supreme Court signposted Ozawa's educational status, religious beliefs, and fluent use of the English language as factors militating against its decision. As the Court irrelevantly remarked, "He was a graduate of the Berkeley, California, High School, had been nearly three years a student in the University of California, had educated his children in American schools, his family had attended American churches and he had maintained the use of the English language in his home."[68] The Court considered Ozawa's embrace of Anglo-American culture, in the form of his education, religion, and language of choice, as providing some proof of performative whiteness. The Court also made sure to acknowledge widespread group assimilation when referencing the "culture and enlightenment of the Japanese people."[69] Similarly, the Supreme Court repeatedly referred to Thind's status as a "high-class Hindu"[70] as a countervailing factor in their decision. Performative criteria therefore played a role in both decisions. Most important, the *Ozawa* Court explicitly created a broad zone of potential whiteness, whereby "[i]ndividual cases falling within this zone must be determined as they arise from time to time by what this Court has called, in another connection, 'the gradual process of judicial inclusion and exclusion.'"[71] The Supreme Court, in effect, gave lower courts the ability to put the Anglo-conformity of individuals and ethnic groups on trial.

Of course, the performative methodology for racial determination set out in *Ozawa* and *Thind* did not emerge sua sponte. Indeed, with its references to intrinsically nonracial characteristics such as education, class, religion, language, and enlightenment, the *Ozawa* and *Thind* Courts invoked a semiology of whiteness and a performance model for racial determination with a longstanding tradition in the United States. The courts also drew on the work of earlier legal scholars who had utilized performative criteria in the determination of racial grouping. John Wigmore, one of the leading evidence experts and treatise scribes of the nineteenth century, wrote an 1894 article in which he contended that the Japanese were indeed white.[72] Although his claim ostensibly rested on the "scientific use of language and . . . [on] modern anthropology,"[73] assimilationist criteria formed the crux of his case. Although Wigmore would have denied white classification to all other Asiatic peoples, he embraced Japanese whiteness on the grounds that the Japanese have "greater affinities with us in culture and progress and facility of social amalgamation than they have with any Asiatic people."[74] Of course, Wigmore's observations on the assimilability of the Japanese have no relevance to an intrinsic and biological conception of race. These traits, however, do provide a performative criterion for the purposes of racial determination. Like Wigmore, the Supreme Court mixed race with class, religion, educational attainment, and linguistic choice in both *Ozawa* and *Thind*. In doing so, the Court effectively rejected any intrinsic and biological notion of race in favor of a constructed one. Since the common-knowledge test put forth by the Court was impractical in its application, performance became the basis for racial construction in the post-*Thind* era.

Litigating the Whiteness of Middle Easterners

The racial-prerequisite cases and the Supreme Court's decisions in *Ozawa* and *Thind* transformed racial-determination jurisprudence into a semiotic exercise, with judges attempting to decipher the hieroglyphics of racial identity. Reading their opinions as narratives, jurists became veritable semiotic sleuths straight out of a postmodern novel, attempting to decipher a complex matrix of signs, imbuing and reifying them with social meaning. Using signposts of assimilation—as expressed through religious practices, educational attainment, marital patterns, and wealth accumulation—the judges found themselves struggling to give definition to race, a concept that belied its ostensible scientific roots and supposed common understanding. Like a transistor radio circuit that Oedipa Mass famously contemplates in a memorable passage from Thomas Pynchon's *The Crying of Lot 49*, the outward simplicity of racial categorization—which seemingly involved just three clear-cut categories—revealed, upon closer inspection, "a hieroglyphic sense of concealed meanings, of an intent to communicate."[75] The meaning of these hieroglyphics was far from certain. They were, in short, in the eye of the beholder, just as the abstract concept of race was imbued with meaning in the interpolative act of the judges who decided the racial-prerequisite cases.

The act of interpretation was not merely from the judge, however; it was from the litigants as well, on both a micro and a macro level. Often, petitioning individuals in the racial-prerequisite cases succumbed to dominant theories of racial supremacy in their litigation strategies by attempting to distinguish themselves from their darker cousins. In this way, the litigants responded to the assimilatory demands of the Republic much like those who came before them. A century and a half earlier, the Irish had transformed themselves from an oppressed, nonwhite race to oppressing members of the white race.[76] Facing nagging questions about their whiteness and suffering from the attendant discrimination that resulted, the Irish responded with hyperperformativity of whiteness. A key step in this transformation stemmed from the vigilance of the Irish in the struggle in favor of slavery and against civil rights for blacks. As Noel Ignatiev documents, the unadulterated embrace of white supremacy paved the way for Irish integration into the White Republic, where citizenship was defined by race. Performance eventually yielded to overperformance: "To become white [Irish immigrants] had to learn to subordinate county, religious, or national animosities, not to mention any natural sympathies they may have felt for their fellow creatures, to a new solidarity based on color—a bond which, it must be remembered, was contradicted by their experience in Ireland."[77] The semiotics of performance dictated a need to act more "white" than whites. Under the panopticonian gaze of the law,[78] which determined social, political, and economic rights and entitlements, the litigants had to perform whiteness, potentially forfeiting other facets of their identity. An examination of the cases both before and, even more significantly, after *Thind* and *Ozawa* reveals the triumph of a performative jurisprudence.

To be sure, when individuals remain outside the realm of racial ambiguity, the courts declared them ineligible for naturalization based on the binding legal precedent of *Ozawa* and *Thind*. In a series of relatively short opinions, federal courts classified Indians, Filipinos, Japanese, and others as nonwhite.[79] But, when they possessed any discretion and leeway in the act of racial determination, the courts drew on decidedly performative criteria in researching their judgments.

Significantly, most of these toss-up cases involved individuals of Middle Eastern descent attempting to be declared white by law.[80] As historical documents, these cases provide rare insight on the degree to which Middle Easterners were able to exercise the rights and privileges of white Americans in the decades prior to the civil rights movement. They also suggest the symbolic indicia of identification on which we still rely in our social construction of race. The actual results of these cases were mixed. Occasionally, and by the slimmest of margins, Middle Easterners were considered white. Often, however, they were not. In the end, it was not biology or any exogenous notion of race that settled the matter; it was assimilability, viewed through the lens of performative criteria, which dominated the jurisprudential calculus.

Indeed, throughout the racial-prerequisite cases, we find evidence of dramaturgy weighing on the minds of the judges. For example, in *In re Balsara*,[81] a U.S. district court held that a Parsee was a white person for the purposes of naturalization. As evidenced by the court's concluding words, performative criteria influenced the decision. "[S]ince the applicant appear[ed] to be a gentleman of high character and exceptional intelligence,"[82] the court elected to grant the petition for naturalization to Balsara. The court therefore utilized performance as a tie-breaker in a borderline case. In *United States v. Pandit*,[83] decided three years after *Thind*, certain critical facts about Sakharam Ganesh Pandit, an Indian immigrant to the United States, played a vital role in the trial court's declaration of

Pandit's whiteness. Such details similarly influenced the Ninth Circuit, which emphasized them in its brief statement of the facts. This information included repeated references to Sakharam Ganesh Pandit's Brahman caste and high social standing, detailed descriptions of his impressive wealth, an extensive résumé of his educational training, and a passing, but all too significant, reference to his marriage to a white woman.[84]

Ultimately, *Wadia v. United States*[85] overturned *Balsara* in light of the Supreme Court's decisions in *Ozawa* and *Thind*. Nevertheless, the court still used performative criteria in making its decision. Judge Augustus Hand even made sure to signpost Wadia's Zoroastrian religion at one point in the brief opinion.[86] Although the court ruled that Parsees cannot qualify as white people since they are too closely associated with the non-white Hindus, it still quoted passages from both *Thind* and *Ozawa* that dictated the use of assimilationist criteria in racial determination and the availability of performative outlets. The court first cited a passage from *Thind* that provided a possible escape for even those of "primarily Asiatic stock" to be considered white.[87] The court then referred to a passage in *Ozawa* stating that there were "some Asiatics whose long contiguity to European nations and assimilation with their culture has caused them to be thought of as of the same general characteristics."[88] Although Parsees, with their allegedly inextricable link to the Hindu people, could not establish legal "whiteness," the court left open the door for other ethnic groups caught between two racial groupings. The court's message was clear: white performance would still be rewarded with white privilege.

Performance and Proximity: The Case of Armenians

For individuals of Middle Eastern descent, the performative quid pro quo was particularly salient in the racial-determination game. The first relevant reported decision in our analysis, *In re Halladjian*,[89] comes from 1909 and takes place in Massachusetts. In the case, the U.S. government vigorously opposed the naturalization petitions of four Armenians on the grounds that they were not free white persons.[90] The attorney general interpreted the word *white* as equivalent to *European* and stated that Congress had reasonably limited naturalization rights to individuals of European descent in order to "describe the variations of domicile or origin which are so closely associated with the mental development of a people."[91] Based on their Asiatic origins, the government concluded that the Armenian petitioners could not be white.[92]

The irony and absurdity of Armenians' veritable "*Caucasian*" origin, as a people residing in the *Caucasus* Mountains, apparently escaped the naturalization officials.

The court disagreed with the government and bestowed the Armenians with U.S. citizenship. In a particularly striking move, especially for its time, the court rejected the very idea of racial purity (if not the entire notion of dividing humanity by race). Noting a long history of intermixing between races throughout the world, especially in the Middle East,[93] the court concluded that "there is no European or white race, as the United States contends, and no Asiatic or yellow race which includes substantially all the people of Asia; that the mixture of races in western Asia for the last 25 centuries raises doubt if its individual inhabitants can be classified by race."[94] Reluctantly charged with the duty to categorize the various races, however, the court deemed Armenians white by law.

In so doing, the court's rationale eschewed any contemplation of the scientific bases of racial classifications. The court's analysis instead focused almost exclusively on the issue of assimilability, tacitly conflating (as the government's position did) the performance of whiteness with the privileges of whiteness. To that effect, the court emphasized the achievements of Middle Eastern civilizations and the close cultural link between the Armenian (and other Middle Eastern) people and the Europeans, pointing out that "a reasonable modesty may well remind Europeans that the origin of their letters was in Phoenicia, the origin of much of their art in Egypt, that Asia Minor claimed, at least, the birthplace of the first great European poet, and that the Christian religion, which most Europeans believe to have influenced their civilization and ideals, was born in Palestine."[95] The court then explicitly endorsed the ability of Armenians to "become westernized and readily adaptable to European standards."[96] With assimilability in mind, the conclusion was seemingly inescapable: the Armenians were white.

Other courts departed from this holding, instead taking a more restrictive view of whiteness, especially as it related to non-Armenians. *United States v. Cartozian*,[97] one of the first racial-prerequisite cases decided after *Ozawa* and *Thind*, is an excellent illustration of the performative aspects of whiteness analyzed by courts and of the ways in which courts interpreted *Ozawa* and *Thind* as precedent. In the 1925 case from Oregon, the government sought to cancel Tatos O. Cartozian's certificate of naturalization on the grounds that his Armenian ancestry precluded his eligibility for naturalization.[98] A U.S. district court ultimately sided with Cartozian.

The court's analysis sheds light on the prevailing view of Middle Eastern-ers, and on concepts of race, at the time.

As *Cartozian* suggests, there was more than a clash between scientific and common-knowledge doctrines at work in the jurisprudence of the era. Rather, the ability of individuals to perform whiteness, regardless of their scientific classification or ability to pass the common-knowledge test, became a critical part of the determination of who was white enough to earn the privilege of naturalization. In so ruling, *Cartozian* reads *Thind* as dictating a court-directed dramaturgy of whiteness, not a common-knowledge test delving into the statutory intent of the framers of the 1790 naturalization laws.[99]

Rejecting both the scientific-evidence inquiry and the common-knowl-edge test, *Cartozian* carefully distinguishes Armenians from other ethnic groups of the Near East. Under the scientific-evidence doctrine, all the people of the Near East would technically qualify as Caucasian and would therefore count as white persons eligible for naturalization. The court steers away from this view, instead choosing to separate Armenians from such ethnic groups as Arabs, Turks, and Kurds.[100] At the same time, the court fails to apply the common-knowledge test as purportedly set forth in *Ozawa* and *Thind*. The court's divide between Armenians and other in-habitants of Asia Minor has little to do with how the average American on the street would view an Armenian vis-à-vis an Arab, Turk, or Kurd. The court even admits that the Armenian province is within the confines of Turkey, which was classified by the average American at the time as an Asiatic society.[101] Moreover, the court never claims that the average Amer-ican, whether from 1790 or 1925, could distinguish an Armenian from an Arab, Turk, or Kurd. Nevertheless, the court draws a clear line between its treatment of Armenians and its potential treatment of other inhabitants of Asia Minor.

Instead, performance of whiteness and perceived assimilatory capacity played a critical role in the court's decision. When determining that Ar-menians were white by law, the court made no true assessment of racial criteria. Instead, the court used white performance as a proxy for white racial belonging. Specifically, the *Cartozian* court used Armenian group assimilation as a surrogate for individual dramaturgy to determine the performative worthiness of Tatos O. Cartozian for citizenship.

First, in the spirit of *Ozawa* and *Thind*, the court conflates the issue of religion with race, inextricably linking racial belonging with the abil-ity of a group to utilize a fundamental tool for integration into the White

Republic. The court also goes out of its way to distinguish Armenians from other individuals of Middle Eastern descent. As the court writes,

> Although the Armenian province is within the confines of the Turkish Empire, being in Asia Minor, the people thereof have always held themselves aloof from the Turks, the Kurds, and allied peoples, principally, it might be said, on account of their religion, though color may have had something to do with it. The Armenians, tradition has it, very early, about the fourth century, espoused the Christian religion, and have ever since consistently adhered to their belief, and practiced it.[102]

The court's prose captures the race-making process in action. Seeking to add precision to the whiteness category, the court resorts to factors wholly unrelated to biology in order to define the category's outer boundaries, shifting seamlessly from an alleged discussion of race to a discussion of religion. Whether the Armenians have historically practiced Christianity is of no relevance whatsoever to any primordial or naturalistic view of racial grouping. Similarly, it is not discoverable to the average person on the street. Nevertheless, the court is constructing race through the lens of religion as a primary component in the semiotics of division. For Armenians, Christianity, instead of color, becomes a proxy for racial belonging. Such an interpolative act undermines the notion of race as an independent truth or exogenously determined fact. Instead, it reveals race as a construct of human institutions and imaginations—a construction and reconstruction that continues to this very day with enormous consequences, especially as the religious affiliation of the Middle Eastern population in the United States has dramatically shifted from Christianity to Islam.

As in *Halladjian*, Armenians' historical affiliation with Christianity and their impressive capacity for assimilation and intermarriage, attested to by expert witnesses, enabled the court to "confidently" proclaim them white by law. Not yet fixed within society's rigid racial categorizations, Armenians could point to their religious affiliation as performative proof of their whiteness. Religious affiliation became an important part of the racial determination for Armenians, as their embrace of Christianity enabled them to assimilate into mainstream Anglo-Saxon culture. Noted the court, "it may be confidently affirmed that the Armenians are white persons, and moreover that they readily amalgamate with the European and white races."[103] Such language is significant since it draws directly from the ruling in *Thind*, in which the Supreme Court denied citizenship to

Thind on the grounds of assimilability. "The children of English, French, German, Italian, Scandinavian, and other European parentage," the *Thind* Court posited, "quickly merge into the mass of our population and lose the distinctive hallmarks of their European origin. On the other hand, it cannot be doubted that the children born in this country of Hindu parents would retain indefinitely the clear evidence of their ancestry."[104] The implication of the Supreme Court's words is clear: Thind and his children did not possess sufficient performative capacity to act white. Thind may have been an upper-class Indian, but he was still a Hindu. Armenians, by contrast, were Christians, not "heathens," as the ancient dichotomy would dictate. Armenians also fell into a sector of the American racial typology sufficiently fraught with ambiguity that they could rely heavily on performative criteria in order to convince the courts that they lay on the white side of the racial divide.

Performance of whiteness was not limited to religious belief. The *Cartozian* court also conflates class with race through the comical use of anecdote and the selective application of demographic evidence. In its ruling, the court cites the work of Dr. Paul Rohrbach, "a scholar of note" who recounts tales of an "Armenian who became a count in Russia, marrying a Russian countess or baroness, and an Armenian missionary who married a German baroness."[105] With these words, performance of aristocracy and membership in the ruling class is made synonymous with whiteness. The court's syllogistic logic is irrepressible: Armenians had freely mingled with the ruling class of Europe, and all members of the European ruling class must be white; ergo, Armenians had to be white. The court's emphasis on social standing belies any ostensible fidelity to either a scientific of common-knowledge interpretation of race.[106] Performance was what mattered.

The court also points to evidence from Dr. Barton, an expert witness who provides the ultimate evidence of white performance—assimilation through marriage—by Armenians. Dr. Barton's anecdotal evidence has nothing to do with any naturalistic formulation of race. "Within his own information," declares the court without any sense of irony, Dr. Barton "knows of ten or fifteen Armenians in Boston who have married American wives."[107]

Meanwhile, the court's analysis is riddled with the kind of scientific analysis that *Ozawa* and *Thind* supposedly did away with. The language of empiricism is employed throughout the court's analysis. The majority opinion makes sure to mention that both key witnesses on which it relies are doctors. And the court attempts to bestow scientific legitimacy on its opinion by resorting to demographic studies rife with purportedly relevant statistical findings. To this effect, the court cites a survey of immigrant intermarriage in New York City that found that first-generation Armenians possessed a similar rate of marriage with individuals outside their nationality (9.63 percent) as other immigrants.[108] From this study, the court endorses the conclusion that there was "no discrimination respecting the intermarriage of men and women of Armenian blood with native Americans; nor has she found that the question of color or race enters as an obstacle."[109] The court's message to new immigrant groups is clear: If you can assimilate yourself into the White Republic, you will gain the privileges of whiteness. Whiteness is not a given, naturally determined, exogenous variable. Instead, it is an outcome, a reward dependent on performance and assimilation.

The *Cartozian* court's analysis also reveals that, although Armenians might qualify as white people, other individuals of Middle Eastern descent were less likely to. In the years both before and after *Cartozian*, courts had opportunities to directly address whether Arabs qualified as white persons for naturalization purposes. The results were decidedly mixed.

Is White, Is Not White: The Case of Arabs[110]

Several courts, including those in *Ex parte Dow*[111] and *In re Hassan*,[112] denied Arabs white status. Later cases from this era further determined that Afghanis and Parsees, who claimed descent from the ancient Persians, were not white.[113] At the same time, a number of cases deemed Arabs white on varying grounds. *In re Najour* (1909) drew on Blumenbach's racial heuristics, rationalizing that, as Caucasians, Arabs must be white.[114] The Court in *In re Mudarri* (1910) uniquely noted the inherent uncertainty in the very term *white*, as embodied in the naturalization statute, and its shifting meaning depending on time and context: "classification by ethnological race is almost or quite impossible. On the other hand, to give the phrase 'white person' the meaning which it bore when the first naturalization act was passed, viz., any person not otherwise designated or classified, is to make naturalization depend upon the varying and conflicting classification of persons in the usage of successive generations and of different parts of a large country."[115] *In re Ellis* (1910) deemed Syrians white on the grounds that they descended from Semitic stock, possessed general acceptance as Caucasians, and had demonstrated assimilability.[116] *Dow v. United States* (1915) granted a Syrian petitioner naturalization rights based on the general ethnological view that Syrians are "Caucasian" and the absence of any more "authoritative construction" of what the word "white" meant in the Naturalization Act.[117] One case, *United States v. Balsara* (1910), even deemed the Parsees, an ancient community of ethnic Persians living in India, white.[118]

All told, the courts' differing conclusions underscore the general uncertainty facing the issue and also serve to undermine the allegedly scientific and rational basis for racial categorization. Take, for example, one particular case from the era: the petition of George Dow, a Syrian man seeking naturalization.[119] The court rejected Dow's plea, declaring him outside the sphere of whiteness. The court ridiculed the reductionism of turn-of-the-century academic literature that had pronounced descendents of European, North African, and Middle Eastern stock as belonging to the same racial grouping, Caucasian: "To speak of the Asiatic inhabitants of Persia or India as 'Aryan' or 'Caucasian' is almost as great a contradiction as to call a negro inhabitant of South Africa a Saxon because he speaks English, or an Indian inhabitant of Peru or Mexico a Latin because he speaks Spanish."[120] Such ethnological and anthropological arguments, Judge Smith reasoned, attempted to reclassify as white those "who have been *always* considered as *not* forming a part of the white race."[121] In short, the court acknowledged a clear rift between popular understanding and technical definitions—a tension that continues to survive in our modern treatment of Middle Eastern racial identity.

In a rehearing that reaffirmed the decision, the court suffered a revealing bout of revisionist history that whitewashed the struggles of the Irish, Italians, Slavs, Greeks, and other recent immigration groups over the issue of racial classification. The court first reasoned that the naturalization statute should be read from the point of view of the average white citizen of the United States in 1790, the date of its ratification. Then, the court confidently pronounced that, to the average male citizen of that era, *white* simply meant *European*, as he was

> firmly convinced of the superiority of his own white European race over the rest of the world, whether red, yellow, brown or black. He had enslaved many of the American Indians on that ground. He would have enslaved a Moor, a Bedouin, a Syrian, a Turk, or an East Indian of sufficiently dark complexion with equal readiness on the same plea if he could have caught him. The opposite west coast of Africa was accessible for the slave supply; the other sources were not, and the trader who went to get his slaves from them was likely to be made a slave himself.[122]

Besides its patently ridiculous notion that enslavement was predicated on a race's "catchability," the court was either ignorant or dismissive of the long and tortuous history of whiteness. As the court explicitly posits, "The broad fact remains that the European peoples taken as a whole are the fair skinned or light complexioned races of the world, and form the peoples generally referred to as 'white' and so classed since classification based on complexion was adopted."[123] Yet as the history of new immigrant groups into the United States reveals, the court's equation of European with whiteness is anything but established fact. As another court had pointed out, if Congress had intended to confer naturalization rights on all Europeans, and Europeans alone, "it would presumably have inserted a more accurate expression than 'free white persons'" in the naturalization statute.[124]

The Fourth Circuit ultimately reversed Judge Smith, holding that congressional intent supported the naturalization of Syrians.[125] After all, reasoned the court, Congress had amended the naturalization statute numerous times since 1790 but never once excluded individuals from "the contiguous countries of Asia near the Mediterranean."[126] This fact is especially significant in light of prior court rulings declaring Syrians, Armenians, and Parsees white. However, the district court's opinion in *Dow*, especially its ethnologic gymnastics, powerfully captures a heuristic that has, in many ways, dominated the American imagination over the past century. Specifically, the new immigrant groups emerging from Ireland, Italy, Greece, and the Slavic countries were slowly but surely integrated into an expanding notion of whiteness that eventually became conflated with the geographical construct of "Europe." Those outside the European/white construct—"whether Chinese, Japanese, Hindoo, Parsee, Persian, Mongol, Malay, or Syrian,"[127] as the court lists for us—did not qualify as full members of the Republic.

The final section of the district court's *Dow* opinion makes clear the ultimate root of this divide: underlying racial hostility. Though the court repeatedly professes the distastefulness of its task ("nothing could be more difficult and invidious for a court to attempt than to determine an applicant's right to naturalization upon any ground of complexion or race")[128] and its hope that the Supreme Court would address "this most vexed . . . question,"[129] the disingenuousness of its palaver becomes clear when one observes the racial invective saturating the rest of the opinion. The court's contempt for individuals of Middle Eastern descent and its selective historical revision are illustrated on multiple occasions. The court refers to the Middle East (without using the term) as an area inhabited by "Turks and Mohammedans of the pernicious and obnoxious nature of the inhabitants of the Barbary states."[130] While in the same breadth acknowledging the Christianity of many Lebanese, the court takes pains to note that they "were the followers prior to their conversion to Christianity of rites and beliefs held up as among the most repulsive (according to modern ideas) of all those of the ancient historical worlds."[131] Here, the court conveniently glosses over the myriad distasteful rites and beliefs of the Romans, the Huns, the Anglos, and the Saxons, along with many other inhabitants of Europe, prior to (and even after) the adoption of Christianity.

Two cases within a two-year span, *In re Hassan*[132] and *Ex parte Mohriez*,[133] addressed whether Arabs qualified as white persons for naturalization purposes. Despite the issuance of contrary rulings, the methodology of both courts was the same, interpreting *Thind*, *Ozawa*, and their progeny as dictating performative criteria in the matter of racial determination. The cases represented two sides of the same coin and followed the dramaturgic trend of racial jurisprudence. They also highlight the peculiar antinomy of Middle Eastern racial classification and the perceived factors pulling both for and against their inclusion in the white category.

In 1942, the U.S. District Court for the Eastern District of Michigan held that an Arab male, Ahmed Hassan, did not qualify as a white person entitled to citizenship through naturalization.[134] Concerns over assimilation and religious difference informed the court's reasoning. As Judge Tuttle argued,

> Apart from the dark skin of the Arabs, it is well known that they are a part of the Mohammedan world and that a wide gulf separates their culture from that of the predominately Christian peoples of Europe. It cannot be expected that as a class they would readily intermarry with our population and be assimilated into our civilization.[135]

Invoking the spirit of *Cartozian*, religion once again becomes a proxy for race. The court adopts the performative interpretation of *Thind*, as epitomized by *Cartozian*. In distinguishing the result of *Cartozian* from the case at bar, Judge Tuttle remarks that Armenians were a

> Christian people living in an area close to the European border, who have intermingled and intermarried with Europeans over a period of centuries. Evidence was also presented in that case of a considerable amount of intermarriage of Armenian immigrants to the United States with other racial strains in our population.[136]

The court therefore bases its ruling not on any scientific notion of race, which might equate Arabs with Armenians, or on any common-knowledge test. Instead, the court assesses Arab racial status in performative terms based on religious practices and intermarriage.

By contrast, a federal court in Massachusetts held that an Arab man, Mohamed Mohriez, qualified as white.[137] However, as in *Hassan*, the court drew on *Thind* and its progeny to delve into a performance-based analysis. Although the court kept its focus on Arabs as a class, rather than on Mohamed Mohriez as a person, the emphasis was still distinctly dramaturgical.

In its short opinion, the court highlights the close link between the Arab people and the West:

> The names of Avicenna and Averroes, the sciences of algebra and medicine, the population and the architecture of Spain and of Sicily, the very words of the English language, remind us as they would have reminded the Founding Fathers of the action and interaction of Arabic and non-Arabic elements of our culture.[138]

Through its cultural-affinity analysis, the court follows its predecessors in equating scientific achievement, cultural sophistication, and the very notion of civilization with whiteness. This represents a far cry from the disingenuous claims of the *Thind* Court that disavowed any espousal of racial hierarchy. In deeming the Arabs white, the court seized on the role of the Arab people in shaping Western civilization by serving as one of the chief vessels through which the ancient Greek philosophical traditions endured to the modern era.[139] Once again, the court's racial calculus is highly performative: To act as a channel for whiteness, or to have whiteness flow through the veins of the culture, is to perform whiteness and therefore to constitute whiteness.

Despite Judge Wyzansky's adoption of performative criteria in the act of racial determination, his opinion in *Mohriez* stands alone among the racial-prerequisite cases in challenging the fundamental constitutionality of the naturalization laws. Wyzansky goes so far as to question the consistency of the white-only naturalization law with the principles of American democracy. Carefully treading the line between carrying out the law and legislating it, he writes,

> And finally it may not be out of place to say that, as is shown by our recent changes in the laws respecting persons of Chinese nationality and

of the yellow race, we as a country have learned that policies of rigid exclusion are not only false to our professions of democratic liberalism but
repugnant to our vital interests as a world power. In so far as the Nationality Act of 1940 is still open to interpretation, it is highly desirable that it
should be interpreted . . . so as to fulfill the promise that we shall treat all
men as created equal.[140]

This critique of the naturalization laws calls into question the immunity of immigration laws from many constitutional safeguards—a judicial
view still in force to this very day.[141] Though courts have consistently held
that the Constitution grants Congress a special plenary power over immigration policies,[142] Wyzansky's words provide a stern warning that certain
policies can cross the line and are fundamentally repugnant to the very
democratic ideals that the Constitution intends to promote. Moreover,
these policies can lead to arbitrary lawmaking. As the prerequisite cases
reveal, policies that rely on racial determination are particularly dangerous, for they seek to reify that which is socially constructed, fluid, and
shifting. Consequently, racial-determination games often produce judicial
opinions riddled with internal contradictions and dadaistic logic that find
Arabs to qualify as white in some situations and nonwhite in others. All
told, the body of racial-prerequisite jurisprudence suggests that the courts
should get out of the determination business altogether.[143]

The Racial-Prerequisite Cases and
Middle Easterners in Broader Perspective

In totality, the naturalization cases reveal profound anxiety about the
racial classification of individuals of Middle Eastern descent. The most
prominent government authority on this matter, the infamous Dillingham
Commission, reflects the resulting state of ambivalence. Under pressure
from lobbying groups such as the Immigration Restriction League, the
Senate formed the Dillingham Commission in 1907 to study the history
of immigration to the United States. Besides reaching its ultimate conclusion—that many of the social and economic problems facing the country
at the time were the direct result of the new wave of immigrants coming
into the country since the 1880s—the commission also sought to parse
out the issue of racial classification. Presented to the Senate in 1911, vol-
ume 5 of the commission's report, the *Dictionary of Races or Peoples*, did
little, however, to settle the issue.[144]

Although the report embraced a broad definition of *Caucasian*, it did so only begrudgingly. The term, wrote the commission, encompasses "all races, which, although dark in color or aberrant in other directions, are, when considered from all points of view, felt to be more like the white race than like any of the other four races [Mongolian, Ethiopian, Malay, and American]."[145] On the other hand, when dealing with individuals of Middle Eastern descent, the report took a divided view: "Physically the modern Syrians are of mixed Syrian, Arabian, and even Jewish blood. They belong to the Semitic branch of the Caucasian race, thus widely differing from their rulers, the Turks, who are in origin Mongolian."[146] The report ultimately concluded that Syrians were barely white and that Turks were categorically not white; other proximate groups remained unclassified.

The crisis of whiteness surrounding early Middle Eastern immigration warrants three broad observations. First, racial classification and naturalization eligibility did not merely impact political rights, such as the franchise; instead, they were instrumental in determining who would be granted full participation in the life of the Republic. Judicial declarations of whiteness affected economic and social freedoms. In California, for example, without naturalization, legal immigrants often could not own land[147] and were disqualified from the practice of such professions as the law.[148] Whiteness also took on heavy symbolic value, as the extensive procedural posture and the arguments in the *Dow* case reveal. Thus, as Cheryl Harris has argued, racial identity and property are deeply interrelated concepts, and whiteness has become the basis for allocating social benefits and entrenching power both in the public and private sectors.[149]

Second, the naturalization suits support one of the central tenets of critical race theory: that race is a construction rather than a biological fact, invented and renegotiated to serve evolving social, political, and economic exigencies.[150] This glimpse into the early contemplations of Middle Eastern racial belonging reveals inconsistent results. In many instances, Middle Easterners were extended white status and its attendant privileges. Often, however, they were deemed nonwhite and suffered the social, political, and economic consequences. The central factor guiding judicial determinations, however, stayed consistent: assimilationist policy considerations dominated the jurisprudence of whiteness, leading courts to dole out white status on the basis of how effectively Middle Easterners "performed" whiteness. Using the panopticonian gaze of the law, courts attempted to decipher the hieroglyphics of racial identity not through any scientific or biological lens (to the extent that it is even possible) but through dramaturgical criteria—wealth accumulation, educational attainment, Christian faith, English fluency, and marriage patterns.

The early years of the Republic witnessed the negotiation of the racial status of myriad immigrant groups. Some groups, such as the Irish, the Italians, and the Slavs were initially deemed nonwhite and denied the privileges of full participation in the Republic. As perceptions of their assimilability changed, however, they eventually received the white designation. The case of Middle Easterners has been no different—perceptions of assimilability have guided the construction of their racial status to this very day.

Although Congress finally abandoned the race-based system of naturalization in 1952[151] and eliminated the quota system based on national origin, which limited annual immigration from each nationality to 2 percent of the nationality's share of the U.S. population, in 1965,[152] performative/white bias continues to exist in the immigration system. The new system's per-country allocations continue to limit immigration from historically excluded countries,[153] effectively limiting immigration by individuals of certain nonwhite races. More importantly, the recent debate over immigration reform has called for greater assimilation of immigrant groups into the United States. The final report of the Commission on Immigration Reform in 1997 called for the "Americanization" of new immigrants through a "process of integration by which immigrants become part of our communities and by which our communities and the nation learn from and adapt to their presence."[154] In particular, the report emphasized the need for these new immigrant groups to conform to white, Christian, Western European norms, especially in their adoption of English as their primary language.

Though the whiteness requirement on the books until 1952 may, at first blush, appear antiquated and derisible to modern sensibilities, we are not as far removed from it as we would like to think. Consider the recent debate over illegal immigration and its pointed focus on our neighbors to the south. Samuel P. Huntington's provocative bestseller *Who Are We? The Challenges to America's National Identity* has epitomized the prevailing discourse, strongly cautioning against any move toward a multilingual and multicultural society. The book, which predicts a calamitous national crisis from the alleged inassimilability of our country's growing Latino population, sternly calls out Mexican immigrants to the United

States for their purported failure to learn English and adopt Anglo values.[155] In short, *Who Are We?* serves as an alarum for the protection of the primacy of white Anglo-Protestant culture in our society. As a critique of the removal of assimilability considerations from American immigration policy over the past half century, the influential tome has led to calls to reintroduce whiteness—at least in its more "honorific" sense—to the immigration calculus. Indeed, the performance of whiteness—through the regulation of behavior unbecoming of whites—has even come to be demanded by law.[156] In 2006, Gwinnett County, home to Georgia's largest Hispanic population, banned mobile taco stands.[157] A city in Kansas banned individuals from sitting on their front porch, an activity closely identified with Latinos.[158] Nativist sentiments have also enforced white performance in the form of language regulations.[159] With the blessing of the courts,[160] many employers have adopted English-only rules at the office place.[161] Meanwhile, initiatives in such states as Colorado have sought to ban bilingual education.[162]

The familiar quid pro quo from the racial-prerequisite cases is once again affirmed: if you can assimilate yourself into the White Republic, you will gain the privileges of whiteness. Without white performance, immigration reform would be necessary and privileges would be revoked from these minority groups. The rhetoric of isolationists and other advocates of tighter borders has even made this quid pro quo explicit. White performance is still a condition of white privilege.[163]

Finally, the cases reveal that Middle Easterners found themselves at the heart of the legal struggle over whiteness. The era when these cases were litigated—the first half of the twentieth century—witnessed the crystallization of modern legal definitions through which Middle Easterners were generally deemed white by law—but just barely. Teetering on the precipice of whiteness, their racial status remained open to contestation. As their performance of whiteness has changed over the years, so has their perceived racial status in the public imagination, to the point where they have become the paradigmatic Other. All the while, however, the government continues to categorize them as white. Chapter 3 explores some of the reasons for this puzzling schism and its profound consequences, especially in the post-9/11 world.

3

From Friendly
Foreigner to Enemy Race

*Selective Racialization, Covering, and
the Negotiation of Middle Eastern
American Identity*

With our nation's racial hierarchy in place, individuals of Middle Eastern descent found themselves on the dividing line. Often, by the thinnest of margins, courts declared them white. Other times, however, courts held otherwise. In either instance, jurists eschewed ostensibly scientific criteria or even common knowledge in determining racial categories. Instead, they utilized a performative heuristic that betrayed the constructed nature of the entire race-making enterprise. As a consequence, Middle Easterners were put on notice: their whiteness was very much in doubt, and as such, their performance would ultimately determine their status and rights. When Congress eliminated the racial prerequisites for naturalization eligibility in 1952, the entire race-determination enterprise appeared poised for relegation to the dark reaches of history. Their irrelevance was short-lived, however, as the government reentered the racial-classification business in the 1960s. Though the government's impetus for racial classification had transformed from the limitation of naturalization rights to the protection of civil rights (through affirmative action and related policies), the doctrines for making these determinations remained the same. For Middle Easterners, the result was their classification as white by law and their consequent exclusion from many of the civil rights measures of the past half century. In recent years, this tack has grown increasingly untenable as public and private discrimination against Middle Easterners has risen dramatically.

To understand the rising tide of discrimination against Americans of Middle Eastern descent, it is first necessary to examine the origins of the terms *Middle East* and *Middle Eastern* and the social meanings assigned to them. In response to broader geopolitical events, Middle Easterners have transformed in the public imagination from friendly foreigners to enemy aliens, and from enemy aliens to a veritable enemy race. Middle Eastern Americans are subject to a twofold, and frequently unconscious, process that has fostered their relative invisibility and absence from the civil rights dialogue. On one hand, society at large has selectively racialized individuals of Middle Eastern descent, thereby unleashing a pernicious stereotyping feedback loop that ossifies the negative connotations associated with the group and the prevalent sense of their Otherness. On the other hand, many Middle Eastern Americans have adopted assimilatory covering measures to downplay their Otherness in the eyes of society. In the process, they have made a Faustian pact with whiteness—both as an unconscious response to and strategic tactic against the forces of racism. Taken as a whole, these forces have simultaneously enabled Middle Easterners to avoid discrimination at an individual level but lessened the ability of the community, as a whole, to systematically fight invidious discrimination and stereotyping in the long term.

The Invention of the Middle East

The term *Middle East* likely emerged in the 1850s from Britain's India Office.[1] It did not enjoy widespread usage in policy circles, however, until the early twentieth century, when it was used in the work of famed American naval strategist Admiral Alfred Thayer Mahan. In an article first published in September 1902, Mahan used the term *Middle East* to refer to a region of growing strategic importance in the emerging conflict pitting Britain and the United States against Germany and Russia.[2] Mahan appeared to define that region as ranging, on a north-south axis, from Turkey to the Arabian Peninsula and, on an east-west axis, from Iran to Egypt. Thus, the designation was borne of geopolitical considerations and its construction wrought with semiotic meaning. As postcolonial theorist José Rabasa has written, a map "functions as a mirror of the world, not because the representation of the earth has the status of a natural sign, but because it aims to invoke a simulacrum of any always inaccessible totality by means of arrangement of symbols."[3] Just as race is a function of social construction rather than inherent biology, the Middle East was invented from political considerations, not any natural geography. This observation is made plain by the region's ostensible boundaries, which encompass at least part of the northern coast of the African continent and typically stretch eastward as far as Iran (a non-Arab country, but one with sizable oil reserves), but not into Afghanistan, Pakistan, and the Indian subcontinent.

The term *Middle East* therefore appears to eschew the typical hallmarks of regional definitions, which are often based on continental, linguistic, or perceived ethnic boundaries. Observes Sedat Laciner,

> This so-called region neighbors two oceans (Indian and Atlantic) and six seas (Mediterranean, Red Sea, Persian Gulf, Black Sea, Aegean Sea and the Caspian Sea). It extends to three continents (Africa, Asia and Europe). It consists of ten sub-regions (Southern and Northern Caucasus, Northern Africa, Arabia, Greater Palestine and Syria, Mesopotamia, the Caspian Basin, Central Asia (Turkistan), Indian Peninsula. Three monotheistic religions (Islam, Christianity and Judaism), with their numerous sects and schools of thought, exist in this region. Thousands of religious and moral faiths, including atheism and paganism, are practiced in this wide geography and thus, it is one of the largest laboratories of the world. Although viewed by the West as all-Arab, the region consists of tens of different ethnic-linguistic communities, with Turks, Arabs and Persians as the main ones.[4]

At the same time, the term is riddled in ambiguity, sometimes encompassing the entire North African coast, from Morocco to Egypt, and other parts of Africa, including the Sudan and Somalia, the former Soviet, Caucasus Republics of Georgia, Azerbaijan, and Armenia, and occasionally Afghanistan, Pakistan, and Turkistan. The Middle East is therefore a malleable geopolitical construct of relatively recent vintage.

Consequently, it was only in the past half century that the term began to refer to peoples of the region. The racial-prerequisite cases that we have analyzed from the first half of the twentieth century never referred to Lebanese, Syrian, Turks, Armenian, or other petitioners as Middle Easterners. Quite simply, they were never viewed as part of a Middle Easterner collective.

A search of all reported federal and state court opinions reveals that there was not a single reference to the terms *Middle East* or *Middle Eastern* until 1946, when a New York court referred to a "European Middle Eastern Service Medal and Victory Medal" given to veterans.[5] Other than scattered references to similar medals, the next mention of the *Middle*

East or *Middle Eastern* came in a 1955 IRS dispute involving the taxation of an oil worker who had taken employment in numerous countries, including Saudi Arabia, Lebanon, Syria, and Iraq. The court synoptically referred to the work as having resided in "Near or Middle Eastern countries."[6] The term was also used in a 1956 breach-of-contract suit in which the U.S. government failed to deliver certain airplane technology to "the Middle East" lest it be used in regional conflicts contrary to American foreign-policy interests.[7] Finally, several federal suits in 1957 linked the term to its most precious commodity, referring on numerous occasions to "Middle Eastern oil."[8] As these cases make clear, in the beginning, the Middle Eastern designation arose in a geopolitical and oil-related context.

In a time-honored process, the racialization of individuals from Turkey, Iran, and the Arab states as "Middle Eastern" came to serve broader economic and political needs. In their influential work on the formation of race, Michael Omi and Howard Winant highlight the "sociohistorical process by which racial categories are created, inhabited, transformed, and destroyed."[9] In prior eras, the racialization and stereotyping of various groups has taken on a distinctly utilitarian flavor.

Take the typecasting of African Americans through the course of history. As we have seen, the demands of the plantation economy helped give rise to the Southern hierarchy and its black-white divide based on skin color (which supplanted the earlier hierarchy based on religious affiliation). As Richard Delgado reminds us, antiblack "prejudice sprang up with slavery. Previously, educated Europeans held generally positive attitudes toward Africans, recognizing the African civilization was highly advanced."[10] As slavery emerged, infantilization became commonplace in media portrayals, as blacks were stereotyped as buffoons unable to survive without the guidance of their masters. Blackface minstrelsy rose to popularity, in the guise of Sambo and other characters, conveying images of blacks as either "inept urban dandies or happy childlike slaves."[11] Following emancipation and the end of the Civil War, however, images became more ominous, with black men portrayed as rapists preying on white women and black women reduced to pliable domestic servants.[12] Stereotypes followed function, first legitimating slavery and later rationalizing lynching, segregation, imperialism, and Jim Crow.

Since "conquering nations generally demonize their subjects in order to rationalize exploiting them,"[13] Latino and Asian stereotypes have undergone a similar trajectory. As Delgado notes, "Anglo settlers in California and the Southwest began to circulate notions of Mexican inferiority only when the settlers came to covet Mexican lands and mining claims."[14] Similarly, early portraits of the Chinese and Japanese cast them as comical and hapless, though they were happily tolerated for their contribution to the American workforce. As economic and assimilatory fears related to these groups heightened, however, Charlie Chan–like stereotypes transformed and gave rise to the clichéd image of the wily, scheming, and menacing "Oriental" criminal mastermind.[15]

Quite simply, concludes Delgado, "Depictions vary depending on society's needs."[16] What then are we to make of the dramatic change in the status of Middle Easterners? It is hardly coincidence that it has occurred over the past generation—a time that has seen the Middle East rise to the forefront of global politics and economic importance due to its ample reserves of the great engine of industrialization: oil.

The Middle Easterner as the Other: The Slippery Slope from Friendly Foreigner to Enemy Alien, Enemy Alien to Enemy Race

Inextricably intertwined with the rising tide of discrimination facing persons of Middle Eastern descent is the mythology surrounding racial construction and related religious and sociocultural perceptions. For prior generations, Middle Eastern Americans came closer to matching our constructed notions of whiteness. They were largely Christian; they came from an exotic but friendly, romantic, and halcyon foreign land imagined to contain magic lanterns, genies, flying carpets, and belly dancers; and they served as a chief vessel of the philosophical and cultural heritage of the West.[17] Thus, in previous generations, people of (what we now call) Middle Eastern descent were, more often than not, blended into the white category. When the Levant was perceived as a desert hinterland, irrelevant to Western interests, its people were not collectivized into a Middle Eastern taxonomy. But once the region took on geopolitical and economic significance, the Middle East leaped into existence as a concept imbued with social meaning. As James C. Scott has argued, the naming process is intricately related to exercise of power.[18] Specifically, the creation of synoptic categories represents an essential step in a state's nation-building process in that it advances the government's ability to track and control both its subjects and those who might pose a threat from without. Race comes into existence only when a group grows sufficiently large, in terms of both numbers and power, as to become a threat.

In an era when we view the most immediate threat to our national security as emanating from the Middle East, it is not surprising that monolithic images of the Middle East and the Middle Easterner have leaped into existence. Middle Easterners have been irretrievably associated with Islam; they appear to hail from a decidedly unfriendly foreign land imagined to contain nothing but terrorists, obstreperous mobs chanting "Death to America," unabashed misogynistic polygamists, and religious fundamentalists; and they seem to represent a wholly different civilization from our own—one with which the inevitable and apocalyptic clash of civilizations is unfolding.[19] Thus, they are the quintessential Other, and the Middle Easterner category, imposed on them by society at large, has become their appellation.

In popular perception, in which the notion of assimilability constitutes the sine qua non of the majority's acceptance of an immigrant group, it is not surprising that Middle Easterners have fared poorly. As Karen Engle has noted, the past century has witnessed a radical transformation in majority perceptions of Middle Eastern individuals: they are, in short, no longer thought capable of assimilation.[20] The changing religious composition of Middle Eastern immigrants to the United States has played a key role in this transformation. As the naturalization cases make clear, perceptions of race are frequently conflated with perceptions of religion. In 1924, about two hundred thousand Arabs resided in the United States. Of these, 80 percent were from Syria and Lebanon, of which group a startling 90 percent were Christian.[21] Many of these immigrants had fled oppression and persecution under the Ottoman Empire.[22] Indeed, an early study of the emerging Syrian and Lebanese community at the turn of the century in New York City found that only 2 of 2,482 residents were Muslim.[23] As the author of the study noted, "The Moslems, Druses and Metâwely are not found in sufficient numbers to warrant more than passing mention."[24]

Given the tendency to conflate race with religious affiliation, and Christianity with assimilability, it is not surprising that, at the beginning of the twentieth century, courts declared Armenians and even some Arabs white by law, thereby entitling them to the privileges of whiteness, including naturalization. However, the composition of the Middle Eastern American population has undergone a dramatic change in recent years, especially in the public imagination. Contrary to popular perceptions, only 23 percent of present-day Arab Americans are Muslim.[25] However, about 60 percent of Arab immigrants arriving in the United States since

1965 identify themselves as Muslim.[26] As it has grown less Christian, the Middle Eastern population in the United States is thought of as less assimilable and, consequently, less white.

As faith in their assimilatory capacity has diminished, Middle Easterners have come to represent enemy aliens, and even an enemy race, in the popular imagination. In the past, the paradigmatic noncitizen was the "Mexican illegal alien, or the inscrutable, clannish Asian."[27] Today, it is the Arab terrorist, and this vision has firmly taken hold of our immigration policies. As Victor Romero argues, "post-9/11, the age-old stereotype of the foreign, Arab terrorist has been rekindled, and placing our immigration functions under the auspices of an executive department charged with 'homeland security' reinforces the idea that immigrants are terrorists."[28] The recent wave of registration and deportation policies aimed at individuals of Middle Eastern descent also highlights this trend. Take, for example, the National Security Entry-Exit Registration System (NSEERS), which was formally announced by the attorney general on June 6, 2002, and then supplemented with a special "call-in" registration in November 2002. The NSEERS singles out a limited class of noncitizens—male, nonimmigrant visa holders over the age of sixteen who are from one of twenty-five Muslim and Middle Eastern countries—for special registration requirements.[29]

The changing perceptions of the Middle East are exemplified with a perusal through one of the earliest reflections on the Middle Eastern population in the United States. At the turn of the twentieth century, Lucius Hopkins Miller, a professor of biblical studies at Princeton University, published a study on the Arab community in New York City. His analysis—which sheds a generally positive light on these new immigrants, embraces their assimilability, and endorses their admission to the Republic—reflects certain stereotypes, both positive and negative, about Middle Easterners that seem quite ill-fitting with contemporary perceptions. For example, Miller's strongest critique of Arabs is their allegedly well-known mendacity. Wholeheartedly acknowledging the duplicitous and perfidious ways of persons descending from the Middle East, Miller notes,

> A main charge brought against the Syrian character is that of sharpness and deceit—a prevalent Oriental strain. Its existence is admitted in the Arabic proverb 'A lie is the salt of man' and in the Arabic story of Satan's journey through the earth. With twelve packs of lies on his back, while

crossing Mount Lebanon, he tripped and fell, spilling the contents of ten bags upon the land of Syria.[30]

To temper the implications of this charge, Miller then argues that Middle Eastern chicanery is not inherent or congenital but a symptom of circumstance:

> When it is remembered that in his own land the only alternative has often been 'lie or die,' it will be seen that Syrian deceitfulness has been largely nurtured by an adverse environment. In this he has shared with every downtrodden race in history. American residence should work improvement in this respect. . . . Nevertheless, the cold fact remains that the inability to tell the truth is the chief blot upon the Syrian immigrant's character.[31]

Interestingly enough, Miller also heaps a number of "positive" stereotypes—unusual by today's popular standards—on the Syrians, particularly emphasizing their law-abiding character. In remarkable language, Miller explains,

> In his love of law and order the Syrian cannot be excelled. Personal inquiry at police stations and among patrolmen, as well as careful search in the reports of the Commissioners of Charities and Correction, failed to bring out the slightest flaw. The Syrians do not become public charges and they mind their own business. The universal testimony of the police authorities is that there is no more peaceful or law abiding race in New York city. The humane spirit is very strong among the Syrians.[32]

Ironically, at the turn of the next century, Middle Easterners would be perceived as the greatest threat to American national security.

Perceptions of the humane spirit described by Miller resonated at least through the eve of the oil embargoes and the Middle Eastern tumult of the 1970s. In an episode of the children's cartoon *Scooby Doo, Where Are You?* that aired in the late 1960s, for example, the gang takes pains to highlight the Persians' renowned kindness, generosity, and hospitality—a message scarcely conveyed by the mass media today. The Persian custom of *tarof*—an elaborate system of ceremonial politeness—was doubtless the inspiration for such a generalization.

As we shall more fully explore in the next chapter, events in the region have led to a dramatic change in media portrayals during recent years.

The image of the Levant as an exotic and charming land has given way to a nightmarish vision of the Middle East as a dangerous, anarchic world teeming with perfidious oil sheiks, Islamic fundamentalists, and maniacal terrorists. But before we document and assess the impact of these changing perceptions, we must consider the particular processes that have fueled this transformation.

The Negotiation of Middle Eastern Identity: Selective Racialization and Covering

The negotiation of the Middle Eastern identity is mediated by a two-fold process that moves both from the top down and from the bottom up. From the top down, society at large engages in a practice that can best be described as *selective racialization*. From the bottom up, Middle Easterners, both privileged and damned by their proximity to the white dividing line, engage in persistent (and frequently effective) covering of their ethnic background. These two social forces combine to create a pernicious stereotyping feedback loop that enervates the political strength of the Middle Eastern community, heightens its invisibility, and leaves little effective resistance to the growing assaults against its civil rights.

A Theory of Selective Racialization

In a landmark article published two decades ago, civil rights scholar Charles Lawrence advanced a powerful critique of existing equal protection jurisprudence and its problematic immunization of unconscious racism from judicial scrutiny.[33] Under existing Supreme Court precedent,[34] plaintiffs cannot raise a cognizable equal protection claim unless they establish that a challenged action purposefully sought to discriminate against a protected group, such as a racial minority. This intent requirement, argues Lawrence, has rendered our civil rights laws wholly inadequate to fight the pernicious systemic racism that pervades our society. As Lawrence explains, "Americans share a common historical and cultural heritage in which racism has played and still plays a dominant role. . . . [This] culture—including, for example, the media, an individual's parents, peers, and authority figures—transmits certain beliefs and preferences . . . [that] seem part of the individual's rational ordering of her perceptions of the world."[35] Lawrence therefore warns us that, by limiting the remedial powers of courts to only those government policies that stem from overt animus, we ignore our broader culture of unconscious racism, its role in shaping our institutions, and its profound impact on our social, political, and economic lives.

The immediate thrust of Lawrence's argument deals with the equal protection doctrine, which attaches solely to state action—governmental regulations and policies. But Lawrence's core insight also has wider implications: to truly eradicate discrimination from our society, we must remedy both intentional and unconscious racism. To accomplish this task, we must scrutinize all forms of unintentional racism, including the social processes by which stereotypes are formed, transmitted, and perpetuated. With respect to individuals of Middle Eastern descent, the act of identification and racialization is laden with tacit associations that fuel negative stereotypes. Drawing on Lawrence's insights on the power of unconscious racism, this section examines the social mechanisms that have exacerbated the rising ride of discrimination against Middle Eastern Americans, fueled their relative invisibility in the body politic and civil society, and frustrated any semblance of a civil rights movement for them.

Specifically, in society at large, Middle Easterners are consistently subjected to a process of *selective racialization*. This largely undocumented and predominantly subconscious mechanism has profound ramifications. Systematically, famous individuals of Middle Eastern descent are usually perceived as white. Meanwhile, *infamous* individuals of Middle Eastern descent are usually categorized as Middle Eastern. When Middle Eastern actors conform to social norms and advance positive values and conduct, their racial identity as the Other recedes to the background as they merge into the great white abyss. By contrast, when Middle Eastern actors engage in transgressive behavior, their racial identity as the Other immediately becomes a central, defining characteristic of who they are. The result is an endless feedback loop that calcifies popular prejudices. Wholesome and socially redeeming activities, which might otherwise subvert public misperceptions of the community, do not get associated with Middle Eastern identity. By contrast, the image of transgression is continually correlated with the Middle Eastern racial category, serving only to reinforce negative connotations with the community.

Our country is filled with individuals of Middle Eastern descent who have contributed constructively to American society. Yet surprisingly few of these Americans are actually perceived as Middle Easterners. Instead, their ethnicity is frequently whitewashed.[36] On one hand, this fact highlights the assimilability of Middle Eastern immigrants in the United States. On the other hand, it creates a problematic signposting of Middle Eastern identity when it becomes associated with transgressive activities.

The long list of Middle Eastern Americans includes individuals from virtually every aspect of American life, including athletes such as tennis player Andre Agassi (Persian/Armenian), Indy 500 champion Bobby Rahal (Lebanese), and NFL quarterbacks Doug Flutie and Jeff George (both Lebanese); entertainers such as actresses Cher (Armenian), Kathy Najimi (Lebanese), Catherine Bell (half Persian), and Gabrielle Anwar (half Persian), actors Danny Thomas (Lebanese) and Tony Shalhoub (Lebanese), radio deejay Casy Kasem (Palestinian/Lebanese), and singer Paul Anka (Lebanese); prominent entrepreneurs such as hoteliers the Maloof family (Lebanese) and Apple CEO Steve Jobs (half Syrian); and politicians and activists such as former New Hampshire governor and White House chief of staff John Sununu (Lebanese), former senator George Mitchell (half Lebanese), and prominent consumer advocate and presidential candidate Ralph Nader (Lebanese/Egyptian). Even "good" Middle Easterners who are perceived as nonwhite are not racialized as Middle Eastern. For example, although they are both half Lebanese, neither Salma Hayek, a famous actress, nor Shakira, an internationally renowned singer, is identified as Middle Eastern. Instead, they are almost universally considered Latina.

Some observers might point to the whitewashing of Americans of Middle Eastern descent as evidence of our evolving colorblindness. But such an argument is belied by the systematic racialization of transgressive individuals. When individuals lie at the cusp of the white/nonwhite divide, we unconsciously categorize them as the Other when they engage in wrongdoing but blend them into the white when they behave within social norms. Andre Agassi is a (white) tennis player, and Ralph Nader is a (white) politician. But Osama bin Laden is labeled an Arab terrorist and the Ayatollah Khomeini was a Middle Eastern Islamic fundamentalist. The act of selective racialization is by no means limited to geopolitical struggles. It occurs on a far more pedestrian, but nevertheless important, level. Take the case of Dodi Al-Fayed, the wealthy businessman who was dating Princess Diana following her divorce from Prince Charles. The escapades of the two, rumored to be engaged at the time of their deaths, were the subject of extensive media coverage. Throughout their relationship, Al-Fayed was repeatedly portrayed as an *Arab* businessman and *Middle Eastern* playboy—not merely an Englishman or a businessman without reference to his race. In other words, he was racialized. And the reason is clear: he was engaging in transgressive behavior, stealing away with the People's princess.

Other examples abound. Recently, Zenadine Zidane, a member of the French national soccer team, viciously headbutted Italian player Marco Materazzi in the finals of the 2006 World Cup. Zidane's violent outburst likely cost his team the championship and has gone down as one of the most infamous incidents in soccer history. While the incident sullied Zidane's previously untarnished reputation, it also did something else: it racialized Zidane in the United States. In the aftermath of the incident, Zidane went from simply being an otherwise ordinary native-born (white) Frenchman on the Gallican national soccer team to becoming an Arab. American media reports highlighted his Algerian roots. The racial subtext was all too clear—there was an implicit association of his apparent predilection for violence with his Arab background. He had brazenly violated social norms with his headbutt and, as such, had become a transgressor. Simultaneously, he went from being white to becoming the Other.

The process of selective racialization occurs with regularity in the mass media, serving to bolster and legitimize existing stereotypes. Although all the characters in the Middle Eastern–themed Disney film *Aladdin* share Arab descent, they are only selectively racialized. The chief wrongdoers— the greedy bazaar merchants, the thief Kazim, and the main antagonist, Jafar—all possess exaggerated stereotypical features. Both Kazim and Jafar sport thick Arab accents, facial hair, and prominent hooked noses. By contrast, the movie's sympathetic protagonists—Aladdin, Princess Jasmine, and the Sultan—possess few of the features traditionally associated with Arabs. Instead, their physiognomy is quintessentially European, and they speak with no trace of a Middle Eastern accent.[37] In other words, the transgressive characters are Arabized and the wholesome characters are Anglicized, thereby heightening negative stereotypes linked to Middle Easterners while concurrently reinforcing positive associations with whiteness.

Another classic example of selective racialization comes from the sitcom *Alice*, which aired on CBS from 1976 to 1983. The show took place at a truck-stop diner named after its affable proprietor, Mel Sharples, who was played by Vic Tayback, an Arab American. Yet Tayback's character was never racialized.[38] Instead, his heritage was whitewashed. This tack did not stop the show from catering to popular prejudices about Arabs during its run. In one episode, Flo, a mouthy blond waitress, is approached by a lecherous oil sheik (played by Italian American actor

Richard Libertini) who wants to marry her in a thinly veiled attempt to add her to his harem as his fourth wife.[39] When presented with a natural opportunity to present someone of Arab descent in a normalized manner, the show demurred, selecting not to Arabize the Mel character. But on the other hand, producers did not hesitate to draw on clichéd images of the misogynistic and gluttonous Arab for a plotline. When asked why they never racialized Mel, the producers of the show stated that "stereotypes take a long time to wither away, and they did not want Mel to have a particular heritage."[40]

The phenomenon is not restricted to Middle Easterners, but can apply any time someone stands at the precipice of whiteness. In the world of baseball, Nomar Garciaparra, a former Boston Red Sox all-star, used to undergo a process of selective racialization with his hometown fans. Garciaparra, who is of Mexican descent, is often mistaken as Italian. Caught at the edge of the white divide, his racial affiliation remains contested and subject to unconscious public perceptions. Whenever he found himself in a particularly hot stretch of hitting, Bostonians would hail him mirthfully on the street, cheering him with the words "Hey, paesano," a greeting popular between Italian Americans. Only when he lived up to his billing as the team captain and perennial all-star was he perceived as an Italian. On the other hand, when he was mired in a prolonged slump, the public not only turned on him but also viewed him in different racial terms. All of a sudden, instead of being acknowledged as a paesano, he would be decried as a "stupid Mexican."[41] Through the process of selective racialization, white continues to be imbued with positive associations while the Other continues to endure negative connotations.

Negotiating Middle Eastern Racial Status in the New America: Covering and Its Implications

The development of a Middle Eastern racial identity is not an exclusively top-down process, contrary to what the racial-prerequisite cases and the selective-racialization process might initially suggest. Racial categorization, and the construction of its social meaning, is the result of an intricate series of negotiations spread over time and space. Definitions and associations are not only promulgated and imposed by the government or public at-large; they are also negotiated in the private sector as a part of the everyday conduct of individuals. And it is in this private arena that Middle Easterners themselves have played a critical role in actively encouraging recognition of their white status through such assimilatory behavior as covering. In the process, Middle Easterners have made a Faustian pact with whiteness that has simultaneously enabled them to avoid discrimination at an individual level but lessened the ability of the community, as a whole, to systematically fight invidious discrimination and stereotyping in the long term.

Theorists have traditionally identified two forms of assimilatory behavior: conversion and passing. Conversion occurs in the act of trying to be something one is not. Passing is accomplished when one acknowledges one's identity but nevertheless attempts to hide that identity. In the context of sexual orientation, for example, a gay man's adoption of a wholly straight lifestyle would constitute conversion. Passing, by contrast, might involve remaining gay but keeping one's sexual preferences entirely hidden from the outside world. In addition to conversion and passing, Kenji Yoshino in his recent work has added to the mix the concept of *covering*.[42]

Drawing from the work of Erving Goffman,[43] who once observed "that persons who are ready to admit possession of a stigma . . . may nonetheless make a great effort to keep the stigma from looming large,"[44] Yoshino calls attention to a rampant, yet relatively unappreciated, consequence of our national impulse toward assimilation—the covering of disfavored identities. Based on pressures to conform to social norms enforced by the dominant culture, a rational distaste for ostracism and social opprobrium can lead individuals to engage in the purposeful act of toning down traits that identify them with a stigmatized group. In keeping with the earlier example on sexual orientation, someone who is a lesbian and says she is a lesbian engages in covering when she "makes it easy for others to disattend her orientation."[45] Specifically, she downplays aspects of her personality that may be associated with lesbianism. Yoshino challenges the fundamental assumptions of the classic discrimination models by arguing that covering can be every bit as pernicious as the two more widely recognized phenomena: conversion[46] and passing.[47] Not only does Yoshino help to define and assess the practice of covering, but he also calls into question our almost universal embrace of the salutary process of assimilation. Assimilation, he argues, can be both an "effect of discrimination as well as an evasion of it."[48]

Applying Yoshino's model in the Middle Eastern context is both revealing and instructive: what, after all, could be more coercively assimilationist than forcibly designating an entire population white de jure while simultaneously treating that population as nonwhite de facto? Not surprisingly,

Middle Easterners have sought refuge in covering as a strategic response to the discrimination they face.

Though Yoshino eschews absolute distinctions,[49] he maintains that all three forms of assimilatory behavior—conversion, passing, and covering—are more available to homosexuals than racial minorities and women.[50] Although there may be general truth to this observation, this is not the case with respect to the Middle Eastern population, which lies on the cusp of the white/nonwhite divide. Like the gay population, and unlike most racial minorities and women, Middle Easterners have the "luxury" of significant covering in multiple ways, enabling them to perform whiteness and assimilate within mainstream American society, but at a tremendous cost to their identity, dignity, and rights.

As with the gay population, Middle Eastern Americans face expectations to engage in self-help to cover up or downplay their Middle Easternness. With the rising levels of intolerance and racial animus against Middle Easterners, covering responses constitute a rational survival strategy. Yet it has a pernicious side effect. The availability of covering (and passing and conversion) strategies reduces the cohesiveness of the group and hampers collective action. African Americans, Asian Americans, and women often enjoy fewer assimilatory options, and this lack of choice forces group solidarity because of their limited alternatives. By contrast, both the gay and Middle Eastern populations "enjoy" a wider breadth of potential responses to assimilatory pressures. In the short run, the promise of freedom from discrimination through mainstream performance inures to their individual benefit. In the long run, however, such responses prevent a group from coalescing around its common interests. Indeed, the much wider latitude of covering options available to both the gay and Middle Eastern populations might explain why both groups have been relative latecomers to the civil rights movement.

Largely due to the existence of distinctive phenotypic characteristics, many African Americans cannot pretend to be anything but African American and many Asian Americans cannot pretend to be anything but Asian American.[51] Many Middle Easterners, however, can realistically opt out of their racial categorization. Middle Easterners are more prone to racial ambiguity because successive waves of diverse populations have passed through the Middle East, making it a veritable racial melting pot since antiquity. Since the stereotypical image of the Middle Easterner is much darker in skin, hair, and eye color than the average Middle Easterner, those who naturally possess lighter skin, hair, and eyes are particularly nimble in their covering. Either way, with the simple change of a revealing first or last name, many Middle Easterners can become Italian, French, Greek, Romanian, Indian, Mexican, Puerto Rican, or Argentine.[52]

The gravitation toward covering is often irresistible, especially through its seductive illusion of simplifying the lives of its purveyors. In the wake of 9/11, Middle Easterners throughout the United States felt under attack and responded with a series of rational covering responses just to survive the wave of hate surging throughout the country.[53] Lebanese and Persian restaurants conspicuously displayed "Proud to be American" signs over their entrances. Cab drivers from the Middle East and South Asia decorated their vehicles with large American flags.[54] A series of hate crimes prompted many Muslim women and Sikh men to remove their head coverings out of fear of being perceived as Middle Eastern.[55]

Four axes of covering—association, appearance, affiliation, and activism[56]—are prevalent in the Middle Eastern community. Consider the phenomenon of association. As one associates more with recognized whites, one better performs whiteness and is therefore perceived as more white. When I first moved to Newport Beach, California, the former hometown of John Wayne and an oceanside hamlet renowned as a bastion of wealth and white conservatism, a friend of mine joked, "Don't worry—I'll be your white sponsor." His wry comment had historical antecedents. A decade after Congress passed the Chinese Exclusion Act of 1882 prohibiting any new immigration from China, Chinese immigrants already residing in the United States had to prove the legality of their presence by providing the testimony of "one credible *white* witness."[57] Mingling with the white is a powerful form of obtaining white bona fides.

In an illuminating passage from her essay *I Grew Up Thinking I Was White*, Iranian American writer Gelareh Asayesh describes the associational covering that she undertakes to assimilate:

> My National Public Radio accent takes me further than my parents' voices, laden with inflections from a faraway land. The options may be limited when it comes to skin color, but it is possible to improve one's status in other ways. I think of it as race laundering: the right clothes, the right car, the right neighborhood can help compensate for that fundamental imperfection: nonwhiteness.[58]

Asayesh's reflections help to explain why Iranian Americans—like many others trying to earn their white stripes—are so often concerned with projecting images of success and wealth. Iranian Americans in Los Angeles are well-known for making their homes in Beverly Hills, driving only a BMW or Mercedes, and dressing in the most high-priced designer fashions. For example, 1995's Alicia Silverstone vehicle *Clueless*, set in Beverly Hills, had an incisive and comical reference to the city's Persian residents. At one point, the lead character points away from the camera and comments, "that's the Persian mafia. You can't hang with them unless you own a BMW."[59] The camera then turns to reveal a throng of Iranian American teenagers outfitted stylishly in black, driving their German imports.

Throughout the Middle Eastern community, the manipulation of appearance also emerges as a quintessential form of covering. Middle Eastern women frequently dye their hair blond or wear colored contact lenses to downplay their more "ethnic" features. Middle Eastern men will go by the name "Mike" for Mansour, "Mory" for Morteza, "Al" for Ali, and "Moe" for Mohammed. Such tactics may appear petty and even futile, but they can be surprisingly effective. I was recently told a story about an Iranian American attorney who went by the name "Moe" instead of his birthname, Mohammed. One day, he was selected for extra screening at the airport. After showing his identification to the TSA workers and undergoing the additional security measures, he calmly protested, wondering out loud if he had been targeted on the basis of his ethnicity. The TSA guard looked puzzled. "It's not like your name is Mohammed or something," he guffawed. Absent the "Mohammed" stigma, Moe had become white.

We also see covering in even the most simple of choices: hair style. It has long been noted that African Americans have a variety of choices on how to wear their hair—including straightened, short, braided, Afro, cornrows, or dreadlocks—each of which ineluctably effects how society perceives them.[60] Hair style functions as a signaling device that determines the degree to which an African American will be racialized as stereotypically "black," assimilable, or something in between. As Devon Carbado and Mitu Gulati observe, coiffing choices can serve as a disturbing marketing device:

> A black person's vulnerability to discrimination is shaped in part by her racial position on this spectrum. The less stereotypically black she is, the more palatable her identity is. The more palatable her identity is, the less vulnerable she is to discrimination. The relationship among black unconventionality, racial palatability, and vulnerability to discrimination creates

an incentive for black people to signal—through identity performances—
that they are unconventionally black.[61]

For a Middle Eastern man, the issue of facial hair is similarly riddled
with semiotic landmines. Since at least the time of Czar Peter the Great,
who in 1698 mandated that all male Russian nobles shave to appear more
Western and civilized,[62] facial hair has held symbolic meaning. Over the
past two decades, as images of the lavishly bearded Ayatollah Khomeini
and Osama bin Laden have flooded the airwaves, the beard, the Middle
East, and radical Islam have grown inextricably intertwined in the American imagination. In the post-9/11 world, I do not go to the airport without
shaving first.

A segment from Sasha Baron-Cohen's brilliant mockumentary *Borat:
Cultural Learnings of America for Make Benefit Glorious Nation of Kazakhstan* exemplifies the link between racial identification and facial hair.
In the movie, Baron-Cohen's Borat character, a purported Kazakh television personality, embarks on a road trip across the United States to gain
a better understanding of American society. In one scene shot in Salem,
Virginia, Borat attends a rodeo. Before delivering his rendition of the Kazakh national anthem, along with some political commentary that almost
gets him killed, Borat chats with the rodeo producer, Bobby Rowe.[63] In the
course of their conversation, Rowe provides Borat with some unsolicited
but friendly advice: change your look to avoid suspicions that you might
be a terrorist or Islamic fundamentalist. "Shave that dadgum mustache
off so you're not so conspicuous," Rowe enthusiastically recommends. "So
you look like maybe an Italian or something."[64]

Affiliation also plays a potent role in covering Middle Eastern identity.
Two prevalent covering methodologies in the Middle Eastern community
exploit society's frequent conflation of religious affiliation and national origin with racial identification. Take the example of a doctor I once knew.
He was born and grew up in Iran. He had then received his medical training in Switzerland, after which he and his wife had ultimately immigrated
to the United States. When people asked where he was from, he would
apparently say "Switzerland." Throughout his community, people thought
of him and his Iranian wife as European. And I suspect that is just how
he wanted it.

What is particularly interesting about this example is that the doctor
and his family never engaged in a wholesale rejection of their ethnicity
or cultural heritage. Their sense of identity and projection of it were far

more complex than that. In fact, the doctor was a dedicated student of classical Persian poetry and prose and hosted a weekly gathering of Iranian immigrants at his house to discuss, in their native tongue, works in the Persian canon. But to the outside world he was Swiss. And who could blame the family for performing this act of covering? There is little doubt that it is a lot easier to be Swiss and deal with the attendant images of temporal precision, chocolate, neutrality, and the Red Cross than to be perceived as Iranian, when people immediately associate your ethnic identity with a host of unpleasantries.

The imprecise relationship between ethnicity and nationality arises in a broader context and represents a particular difficulty in conducting affirmative-action programs. Latin America has witnessed several waves of migration from Europe. Some of these immigrants have subsequently relocated to the United States. However, they sometimes draw on their intermediate stop in Latin America as a basis for claiming "Hispanic" heritage on school and job applications. In one sense, their choice is entirely warranted. *Hispanic* is generally not characterized as a "race" at all. The University of California at Los Angeles exemplifies this idea in its definition of Hispanic/Latino as "[p]ersons of Latin American (e.g., Central American, South American, Cuban, Puerto Rican) culture or origin, regardless of race."[65] In another sense, if identification of Hispanic heritage is used for affirmative-action purposes and is meant to offset both past and present discrimination, such a practice dilutes the means-ends fit of remedial programs.

Many Iranians or Arabs of Jewish background cover by rationally exploiting mainstream (mis)perceptions of "Jewishness" as both a religion and an ethnicity. For example, although the Jewish Iranian population is relatively large, especially in Los Angeles, the very existence of a Jewish Iranian population is a surprise to the many people who view Iran as an Islamic monolith. By identifying themselves to the world as Jewish, these Jewish Iranians tend to avoid any further questions about their ethnicity, as people assume their ethnicity is Jewish and that they therefore are white (i.e., Ashkenazi Jewish) and not Middle Eastern. A Jewish Iranian poet I once knew demonstrated her profound awareness of the way in which this popular misperception could be exploited for assimilatory purposes. Explaining the extent of her Persian pride, she pointed out that she had embraced her Iranian heritage despite the obvious covering tactics at her disposal. "Since I'm Jewish, I don't have to be Iranian," she remarked. "Yet I choose to be."

Finally, with respect to activism, we have witnessed profound covering in the Middle Eastern community. As Kenji Yoshino argues, many minorities are reticent to become involved in the fight to protect their civil rights, lest they be associated with militant ethnics and become racialized. In the Middle Eastern American community, there is a profound wariness of political involvement, a fact revealed by the dearth of elected officials of Middle Eastern descent, even in areas with large concentrations. For example, it is believed that the highest ranking Iranian American public officeholder in the United States is Jimmy Delshad, the mayor of Beverly Hills.[66] Delshad was only elected to his post in 2007.[67]

Besides covering based on association, appearance, affiliation, and activism, the downplaying of racial identity occurs in numerous other ways in the Middle Eastern community. A classic form of covering occurs when you ask Iranian Americans about their ethnicity. Often, they will respond "Persian," not "Iranian." The reason is easy to understand. Persia evokes images of an ancient empire, a proud history, magnificent rugs (and cats), and a rich culture. Iran, by contrast, evokes images of the hostage crisis, the Axis of Evil, radical fundamentalism, jihad, and fatwas.

My own last name, despite its apparent in-your-face declaration of my likely ethnic origins, often creates an exploitable ambiguity. The "Tehran" seems to designate Iranian roots, but the suffix "-ian" connotes Armenian descent. Read literally, therefore, it might mean "Armenian from Tehran." And perceptions of where I fit in someone's worldview vary radically depending on whether someone chooses to focus on the first or last part of my surname. Individuals who are familiar with Armenians will highlight the "ian" and categorize me as an Armenian. As an Armenian, I am perceived as Christian, white, and an American ethnic, much like an Italian or Greek. As an Iranian, I am perceived as Islamic, nonwhite, and a perpetual foreigner. As an Armenian, I have no link to terrorism and I do not have to answer for the problems in the Middle East. For those in the know, my ancestors were the victims of the first genocide of the twentieth century—the Turks' slaughter of the Armenians—and my ancestors founded the first Christian nation. As an Iranian, my roots are decidedly less sympathetic.

Recently, this striking dichotomy presented itself with disarming clarity. At an academic function, I met a fellow law professor who, upon seeing my last name, remarked, "So you're Armenian." I nodded. He proceeded to tell me about his fondness for and professional ties to the Armenian community and how several of his close friends were of Armenian descent.

The next day, I had an appointment with a new primary-care physician. After completing the necessary paperwork, I waited for the doctor in one of his examination rooms. After several minutes, he walked in, grabbed my file, and, without missing a beat, queried, "So you're Iranian?" He was staring at my name on the patient-information form that I had filled out. I nodded, and then he dropped the following curious line: "Boy, I hope *we* don't have to go to war with *you* soon." I was speechless, though I thought about sarcastically apologizing to him (he had a Germanic surname) about how we had to go to war with him a few years back during World War II. But I was there for health care, not a political debate. "I hope we don't have to go to war with *them* either," I replied. The divide could not be more pronounced: as Armenian, I am a friend; as Iranian, I am a foe.

Beyond covering, Middle Eastern assimilation also crosses into the realm of passing and even conversion. As a matter of pride, many Middle Easterners (especially those from older generations, for which the importance of whiteness was perhaps more accentuated) insist on actually being considered white. In this regard, they are no different than prior immigrant groups. For example, in all but one of the many reported racial-prerequisite naturalization cases,[68] the petitioners claimed to be white, despite the fact that it was much harder to establish white, rather than black, status. At the time, many states had laws on the books declaring any individual with a single quantum of black blood to be black by law.[69]

There are, of course, some exceptions to the inexorable gravitation of American ethnics to seek white recognition. Where nonwhite groups dominate, performance of nonwhiteness can be a condition for nonwhite privilege. For example, Italian American teenagers in the inner city frequently perform nonwhiteness to distance themselves from the white hegemon and to facilitate their assimilation with other urban youth. Similarly, in a world where racial diversity is not only increasingly tolerated but celebrated, a veritable ethnic-chic movement has emerged. One example of increasing nonwhite identification comes from Hawai'i, where the past few decades have witnessed a remarkable surge in the percentage of individuals who claim native Hawaiian identity—a surge that cannot statistically be explained by natural growth patterns. For one, native Hawaiians qualify for numerous social, economic, and political privileges not extended to non-Hawaiians.[70] Even more significantly, the rise of the Hawaiian-pride movement, the wake of Hawaiian sovereignty politics, and a revitalization of Hawaiian institutions, including the ancient language, has led to a celebration of all things Hawaiian.[71] At Punahou School, a college-preparatory academy long viewed as the bastion of *haole*[72] missionary power, white students dub themselves with polysyllabic Hawaiian middle names just to have a claim, however tenuous, to the Hawaiian culture.[73] It is therefore not surprising that recent census numbers show that, compared with a decade ago, almost 50 percent more Hawaiian residents now consider themselves descendants of native Hawaiian stock. The 1990 census counted 162,279 individuals of Hawaiian descent in Hawai'i; the 2000 census counted 239,655.[74]

In the continental United States, however, white privilege still reigns supreme, and, naturally, immigrant groups still seek white recognition.[75] This is certainly true for the Iranian American population. The United States has seen a huge wave of immigration from Iran since the 1979 revolution. In 1996, it was estimated that almost 1.5 million Iranians resided in the United States, a figure that had grown from just a few thousand in the 1970s.[76] However, despite changes to the 2000 census, which allowed Middle Eastern individuals such as Iranian Americans to identify themselves as something other than just "white," it appears that very few Iranian Americans took the opportunity to do so. In fact, only 338,266 individuals in the United States identified themselves as Iranian.[77] The majority of Iranians, it seems, chose conversion. Any visitor to Los Angeles (often referred to as Tehrangeles or Irangeles) can attest that there are probably 338,266 individuals of Iranian descent living in Southern California, let alone the rest of the country.

The reason for this statistical discrepancy is not too difficult to ascertain: having fled a severely repressive government in their homeland, many Iranians have a profound mistrust of government. As a result, it is hardly surprising that they would balk at the chance to single themselves out conveniently to the government for identification and tracking purposes. Additionally, there is a strong desire within the Iranian community to assimilate. Ask typical Iranian Americans if they are white, and they will say, "Of course." Then, inevitably, they will tell you that the word *Iran* comes from the Sanskrit word meaning "Land of the Aryans" and that they, not the Germans, are the original Aryans.

When I was in grade school, my mother provided me with some goodnatured but potentially disastrous advice: if anyone approaches you with racial hostility, calmly explain to them that, as a Persian, you are the true Aryan. I remember telling her that skinheads were unlikely to pause to have a discussion with me about nomadic migration patterns and racial genealogy dating back to antiquity. My mother's posture, however, was widely shared. As poet Lelah Khalili observes, Iranian Americans frequently

> pride [them]selves for being so closely related to the Hansels and Gretels of Europe, . . . defend [their] 'Aryan' blood vociferously . . . [and] introduce [them]selves as descendants of a race of Indo-Europeans (or Indo-Aryans)—whatever that is—who came across the Eastern planes [*sic*] to Iran and who are the ethnic cousins of those healthy and strapping blond-and-blue-eyed Germanic people populating Central Europe.[78]

When this claim of lineage is combined with Iran's geographical proximity of the Caucasus Mountains, the inescapable conclusion might appear to be one of whiteness. A recent Ninth Circuit case involving an asylum seeker from Iran epitomizes this mindset. The 1996 decision notes that the asylum seeker designated his ethnicity as something curiously (feline or libationary?) called "White Persian."[79]

The craving for such judicial affirmation of whiteness mirrors the events of a century earlier, when in *Ex parte Dow* a federal district court held that Syrians were not white.[80] Denied membership in the racial category needed for naturalization, the petitioners motioned for a rehearing, which the court sympathetically granted.[81] The request for, and acceptance of, the rehearing are particularly salient since they were not grounded in the potential economic or political injury that such a racial judgment would cause Syrian Americans. Instead, the rehearing petition and grant rested on the profound psychological trauma that a formal designation of nonwhite status would inflict on Syrians as a group. As the court later wrote,

> Deep feeling has been manifested on the part of the Syrian immigrants because of what has been termed by them the humiliation inflicted upon, and mortification suffered by, Syrians in America by the previous decree in this matter which they construe as deciding that they do not (as they term it) belong to the "white race."[82]

Iranian American writer Gelareh Asayesh recalls the radical change in racial self-perception that she underwent upon arrival in the United States. In Iran, she was indisputably white. In the United States, however, both friends and strangers informed her that she was not. The transformation, she candidly admits, was painful. "If I was having trouble making the transition from one racial framework to another, it was not because I was above the fray but because I did not want to relinquish the privileges accorded me in one framework and denied me in the other. What passed for white in Iran was colored in America; and I didn't like being demoted."[83] Not surprisingly, this appetite for whiteness is prevalent throughout Middle Eastern culture. No group escaped the desire for whiteness, as even the Egyptian royal family traditionally associated itself with Europe by claiming Albanian descent.[84] Whiteness, among Middle Easterners, is almost uniformly considered a mark of beauty. Although the college textbook by Daniel Bates and Amal Rassam, *Peoples and Cultures of the Middle East*, oddly claims that "there is no prevailing ideology of race based on color," it readily admits that "in much of the [Middle East] light skin is considered a mark of beauty and higher status."[85]

Of course, not everyone seeks white recognition. The younger generation of Middle Eastern Americans is much more likely than prior generations not only to eschew covering techniques but to celebrate actively their ethnicity and even insist on their nonwhiteness. Nevertheless, the gravitation toward whiteness remains a dominant social force. It is frequently so doggedly pursued that it actually serves to a group's long-term detriment.

Mexican Americans provide an instructive example of the tension between individual and collective interests, and of short- and long-term consequences. Like Middle Easterners, Latinos have suffered a problematic dualistic ontology of racial identification and a craving for whiteness that, in prior eras, has frustrated the vindication of their civil rights. Mexican Americans have often sought refuge in covering activities. Rodolfo Acuña, for example, notes the tendency of the Mexican American community in Los Angeles to emphasize its Spanish (i.e., European and white) roots.[86] As he argues, many Mexican Americans have internalized an "anything but Mexican" mindset, or colonial mentality, that fuels their desire for white recognition and leads them to emphasize their Spanish, Italian, or French ancestry.[87]

In prior eras, this irrepressible claim to whiteness has actually undermined civil rights efforts. In the landmark suit *Hernandez v. Texas*,[88] Pete Hernandez challenged the systematic exclusion of Mexican Americans from juries in Jackson County, Texas. In response, the State of Texas claimed, among other things, that there was no racial discrimination occurring since individuals of Mexican descent were not a separate class from whites. The Supreme Court ultimately sided with Hernandez, holding that Mexicans were a distinct race from whites for equal protection purposes and that the Equal Protection Clause applied to all forms of race discrimination, not just discrimination against blacks. Surprisingly though, Hernandez faced strong opposition to his position from within the Mexican American community. Gustavo Garcia, a civil rights litigator of the time, commented, "Caucasians were on the jury. Mexicans are Caucasian. So what's all the fussing about?"[89] To Mexican Americans such as Garcia, the recognition of their whiteness trumped the vindication of their legal and political rights or the preservation of equal protection under the law. This "Faustian pact with whiteness"[90] parallels the extant Middle Eastern hunger for judicial affirmations of whiteness, even when it inures to the group's long-term detriment.[91]

In sum, like the Irish, Slavs, Italians, Greeks, and Mexicans before them, Middle Eastern immigrants have sought to secure their position in American society through the ultimate prize of white recognition. The struggle, however, has not been easy. Formal recognition of whiteness by state and federal governments belies a history of discrimination against Americans of Middle Eastern descent. The wide range of both passing and covering strategies adopted by Middle Easterners reflects the response to this discrimination. Combined with the process of selective racialization, it is a practice that has grown increasingly problematic. The rewards for effective covering are, in the short term, positive. But in the aggregate, the phenomena of covering and selective racialization have helped to perpetuate negative stereotypes about Middle Easterners while frustrating the development of an effective community response to issues of concern for Middle Eastern Americans.

Thus, in order to combat the discrimination facing Middle Eastern Americans, we must look not only without but within. Perhaps this is the most lasting contribution from Charles Lawrence's seminal article: because of our shared experiences as Americans, we

> inevitably share many ideas, attitudes, and beliefs that attach significance to an individual's race and induce negative feelings and opinions about nonwhites. To the extent that this cultural belief system has influenced all of us, we are all racists. At the same time, most of us are unaware of our racism.[92]

We must therefore all engage in vigorous analysis of the broad psychological mechanisms at work in the racialization and discrimination process. In the end, as Lawrence concluded some twenty years ago, "[a] difficult and painful exploration beats death at the hands of the disease."[93] Recognition of the unconscious dynamics at play in the race-making process is a necessary first step in dismantling racial hierarchy for all Americans, both Middle Eastern and otherwise.

Unfortunately, however, the pervasion of increasingly hostile media portraits of the Middle East and of Middle Easterners has further exacerbated the problem. Visual representations of the Middle East and of Middle Easterners are, therefore, the focus of our next chapter.

4

The Last Minstrel Show?
Middle Easterners in Media

Art is the means through which we order the universe. Images play an instrumental role in both reflecting and constructing our notions of reality. As a result, they inextricably affect racial perceptions. Bearing this in mind, we turn our attention to the depiction of Middle Easterners in popular culture and the mainstream media. In the past, Hollywood—the world's most influential producer of images—has endured severe criticism for its part in perpetuating invidious racial stereotypes. The entertainment industry has responded by encouraging the casting of individuals from historically underrepresented groups and eschewing the most egregious and cardboard portrayals of ethnic minorities, with one notable exception: Middle Easterners. Representations of Middle Easterners as barbaric terrorists, loathsome misogynists, and religious lunatics continue to dominate the silver screen. In part, such portrayals are tolerated because of negative public opinion toward the Middle East. At the same time, these images not only reflect existing stereotypes, but they also help to ossify and further perpetuate them. With flawed deductive extrapolation, the public reifies these representations of Middle Easterners as a fair and balanced reflection of reality. The resulting impact on policy—both in the practice of racial profiling and elsewhere—is alarming, and the psychological toll on the Middle Eastern American community is grave and underappreciated.

Cinema and Stereotype

As numerous scholars have argued, minority groups have long faced the problem of insidious typecasting on the silver screen.[1] Two recent empirical accounts epitomize the compelling research on this issue. In his study *Greasers and Gringos*, Steven Bender details how media depictions have influenced public policy toward the Latino community over the past century. Specifically, Bender documents the ways in which images of indolent, mendacious, hot-headed, and hypersexual Latinos have perpetuated certain stereotypes. The stereotypes, he argues, have adversely affected the treatment of Latinos by police and prosecutors, the course of immigration reform, and the scope and exercise of Latinos' legal rights. Similarly, in *The Slanted Screen*, director Jeff Adachi exposes the rampant deployment of invidious stereotypes of Asian Americans in film throughout the years. Hollywood has persistently abetted the emasculation and desexualization of the Asian male by assiduously averting depictions of them in romantic situations. *Romeo Must Die*, a rare blockbuster featuring an Asian American lead, starred Jet Li opposite actress/singer/sex-symbol Aaliyah. Despite the fact that the storyline derived from *Romeo and Juliet*, the movie carefully avoided any intimacy, let alone a love scene, between the stars. In the movie's most explicit moment, Li and Aaliyah briefly share a hug. The film suggests the continued survival of an implicit, racially grounded Hays Code[2] in Hollywood.[3]

At the same time, few Hollywood movies feature nonwhite lead protagonists,[4] and the subject matter of mainstream releases infrequently involve minority groups. Even in the instances when a storyline treats a minority-related theme, the action is predominantly driven by a white character. As legal scholar Keith Aoki has asked, "Why do filmmakers generally seem to assume that a mainstream audience wants, indeed needs, a white character as an avenue into any story about an Asian American, or for that matter any other minority community?"[5] Take the recent wave of Hollywood movies focusing long overdue attention on the African continent. *The Last King of Scotland*, a purported biography of Ugandan dictator Idi Amin, used a wholly fictional young Scottish doctor, played by James McAvoy, as the central character and the propelling protagonist.[6] *Blood Diamond*, an exposé of the horrors of the diamond trade, uses Danny Archer, a white mercenary from Zimbabwe played by Leonardo DiCaprio, as its chief protagonist and Maddy Bowen, a white American journalist played by Jennifer Connelly, as his love interest.[7] In the few instances when this trend has not held true, it has taken the insistence of a minority in a significant position of power to force the issue. For example, Justin Lin, the director of both *Better Luck Tomorrow* and *The Fast and the Furious: Tokyo Drift*, found studio executives pressuring him to recast the movies with Caucasian characters in lead roles, despite the fact that both movies featured plotlines that inextricably involved Asian characters. It was only at Lin's insistence and when he exercised his leverage as the films' director that the features were made with Asian leads.[8]

Sadly, it is still a notable victory for minority groups when a Hollywood movie does something as simple as casting a minority in a non-stereotypical role that acknowledges his or her ethnicity without calling undue attention to it. As Steven Bender notes, a youth-oriented blockbuster as seemingly apolitical as Robert Rodriguez's *Spy Kids* represented a momentous occasion for Latinos in film: "By placing Latino characters at the forefront and not depicting them as outside the mainstream, Rodriguez may achieve more than he would by raising a cinematic fist for racial equality."[9] The profound impact of such a seemingly mundane casting decision should not be underestimated.

There is much to criticize about Hollywood's historical treatment of minority actors, its perpetuation of invidious racial stereotypes, and its failure to address diverse subject matter. On the other hand, there has been significant outcry against Hollywood's history of unfavorable portraits and treatments of numerous minority groups. To its credit, the entertainment industry has begun to respond constructively. In recent years, more mainstream movies have subverted and even actively mocked stereotyping of Asians[10] and African Americans.[11] Consider the movies *Better Luck Tomorrow*, released in 2002, and *Harold and Kumar Go to White Castle*, released in 2004. Both features delivered resounding blows to the pernicious and oppressive "model minority" myth by casting Asian Americans in leading roles portraying characters that are sexual, prone to hedonistic bouts of drinking and drug abuse, and yet simultaneously ambitious, witty, and intelligent. At the same time, the public has also grown less tolerant of the demonization of minority groups. There is still, however, one notable exception to this trend: Middle Easterners.[12]

The Treachery of Images

With alarming regularity, the entertainment industry continues to cast Middle Easterners in a largely stereotypical light. Jack Shaheen's analysis of popular films documents the consistent vilification of individuals of Middle Eastern descent on celluloid.[13] Hollywood does not typically feature Middle Easterners in starring roles. When they do appear onscreen, the men are typically portrayed as wife beaters, religious zealots, and terrorists.[14] Meanwhile, the women are often represented as cowering, weak, and oppressed. The most recognized Iranian American actress is Shohreh

Aghdashloo, and her two most prominent roles have covered both terrains: she played a reticent and abused Iranian American wife in *House of Sand and Fog* (a role for which she received an Oscar nomination) and an Islamic matriarch of a domestic terror cell in the Fox drama *24*.

The blockbuster *Rules of Engagement*, which was released a year and a half before 9/11, epitomizes Hollywood's deeply troubled handling of Middle Eastern portrayals. In a key scene in the movie, an angry Arab mob gathers outside the American embassy in Yemen. Filled with profound hatred of the United States and animated by a barbaric thirst for blood and violence, numerous Arab women and children—both boys and girls—appear to be threatening the Marines sent to protect the embassy. When snipers open fire on the Marines, the Marines decide to retaliate by opening fire on the crowd, killing eighty-three Yemenites in all. In one closeup, we see a five-year-old Yemeni girl shooting an automatic pistol at the Americans. As Jack Shaheen observes,

> no Hollywood WWI, WWII, or Korean War movie has ever shown America's fighting forces slaughtering children. Yet, near the conclusion of *Rules of Engagement*, US marines open fire on the Yemenis, shooting 83 men, women, and children. During the scene, viewers rose to their feet, clapped and cheered. Boasts director Friedkin, *"I've seen audiences stand up and applaud the film throughout the United States."*[15]

The American-Arab Anti-Discrimination Committee deemed *Rules of Engagement*, with its ludicrous portrait of young Arab girls (even an amputee) attempting to kill Americans, as "probably the most vicious anti-Arab racist film even made by a major Hollywood studio."[16] Critics from numerous mainstream media outlets—including CNN, *Entertainment Weekly*, the *Los Angeles Times*, *Time*, and the *Christian Science Monitor*—condemned the film's blatant bigotry.[17] As reviewer Mark Freeman noted,

> The Yemeni people are painted in the broadest, most racist terms imaginable. Friedkin lets his camera linger over their angry faces, exaggerating their difference: the robes, the veils, the beards, the bizarre, harsh language, and their keen desire for violence. . . . The message of *Rules of Engagement* is the necessity to kill all those who actively oppose the United States and that the murder of women and children is acceptable in such cases. The implicit suggestion is that no matter what, these

Middle Eastern fanatics will be carrying a gun and a desire to shoot you dead first—even innocent looking six year olds—so their annihilation is in the best interests of the "civilised" world. This hysterical, paranoid fear of the Other pervades every scene in *Rules of Engagement*, it celebrates the death of these Yemeni people because they do not share a love for the USA. Much like the absurd representation of the Russians in the McCarthyist '50s (and again in the Reaganite '80s) those from the Middle East, those not sharing a Christian background, those who dress, speak, act differently to the shining example of America are an instant threat. Wiping them out, despite their guilt or innocence, age or attitude, is *Rules of Engagement*'s solution to the problem.[18]

Despite its virulent racism, the film topped the U.S. box office for two weeks and earned its studio tens of millions in profit. The regular applause and cheer that the slaughter of the Arab crowd by the Marines garnered from audiences typified *Rules of Engagement*'s resonance with the public and the film's appeal to our most jingoistic tendencies. The movie also bucked the trend of increased sensitivity toward minority groups in recent mainstream features. Compare, for example, the treatment of the Arabs in *Rules of Engagement* with the portrait of the Japanese in Clint Eastwood's recent World War II drama *Letters from Iwo Jima*, which received criticism for what some observers felt was an overly *sympathetic* portrayal of Axis Japan.[19]

In contemplating the enduring acceptability of anti–Middle Eastern sentiments, I am reminded of an incident from my youth. In December 1988, the world's biggest band at the time, Guns N' Roses, had just come out with their eagerly anticipated follow-up to *Appetite for Destruction*, their multiplatinum major-label debut. The new album, *G N' R Lies*, was no disappointment. Partly acoustic, *Lies* spawned a decade's worth of unplugged performances on MTV and solidified the band's status as the era's both most popular and most critically acclaimed hard-rock band. Guns N' Roses stood alone in bridging the gap between the cross-dressing, spandex-wearing, big-haired bubblegum metal of the mid-'80s and the alternative, darker grunge that supplanted it in the early '90s. All my closest high-school friends were fans of their music, and this appreciation for the band had always brought us together. So it was with great anticipation that, one Friday, we headed to the record store en masse to pick up a copy of *Lies*. We then went back to the house of one of my friends, where he placed the album on the turntable (those were still the days of vinyl) and we listened, in a single sitting, to the work from beginning to end. We were all taken aback by the musicianship of the entire album. But it was the final song, "One in a Million," that brought us to a complete silence. A dark, haunting melody, it played on my friend's stereo. Its guttural, searing guitar line foreshadowed the ominous first-person lyric, the inner monologue of a small-town, midwestern white teen arriving for the first time in Los Angeles—portrayed, as in *Blade Runner,* as an apocalyptical multiracial inferno burning at the edge of the continent, one quake, mudslide, flood, fire, or riot away from Armageddon. True to the subject matter, the lyrics took a disturbing and troubling turn. With callous, unremorseful bravado, Rose sang,

Police and Niggers, that's right
Get out of my way
Don't need to buy none of your
Gold chains today

Moments later, with a reference to Iran, the lyrics became personal to me:

Immigrants and faggots
They make no sense to me
They come to our country
And think they'll do as they please
Like start some mini Iran
Or spread some fucking disease
They talk so many goddamn ways
It's all greek to me

I looked around to watch my friends' reactions. Like typical teenagers, they appreciated Axl's unapologetic rant, as racist and homophobic as it was. But just as the guys were bonding over the album, replaying the song and even singing along with its lyrics, smiling, in an odd acknowledgment of me, at the line about Iran, I felt a profound sense of Otherness. To this day, I listen to the song with deep ambivalence and an unease born both from the lyrics and the chilling sensation of separateness I felt that day twenty years ago.

Rose argued that he had taken poetic license to express the innermost thoughts of what any mild-mannered midwesterner might think upon arriving, for the first time, in the heart of the big city. Yet Rose's poetic-license defense was belied in an interview he did with *Rolling Stone*, in which he revealed that the inspiration for his Iran stanza was not the perspective of some fictional character but was born of his own personal experience. In an earlier incident, he and guitarist Slash reportedly entered a convenience store only to be chased out by the Iranian clerk, who was wielding a knife and swinging it wildly at them. Commented Rose,

> When I use the word immigrants, what I'm talking about is going to a 7-11 or Village pantries—a lot of people from countries like Iran, Pakistan, China, Japan et cetera, get jobs in these convenience stores and gas stations. Then they treat you as if you don't belong here. I've been chased out of a store with Slash by a six-foot-tall Iranian with a butcher knife because he didn't like the way we were dressed. Scared me to death. All I could see in my mind was a picture of my arm on the ground, blood going everywhere. When I get scared, I get mad. I grabbed the top of one of these big orange garbage cans and went back at him with this shield, going, "Come on!" I didn't want to back down from this guy.[20]

Naturally, the song generated a storm of controversy, as serious concerns were raised over Rose's use of the N word and even about the blatant homophobia. The voluminous coverage dedicated to the troubling lyrics, however, scarcely mentioned Rose's anti-Iranian commentary or his immigrant bashing. Indeed, the extensive Wikipedia entry for the song focuses on the controversy surrounding the antiblack and antigay sentiments in "One in a Million." Not a word is mentioned about the anti-Iranian hatred.[21]

As the final available frontier for blatantly racist portrayals in mass media, it is almost as if Middle Easterners have become the target of the sublimated wrath that was previously (and acceptably) directed in film, television, music, and books against African Americans, Latinos, Native Americans, Asians, and gays. Worse yet, the problem is growing. Paralleling the changing view of Middle Easterners in the American imagination, the portrait of Middle Easterners on celluloid and elsewhere has also undergone a fundamental transformation, growing even more pernicious through time. In prior decades, depictions of the Middle East focused on the exotic and mysterious, whereas the releases of recent years have increasingly emphasized the perfidious and barbarous. Laurence Michalak's study of mainstream movies with Middle Eastern themes carefully documents this disturbing trend. Comparing 87 such films from the 1920s with 112 made in the 1960s, Michalak finds that the earlier depictions primarily romanticized the Middle East and high-lighted the charm and allure of its people, whereas movies of the later era increasingly associated the region and its inhabitants with violence and a panoply of illicit practices, including torture, prostitution, money laundering, and treason.[22] On television, the stereotypical treatment is similar. As David Prochaska observes,

> On TV, almost all of the fictional "Arab" figures—who are not even played by Arab actors—are typecast as villains and buffoons, ranging from oriental despots, backward sheikhs, and terrorists, to wealthy playboys, assassins, and white slavers. Negatively stereotyped Arabs have appeared on *Vegas, Fantasy Island, Bionic Woman, The Six Million Dollar Man, Police Woman, McCloud, Hawaii Five-O Cannon, Columbo, Medical Center, Wonder Woman, Trapper John, M.D., Charlie's Angels,* and *Rockford Files.*[23]

Hollywood is by no means alone in perpetuating such stereotypical images. According to Suha Sabbagh's study *Sex, Lies and Stereotypes: The Image of Arabs in American Popular Fiction*, Arabs were prominently featured in thirty-three best-selling works of American fiction during the 1970s and '80s. Only one, John le Carré's *The Little Drummer Girl*, depicted them in a favorable or historically accurate light. Advertisers have also done their part. A few years ago, Thomson & Thomson, a prominent trademark research firm, ran an unsettling advertisement in no less than the official publication of the American Bar Association, the *ABA Journal*. The spread depicted an Arab raising a sword to decapitate a man and featured the following tagline: "Without Expert Trademark Research You Could Be Put in a Compromising Situation." Taken by itself, such an image would be suspect, not to mention in poor taste, especially given the horrifying recent round of widely disseminated videos depicting actual terrorist executions of hostages. But in a society in which Middle Easterners rarely appear in advertising, their sudden presentation, when cast in the most stereotypical of lights, becomes deeply troubling.

Besides enduring consistently negative portrayals on the screen and in the media, Middle Easterners also suffer from relative invisibility in two different ways. First, mainstream filmmakers often cast non–Middle Eastern actors in Middle Eastern roles. Second, Middle Easterners remain largely absent from the screen even when the setting or plot warrants, or even necessitates, the inclusion of a Middle Eastern character.

In a time-honored practice, the movie industry has traditionally insisted on casting white actors, even when a role involves a person of color. In days of yore, Hollywood would hire an Italian man, slap on some war paint, and have him play a Native American,[24] or would take a raven-haired white female, offensively slant her eyes, and cast her as an Asian.[25] Of course, there is nothing inherently wrong with race-blind casting, as long as it works both ways. But in reality, it never has; one rarely sees, for example, an African American, Latino, or Asian actor cast as a white character.

Yet with the lobbying efforts of such organizations as the NAACP, Hollywood has recently abandoned such racially insensitive practices,[26] except with respect to Middle Easterners. As far back as the silent movies, Hollywood has cast non–Middle Easterners as Middle Eastern characters. Rudolph Valentino played the lead Arab roles in several silent movies, including *The Sheik* and *Son of the Sheik*. Numerous white actors have followed suit through the years, including Douglas Fairbanks (*The Thief of Baghdad*), Sean Connery (*The Wind and the Lion*), and Albert Molina (*Not Without My Daughter*). However, unlike the change we have witnessed with respect to other ethnic groups, the practice continues unabated to this day. Take the recent international blockbuster *300*, a retelling of the ancient Battle of Thermopylae between King Leonidas's ragtag crew of 300 Spartans and Emperor Xerxes's 120,000-strong Persian army. The movie raised a considerable stir in Iran, where the government issued a press release condemning its savage portrait of the Persians and denouncing the movie as a form of "psychological warfare" by the United States. Whatever the merits of such an argument (though it should be pointed out that few Americans even associate Persia with Iran), there was a problematic aspect of the film that remained completely ignored: most of the "Persians" in the movie were actually played by Hispanic or African American actors. In fact, not a single major character was actually played by a Middle Easterner, let alone a Persian—a particularly shocking fact when one considers how it easy it would have been to cast a Middle Easterner in the movie, especially given the large Persian population living within close proximity of Hollywood.[27]

Just as perniciously, Middle Easterners have been whitewashed from the screen even in settings where reasonable and normalized portraits of them would have made eminent sense. Take the long-running Fox series *Beverly Hills 90210*, which followed the lives of a fictitious group of teenagers residing in the wealthy West Los Angeles enclave. In the name of research, and research alone, I have personally viewed all 296 episodes of the series during its decade-long run and never witnessed a single Persian character depicted. In fact, the closest the show came to having a Middle Eastern character was an episode guest-starring Matthew Perry, long before his days on *Friends*.[28] In the episode, Perry plays Roger Azarian, a successful student-athlete at West Beverly High. The only indications of Azarian's Middle Eastern origins are his Armenian last name and several veiled references to his father's status as a first-generation American. While Azarian is on his way to a good college and a potential run on the professional tennis tour, he deeply resents the pressure that his successful father has forced on him. Unable to deal with the crushing burden of living in his father's shadow, Azarian plans to kill his father in a murder-suicide. Brandon Walsh, the good-natured Anglo-Minnesotan lead protagonist, naturally saves the day at the eleventh hour.

The wholesale evisceration of any Middle Eastern presence from the television show is utterly perplexing when one considers the fact that at least 40 percent of the teenage population in Beverly Hills is Persian.[29] It would be absurd to set a television show in Harlem and not depict a single black person, unthinkable to cast a program in rural Idaho and not have a single white person in the cast. Yet, for ten years, *Beverly Hills 90210* never featured a single Persian character. With the absence of any terrorist-related themes, it appears, the series had no use for one. For a show with several thousand characters, the complete absence of a group that makes up almost half the real Beverly Hills teenage population is nothing short of stunning.

Of course, the wholesale whitewashing of an entire ethnic group is not an entirely new phenomenon. As Steven Bender points out, Latinos have similarly faced systematic exclusion from many television programs—including *Friends*, *Seinfeld*, and *Will & Grace*—set in cities with large Latino populations.[30] While strides have been made in more fairly representing other ethnic groups, Middle Easterners have made little progress. In recent years, political pressure has convinced various media arms to adopt diversity initiatives to rectify the systematic underrepresentation of minorities in television and film.

One example of such an initiative is the Screen Actors Guild's Diversity-in-Casting Incentive (DCI). Touted prominently in SAG's public-relations materials and on its website, the DCI incentivizes filmmakers to cast minorities and other historically underrepresented groups by offering lower minimum wage rates under the Master Agreement if a certain percentage of speaking roles go to diversity actors. Although SAG's DCI represents an important step, it suffers from several significant shortcomings.

First, the initiative only applies to low-budget movies—movies that rarely achieve broad mainstream distribution and audiences. SAG is therefore providing breaks for the films that are generally the least viewed. As such, it fails to rectify the exclusion of minorities from the highest paid acting gigs and does nothing to improve diversity in the mainstream media. Second, by setting lower minimum wage rates on diverse productions, it arguably creates a problematic two-tiered minimum-wage system: a higher rate for white male productions and a lower rate for diversity productions. To encourage greater casting of underrepresented groups, the initiative is allowing filmmakers to pay members of those underrepresented groups lower rates than they would ordinarily receive.

Finally, and most pressingly for the purpose of our discussion, the DCI's scope has some notable limitations. The reduced minimum wage rates on qualifying DCI productions only apply to casts for which a threshold percentage of speaking roles go to performers from one of four "protected" groups: women, senior performers, performers with disabilities, and people of color.[31] The initiative defines people of color as individuals who are "Asian/Pacific Islander, Black, Latino/Hispanic and Native American Indian."[32] Consequently, Middle Easterners, who represent a significant victim of Hollywood stereotyping, are wholly excluded from protection under the DCI. At the same time, the inclusion of other minority groups in the DCI creates a perverse casting incentive. When the rare treatment of Middle Eastern subject matter does hit the screen, filmmakers are effectively encouraged to cast Indians (who count as Asian), light-skinned blacks, Hispanics, and Native Americans in those roles instead of Middle Easterners so that they might qualify for the special DCI rates.

SAG's data on casting trends, which industry analysts use to monitor progress of minorities in the acting profession and diversification of content, are similarly flawed. They capture race as one of five categories: Caucasian, African American, Native American, Asian/Pacific Islander, and Latino. As usual, Middle Easterners find themselves in the Caucasian box.[33] Additionally, SAG has an Asian Pacific American Caucus, an African American Caucus, a Native American Caucus, a Latino/Hispanic Caucus, a Women's Caucus, a Performers with Disabilities Caucus, and a Senior Performers Caucus. Surprisingly there is no Middle Eastern caucus.

SAG likely does not manifest overt concern about Middle Eastern casting issues because there is not enough pressure surrounding the issue. In large part, there is a widespread public tolerance for stereotypical portraits of Middle Easterners. Even as depictions have grown increasingly absurd, there has been little public outcry. As Akram and Johnson observe, "The stereotyping and demonizing of Arabs and Muslims by American films may well have gone largely unnoticed because they are entirely consistent with widespread attitudes in U.S. society."[34] Maz Jobrani, an Iranian American actor who has made guest appearances on numerous television shows, including *Law & Order* and *24*, poignantly describes the troubling portrayal of Middle Easterners in the mass media. "We are always depicted as lunatics," he comments. "I've guest-starred on TV shows and several times, even if I'm playing a good guy, there is someone on the show being accused of some terrorist act. If that's in people's minds and nine times out of ten they see you on TV and it deals with terrorism, then it's going to stick."[35] In the words of movie critic Godrey Cheshire, the portrait of Middle Easterners as bloodthirsty terrorists appears to be "the only vicious racial stereotype that's not only still permitted but actively endorsed by Hollywood."[36]

Indeed, in a haunting recycling of the past, the racist tropes historically employed against blacks, Jews, and other persecuted minorities are now pointed against Middle Easterners, culminating in a discourse that juxtaposes our Western values against their Oriental barbarism. Such portrayals depict the Middle Easterner as a devious, hook-nosed perpetual foreigner who presents a continuous threat to our national security and way of life.[37] As political scientist Ronald Stockton suggests, the use of such imagery has frequently come at moments of crisis and unrest, such as the oil embargo in the early 1970s and the instability in the Middle East during the late '80s and early '90s. One salient example comes from an American national monthly that, in 1989, published a cartoon entitled "Reading the Arab Mind." "Vengeance," "fanaticism," "double talk," and "blackmail" formed prominent compartments in the illustration. Interestingly, the work mimicked (perhaps subconsciously) a viciously anti-Semitic cartoon from nearly a century ago. The earlier image divided the "Jewish mind" into such categories as "worship of money," "cowardice," and "theft."[38] The striking commonalities—the portrayal of both Arabs and Jews as possessing "socially hostile orientations to the world and rigid mental compartmentalization with thought processes alien to normal humans"[39]—constitute a key lynchpin for racist ideologies, which condone hatred by dehumanizing members of a targeted minority.

Representation Becomes Reality: Ceci N'Est Pas Un Arab

In his deceptively simple painting *La Trahison des Images*, René Magritte depicts a pipe with the words "Ceci n'est pas une pipe" (This is not a pipe) written below the image in neat cursive. Magritte's seemingly paradoxical statement challenges our dangerous tendency to conflate mimetic representation (the painting of a pipe) and object (a pipe).[40] The treachery of images results when we internalize these coded visual messages as reality. Similarly, Hollywood not only reflects certain stereotypes about Middle Easterners but also recursively perpetuates and spreads those stereotypes. The memorable 1991 drama *Not Without My Daughter* provides a powerful example. The movie, starring Sally Field fresh off her Oscar win in 1985, tells the story of Betty, an American woman of European descent who falls for the charming Moody Mahmoody, a seemingly Westernized, well-educated Iranian American doctor living in Michigan. The two marry and, shortly thereafter, have a daughter. But all is not well for Dr. Mahmoody. He experiences recurrent racism at his workplace and grows increasingly homesick. In response, he convinces his wife that they should take their daughter for a visit to Iran. Unfortunately, once they arrive in Iran, the latent misogynistic and violent Muslim apparently lurking within Moody is unleashed with gusto. An erstwhile model of American assimilation, he transforms within a few weeks into a fanatical Islamicist who brutally assaults his wife, forces her to wear traditional head coverings, and monitors her every movement under capital threat. He then unilaterally announces that his family will be living in Iran permanently and then beats Betty as he informs her that, in Iran, men exercise despotic control over every aspect of their spouses' lives. His insular, ganglike family members serve as co-conspirators, placing Betty under virtual house arrest. Ultimately, Betty plots her escape—but not without her daughter in tow.

Throughout the movie, Betty prominently dons a gold-cross necklace, a stark symbol of the clash-of-civilizations motif present throughout the movie. The one benign Iranian who assists Betty in escaping dresses impeccably in fine Italian suits, always has the delicate sounds of classical music wafting throughout his house, and sports a perfect Oxford accent. As a whole, however, the Iranian men are consistently portrayed as militant fundamentalists. Meanwhile, the women are depicted as cowering conformists unable to speak their minds or resist male authority. A heavy specter of Iranian anti-Americanism runs rampant throughout the movie.

Despite its attempt at serious narrative, the movie degenerates into absurdity with the melodramatic title, sensationalist subject matter, Moody Mahmoody's ridiculous appellation, Sally Field's typical histrionics, and the movie's farcical tagline: "In 1984, Betty Mahmoody's husband took his wife and daughter to meet his family in Iran. He swore they would be safe. They would be happy. They would be free to leave. He lied." There is no denying the harrowing story of the real Betty Mahmoody, who bravely managed to escape Iran with her daughter in 1986.[41] There is no doubt that fundamentalist Islam, as practiced in Iran and elsewhere, is an absolute affront to the basic rights of women. But the movie draws on and heightens the worst stereotypes about Iranians: their purported religious fanaticism, misogyny, and inassimilability. For example, at one point, Moody forcibly enrolls his wife in a Koran study class, where she befriends a naive midwestern housewife who was brought to Iran under similar circumstances by her Iranian American husband. In a brief moment away from their husbands, Betty asks her, "Was he ever violent?" "Not in the States," her friend confides as Betty nods knowingly. The message to the viewer is clear: no matter how seemingly Westernized an Iranian American man might seem, under the veneer lies a violent, unrepentant jihadist.

Surprisingly, the movie received little condemnation or criticism. In an era when the slightest hint of racism can sometimes generate a massive controversy and result in numerous corporate apologies and firings,[42] the movie produced little dissent over its blatant racism or quibbles over its sensationalism and panderage. Popular reviews at the time of the movie's release were largely favorable, with critics even lauding its instructive insights into Iranian culture.[43] To this day, the movie continues to enjoy a successful syndication run on cable channels.

On occasion, portraits of any ethnicity will inevitably conjure up and reiterate certain stereotypes. There is nothing inappropriate about a writer or director, in isolation, making a movie about terrorism that predominantly features Middle Easterners. That said, media portrayals should not always (or almost always) perpetuate stereotypes. The problem becomes clear upon examination of the overall trend. When virtually every single piece of mainstream media that features Middle Easterners inextricably involves themes of terrorism, violence, misogyny, and/or religious extremism, one must conclude the presence of a systematic failure to portray Middle Eastern peoples with accuracy. As Steven Bender posits in the Latino context, "One might ask, what harm was done by . . . telling a factual slice of Puerto Rican life in New York City" or, for that matter, by making a movie based on the terrifying ordeal of Betty Mahmoody? Bender persuasively responds,

> The answer stems from the insignificance and illegitimacy of Latina/o stories in the culture of American mass media. Anglo borrowing of Latina/o influences and Anglo telling of Latino stories would be more tolerable and even welcome if they occurred against a backdrop of Latina/o relevancy and positive visibility. Surely, stereotypical images will lose their sting if they are balanced by a steady depiction of Latina/o characters in honorable roles. Against such a backdrop, *West Side Story* would not be the only media representation of Puerto Ricans, and thus their portrayal as a murderous but perhaps misunderstood thug in *Capeman* (or as an unruly mob in *Seinfeld*) could be viewed more properly as one man's misdirected life than as a cultural blueprint for Puerto Ricans and other Latinas/os.[44]

Similarly, Moody Mahmoody's dark descent into Islamic fundamentalism and misogyny would be viewed as one man's misdirected path rather than the blueprint of the Iranian American male. Unfortunately, since such portrayals of Middle Easterners are inevitably the only portrayals of Middle Easterners that make their way into the mainstream media, existing prejudices only worsen with exposure to such one-sided depictions.

The media mediates, cultivating perceptions that have a profound and direct real-world impact.[45] As Michael Omi and Howard Winant note in their seminal work on the subject, racial formation is a function of "social structure and cultural representation."[46] Hollywood serves as both reflector and cultivator of cultural representations, and its images directly influence constructions of race, which "becomes 'common-sense'—a way of comprehending, explaining, and acting in the world."[47] This concept, abstract to many, becomes eminently tangible to its unwitting victims. When I was discussing *Not Without My Daughter* with a friend recently, he recounted a memorable incident from his adolescence. At that time, he had been dating a girl for several months. One day, concerned about the relationship, she confronted him about some anxieties that she had been experiencing. When pressed to share her feelings, she revealed the source of her apprehensions: "You're not going to be like that guy in *Not Without My Daughter*, are you?" she asked. My friend, who is only half Iranian and typically passes for a white European, carries the badge of his father's Iranian surname and, with it, the inevitable associations. I could not help but laugh painfully at his tale; it was a fate with which I was all too familiar. On numerous occasions, I have also been forced by a girl-friend or her parents to answer for the sins of Dr. Moody Mahmoody. My Christian first name, Catholic upbringing, and otherwise "excellent" performance of whiteness (no matter how unconscious or unintentional) tempered the scrutiny I faced, but only slightly.

The media's increasing ubiquity has only exacerbated its negative impact on public perceptions of Middle Easterners. As Edward Said once noted, "One aspect of the electronic, postmodern world is that there has been a reinforcement of the stereotypes by which the Orient is viewed. Television, the films, and all the media's resources have forced information into more and more standardized molds. So far as the Orient is concerned, standardization and cultural stereotyping have intensified the hold of the nineteenth-century academic and the imaginative demonology of the 'mysterious Orient.'"[48] With these words, Said highlights a dangerous consequence of the information age. While we have multiplied our rate of data access, we have not enjoyed a commensurate rise in data quality. More information is not necessarily better information, especially when that information is based on invidious, wholesale stereotyping of an ethnic group. Through the consumption of media, individuals who have had no personal experience with Middle Easterners receive and internalize a clichéd image of the group as a whole. That tabula rasa has now disappeared, replaced with a flawed maquette of the quintessential Middle Easterner that resides in the minds of many.

It should therefore come as no surprise that the images of Middle Easterners, as reflected in mainstream media, are not innocuous. They play a role in animating public policy and contribute to the harsh realties that Middle Eastern Americans must endure: hate crimes,[49] special registration requirements,[50] arrest with indefinite detention,[51] racial profiling,[52] and job discrimination.[53] And the psychological tolls from this attack against the civil rights of Middle Easterners cannot be underestimated.

Flying the Unfriendly Skies

Perceptions ineluctably influence reality. According to the tenets of cultivation theory, a concept first devised by communication scholar George Gerbner, media exposure cultivates viewers' perceptions of reality by "mass-produc[ing] messages and images [that] form the mainstream of a common symbolic environment"[54] and by socializing viewers into "standardized roles and behaviors."[55] The process of enculturation from the visual images and symbolic cues that are widely disseminated by the media influences racial perceptions. For Middle Easterners, the power of cultivation theory is most readily apparent in one particular public space: the airport. When examining the treatment of Middle Easterners at airports, we are provided a poignant reminder of the way stereotypical media portraits can perpetuate racism and wreak a particularly devastating toll on the regular lives of targeted groups.

News coverage of Middle Eastern issues and fictional portraits of Middle Easterners in films and on television have combined to cultivate a fear of terrorism anytime someone of Middle Eastern descent boards the same flight we do. In numerous recent incidents, mere crew and/or passenger discomfort has triggered the forcible deplaning of individuals with Middle Eastern features. Often predicated on nothing more than the abstract association of Middle Eastern physiognomy with violence and terrorism—no doubt spurred by the endless blitz of media images reinforcing this stereotypical linkage—these evictions have a devastating impact on their victims. Airports serve as a remarkably public arena where individuals exercise a right deemed fundamental by the Supreme Court in *Saenz v. Roe* (1999)[56]—the right to interstate travel. Discriminatory incidents at the airport are therefore particularly humiliating and implicate a denial of basic civil rights.

Section 44902 of the Federal Aviation Act, originally enacted by Congress in 1961, grants airlines the unilateral right to permissive refusal, defined as the ability to deny "transport [to] a passenger or property the carrier decides is, or might be, inimical to safety."[57] Under federal aviation regulations, this right flows to a pilot as well.[58] Although courts have held that this right is "decidedly expansive, [it] is not unfettered."[59] As such, arbitrary or capricious refusal to allow a passenger to fly can theoretically give rise to a claim for damages. In practice, however, pilots have repeatedly exercised their unilateral right to refuse to fly a plane if they do not feel comfortable with any passenger. Virtually no cause need be demonstrated—often, it seems, appearing Middle Eastern is cause enough.

Such a posture flies in the face of our most cherished values and legal norms. The segregationist South had many white individuals who felt profound discomfort at the very sight of a black person in the same bus, restaurant, or school as them. Yet we have long since universally condemned the practice of segregation. The *Brown v. Board of Education* decision rested, in large part, on the Supreme Court's view that such systematic separation inflicted tremendous psychological wounds on the black community. Citing several academic studies, the Court concluded that "[t]o separate [blacks] from others of similar age and qualifications solely because of their race generates a feeling of inferiority as to their status in the community that may affect their hearts and minds in a way unlikely ever to be undone."[60] The practice of forcibly deplaning Americans of Middle Eastern descent solely on the basis of crew and/or passenger discomfort inflicts a badge of inferiority on the entire Middle Eastern community and undermines our basic tenets of equality.

Take the case of Jehad Alshafri, a thirty-two-year-old Arab American.[61] On November 3, 2001, American Airlines refused him the right to board a flight from Boston to Los Angeles. As the airline explained, Alshafri looked "suspicious." It apparently did not matter that Alshafri worked as defense contractor and possessed secret-level security clearance from the government. He was still considered such a threat that his civil rights were unilaterally trampled in the name of security. To add a strong dose of humiliation to the incident, Alshafri was escorted from the boarding area by a state trooper in full view of his fellow passengers.

Arshad Chowdhury, a Bangladeshi American, simply looked too Middle Eastern when he attempted to board a Northwest Airlines flight from San Francisco on October 23, 2001. An American-born citizen, Chowdhury grew up in Connecticut, attended Wesleyan University, and was an MBA candidate at Carnegie Mellon University at the time of the incident. Before entering business school, he was an investment banker for Deutsche Bank and worked at the World Trade Center. Without any tangible security rationale, the pilot declared that he would not fly with Chowdhury aboard. Both the FBI and the local law enforcement quickly arrived on the scene, and although they cleared Chowdhury to fly, the crew's decision stood.[62] For good measure, Northwest Airlines placed Chowdhury's name on a security block list distributed at all American airports, thereby frustrating any of his future attempts to fly.[63] As Chowdhury later argued, "Allowing pilots to trump law enforcement does not have anything to do with security. It's not even rational. The result of this system is that my parents and my friends in the Bangladeshi American community are too scared to fly. While we share with all Americans a fear of the statistically slim chance of terrorism, my community has the additional fear of almost certain harassment from our fellow Americans."[64]

In late 2001, Tony Zohrehvandi, a forty-one-year-old Iranian American software developer was denied the right to board an American Airlines flight from Seattle to his home in Dallas. The decision was particularly ironic since it was made by Zohrehvandi's *own employer*. At the time of the incident, Zohrehvandi happened to be a twelve-year veteran of American Airlines. American Airlines officials informed him that "he had done nothing suspicious but that he was being refused transport solely because the crew did not want to fly with him."[65] Specifically, he was told that the pilot "didn't like the way [he] looked."[66] In response, Zohrehvandi asked his company to limit his business flying and went on anxiety-suppression medication.

The dehumanization and psychic pain inflicted after suffering such a humiliating fate becomes evident upon consideration of Zohrehvandi's heartrending thoughts after the incident: "When I became a citizen and said my pledge of allegiance," he noted, "I said liberty and justice for all— not just for white, blond and blue eyes. It shatters your dream. Is it going to be like this from now on—every time some idiot takes an action against the U.S., are we going to be singled out again?"[67] Unfortunately, one cannot help but conclude that the answer to Zohrehvandi's question is a resounding yes. Yet we fail to contemplate the inexorable sense of ostracism, isolation, and belittlement felt by the victims of such racism. Commented Zohrehvandi, "In this country when I became a citizen, they said, 'You're an American.' On [the day of removal from the flight, I realized] I will never be an American in this country as long as I look like this."[68] At the core, the experience suffered by Zohrehvandi and countless other Middle Eastern Americans represents a fundamental betrayal of the promise of America and the values of the Constitution. Zohrehvandi's fear—that he will never be viewed as a full-fledged American—is harbored by all individuals who suffer the humiliation of unchecked, and even socially condoned, discrimination such as profiling.

It is also a pang I have shared on numerous occasions, especially after 9/11. In early 2002, while waiting to check in for a flight from Orange County to Chicago, I noticed a middle-aged woman of European descent looking nervously over me. After several minutes, she engaged me in conversation, quickly getting to the point: "Where are you going?" she asked. I told her I was on my way to the East Coast, via Chicago, for a business trip. At my mention of Chicago, I could see her wince ever so slightly, as she realized we were going to be on the same flight. She pressed on, asking me what I did for a living. I told her.

"You don't look like a lawyer," she challenged.

"Thank you," I replied.

"My dad's a lawyer. And he always wears a suit," she countered. "Where's yours? You only have a backpack with you." The rapid-fire questions went on for several more minutes.

A few months later, I found myself on a flight from Los Angeles to Salt Lake City. I recognized the by-now-familiar nervous gaze from the passenger, an older woman of European descent, sitting next to me. After fidgeting skittishly for several minutes, she worked up the nerve to talk. Like her predecessor in Orange County, she quickly got to the point and, within three questions, began to cross-examine me about my religious background.

Neither of these experiences was as traumatic as anything suffered by Alshafri, Chowdhury, or Zohrehvandi. But each had its painful psychic toll. No matter what I do, it reminded me, I may never be a true equal in my country. As much as I would like to disarm the stinging query "Where are you going?" with a deadpanned quip "To see Allah," such a response would likely land me on the evening news. I am profoundly aware that, as a Middle Eastern male, in many public spaces such as airports, I enjoy substantially fewer rights, First Amendment or otherwise, than others.

Although 9/11 has exacerbated this state of affairs, it did not create it. I can remember one of the first trips I took abroad as an adult. It was the spring of 1993. A sophomore in college, I was traveling with a group of my Harvard classmates in Amsterdam. As we checked in for our flight to return to the States, I was taken aside by security officials for KLM Airlines. For the next twenty minutes, the fabled racial tolerance of the Dutch betrayed me as I was subjected to a demeaning interrogation by security, forced to recount my life story and justify every detail of my short trip. The reason I was singled out for special treatment was quite clear, and the guards shamelessly made no attempt to hide it. All was well and I was just another American traveling with my American passport until one of the guards got to the box naming my place of birth: Tehran, Iran. At that moment, I became very different from my classmates, and I could feel the badge of inferiority pinned on me. Eventually, the security officials let me go and allowed me to board my flight just in the nick of time. But I will never forget the humiliation I felt as my classmates looked on and wondered what I had done to warrant such disparate treatment.

I am reminded of the words of Franz Fanon, who captured the profound psychological impact and sense of helplessness that racial prejudice inflicts on its victims. Describing how individuals of African ancestry succumb to a heightened level of self-consciousness over their bodies, he writes, "I am given no chance. I am overdetermined from without. I am the slave not of the 'idea' that others have of me but of my own appearance. . . . I am being dissected under white eyes, the only real eyes. I am *fixed*. . . . Why, it's a Negro!"[69]

Middle Eastern Americans can never escape their skin. Under the dominant gaze, they remain perpetual foreigners, never quite equal, always a part of the Other. In *Covering*, Kenji Yoshino's autobiographical contemplation of race and sexual orientation, Yoshino flags the problem of perpetual foreigner status: "I came to hate the question 'where are you from, really?' that followed my assertion that I had grown up in Boston."[70] For certain groups, this question inevitably emerges in daily conversation and serves as a constant, nagging reminder of one's presumptive un-Americanness. Even more perniciously, it acts as an unconscious but powerful inducement toward assimilatory behavior, in the (perhaps futile) hope of one day escaping the inquiry. Finally, it is a tragic reminder that one is never fully an equal part of the American body politic. This fact causes more than just psychic damage. Indeed, at times of crisis, it has very real effects.

Consider the impact that the perpetual-foreigner notion has had on Asian Americans in recent years. In the high-profile Wen Ho Lee scandal, the Chinese American scientist working at Los Alamos National Laboratory was charged with espionage for allegedly selling nuclear secrets to the Chinese government. Lee professed his innocence all along but was denied bail and held in solitary confinement. Most media outlets immediately assumed his guilt, a position all too easy to believe given the status of Asians as perpetual foreigners in the American subconscious.[71] Ultimately, however, Lee was vindicated when the case against him imploded. Years and millions of dollars worth of investigation turned up no evidence of spying, and charges of espionage were dropped. In the end, the presiding judge in Lee's trial issued a remarkable personal apology to him for "the unfair manner in which you were held in custody by the executive branch" and deemed the prosecution "an embarrassment to the nation."[72]

Shortly after 9/11, Captain James Yee, a Muslim Chinese American chaplain serving with the Army, faced charges of espionage for allegedly using his position at Guantánamo Bay to spy for Islamic extremists. While awaiting trial, Yee spent three months in a maximum-security military prison, and his lawyers began to prepare a death-penalty defense.[73] Ultimately, the government dropped the charges for lack of proof. In the end, adultery and the downloading of pornography—hardly the stuff of national security—were the most significant allegations the government could muster against Yee.[74]

The tales of both Lee and Yee are instructive on several levels. First, they demonstrate that the problem of the perpetual foreigner and the impact of the war on terrorism reach beyond the Middle Eastern population and affect all individuals on the darker side of the white/black divide. Second, their experiences are tragic reminders that we still endure a dual-tiered system of citizenship, in which minorities, no matter how assimilated, still face questions about their loyalty. As Harvey Gee points out, both Lee and Yee possessed all of the standard model-minority qualifications: they were both highly educated individuals who had achieved the American dream through hard work and perseverance.[75] But they could never escape their heritage. Focusing on their foreignness and Yee's ties to Islam,[76] the government and the press all too readily believed the tenuous allegations of treason mounted against the two men.

In arguing that the use of remedial race-conscious policies to redress past discrimination is never constitutional, Justice Scalia once posited that, "in the eyes of the government, we are just one race here. It is American."[77] As the tribulations of both James Yee and Wen Ho Lee indicate, Scalia's optimism was, at the very least, premature. My own personal experiences also cast doubt on Scalia's one-race hypothesis. Ironically, when I travel abroad, I am viewed as an American. In my own country, I am presumptively viewed as an outsider.

My status as a perpetual foreigner became shockingly clear during two episodes that should have had no racial subtext. The first episode took place during high school, after a flirtatious conversation with an attractive classmate. After she had left, one of my other classmates, a person whom I considered a friend, turned to me and asked, "You think she likes you?" I shrugged my shoulders, not quite sure what he was getting at. "Well, don't forget, you're Iranian," he reminded me, making sure to emphasize the long "a" in his pronunciation. He then put the nail in the coffin: "and you always will be."

The second episode occurred more recently. In my nonacademic life, I am an intellectual-property and entertainment litigator. Recently, I represented one of the world's largest celebrity-photography agencies (a.k.a. the paparazzi) in a copyright-infringement suit against a prominent Internet gossip blogger named Perez Hilton. The litigation generated immediate headlines, partly due to the novel cyberlaw issues at stake, but mostly due to the fact that it pitted a controversial gossip reporter known popularly as the Most Hated Man in Hollywood against the controversial paparazzi. My client received numerous comments from the general public about the suit—mostly remarking on its merits. One comment, however, had nothing to do with the substance of the litigation. Curiously, it dealt with my client's choice of counsel. "I see that you have an Iranian attorney," the note read. "USA classifies Iranians as residents of the Axis of Evil. Isn't it funny that you had chosen an Iranian to represent American beliefs?" Sadly, the comment was not a radical outlier or an errant data point in an otherwise race-blind world. Nor was it just the random musing of some uneducated moron. Eerily, it recalled a strikingly similar series of comments that were made to me from a far more educated source.

One day during my third year in law school, I had a meeting with a group of newly admitted students who were visiting Yale to determine if they would matriculate. While several of us were immersed in banter, one of the newly admitted students appeared to be staring at me with a confused glare. When she could finally seize on a break in the conversation, she turned to me and asked, "What are you?" After ascertaining what she meant (she wanted to know my ethnic background), I told her that I was Persian, Armenian, and Irish. She came from mixed European descent.

"Yeah, I thought you looked Iranian," she replied. Then she said something rather curious. "So, what's it like, you know, studying our law. It must be strange, huh?" I looked at her perplexed, shocked that she would ask such a question.

"What do you mean?"

"Being Iranian and all. It must be weird and so different to study American law." Although there was no rational basis for her to surmise that I was not American (or even native born, for that matter), the internal calculus in her mind was irrepressible: being of Middle Eastern descent meant that I could not be American.

I explained to her that I had grown up in the United States and that I was an American citizen. I was, therefore, studying *my* law. But the natural conception of the Middle Easterner as "the Other" is so indelibly and widely imprinted in the American mind that even the best and brightest young adults in our country fall victim to it.

Stereotypical depictions reinforce clichéd perceptions that, in turn, produce discriminatory conduct. Middle Easterners are portrayed as the perpetual foreigner, the enemy, the Other, the terrorists, the uncivilized heathens who threaten the American way of life with their inhumane thirst for violence. The impact of such prevalent prejudice is grave.

Historically we have witnessed the profound psychological toll that slavery, segregation, and discrimination have had on the African American community. As Alvin Poussaint and Amy Alexander have argued in their study *Lay My Burden Down*, systemic racism has mired the community in an underappreciated mental-health crisis. Quite simply, racism can result in the internalization of self-loathing and feelings of hopelessness that often express themselves in the ultimate form of self-devaluation: suicide.[78] Anecdotally, there appears to be a similarly grave mental-care crisis in the Middle Eastern community. I use the word *appears* because the crisis remains wholly undocumented, largely due to the unavailability of health-care data that extricates Middle Easterners from the white category. Still, it is well established that depression and isolation are the two most prevalent factors that predicate suicidal ideation.[79] There can be no greater isolation than one's status as the perpetual foreigner in a society and the persistent demonization of one's ethnicity in the mainstream media. Images can be treacherous indeed.

All told, the media reflect and help to perpetuate stereotypical conceptions that fester in the imagination of the public and, ultimately, legitimate invidious policies targeting Americans of Middle Eastern descent. Profiling at the airports is but a small example of this larger trend. The next chapter documents the rising tide of hate facing Middle Eastern Americans: the racially bent war on terrorism, targeted immigration policies immunized from equal protection scrutiny, unabated job discrimination, and hate crimes. As we shall see, the media, combined with broader social, economic, and geopolitical forces, have laid the groundwork for the growing attack on Middle Eastern civil rights.

5

Threat Level Orange

The War on Terrorism and the Assault on Middle Eastern Civil Rights

De jure segregation ended several decades ago. Majority attitudes toward racial minorities have, by most measures, improved dramatically in the past generation. And rates of discrimination and hate crimes have declined precipitously in recent years. Though its work is not nearly complete, the civil rights movement has bettered the lives of millions of Americans and made our society more just and egalitarian. In one particular area,[1] however, the civil rights movement has not done nearly enough: the protection of Middle Eastern Americans. This chapter seeks to identify and explain this major shortcoming in the modern civil rights movement.

Unlike many other groups, Middle Eastern Americans appear to be suffering from growing rates of discrimination, both in the private sphere and through government policies. Recent years have witnessed a remarkable transformation in the public image of Middle Eastern people, as they have transitioned from (possibly white) assimilable ethnics to the quintessential Other. This trend has only accelerated with the tragedy of 9/11. As a result, Middle Easterners have endured a veritable assault on their civil rights. The following analysis documents this rising tide of hate, locates it within the broader context of international events, and critiques the inadequate responses to it by our legal and political institutions.

The Historicization of Racism

In popular thought, racial prejudice is increasingly viewed as a historical relic. Take, for example, the political discourse on remedial government programs such as affirmative action. Proponents often rationalize affirmative action as a means to rectify the impact of past discrimination on minority groups, while opponents condemn the policy for creating new discrimination against the majority in order to make up for the sins of our forbears.[2] This polemic, however, paints an incomplete picture of social realities. The stronger case for affirmative action is as a remedy for present, rather than past, discrimination. Moreover, in criticizing affirmative action and in debating broader social issues, we overlook the still widespread phenomenon of discrimination, both conscious and unconscious. Nevertheless, we maintain a false veil of colorblindness that whitewashes not only centuries of oppression but also the pervasive racism that continues to exist in our own society.

The case of John Rocker, the former Atlanta Braves reliever who was derided in the media several years ago for his racist, homophobic, and xenophobic comments, illustrates the common social dynamic in confronting racism. In an interview conducted by a *Sports Illustrated* reporter, Rocker turned his hatred for New York and its residents into an assault on various minority groups:

Imagine having to take the [Number] 7 train to the ballpark [in New York], looking like you're [riding through] Beirut next to some kid with purple hair next to some queer with AIDS right to some dude who just got out of jail for the fourth time next to some 20-year-old mom with four kids. It's depressing.[3]

Unabashed, he explained that

[t]he biggest thing I don't like about New York are the foreigners. I'm not a very big fan of foreigners. You can walk an entire block in Times Square and not hear anybody speaking English. Asians and Koreans and Vietnamese and Indians and Russians and Spanish people and everything up there. How the hell did they get in this country?[4]

Immediately upon publication of the interview, Rocker faced a maelstrom of public criticism and universal condemnation for his views. He was quickly punished by Major League Baseball and his team, and within two years he found himself entirely removed from professional baseball. Publicly, Rocker's comments were sternly rebuked as ignorant, and Rocker was portrayed as a transgressive outlier.

On one level, our swift response to certain forms of racial intolerance in the public sphere is admirable and illustrates the remarkable improvement in racial attitudes over the past few decades. But the response also suggests that the war against racism has not yet been won and that much work remains. Unfortunately, Rocker's comments were not as extraordinary or deviant as many people would suggest. Indeed, viewed with any degree of candor, his comments are the kind of intolerant and uneducated bigotry that one can hear all too frequently in private conversation. As a society, though, we pretend that Rocker is a thorough outlier or a rogue madman, not a representative of the viewpoints of a sizable minority of Americans. So, we publicly lambaste racism, punish purveyors such as Rocker, pat ourselves glibly on the back for being enlightened citizens, and move on without exploring the extant wellspring of such thought. Only 38 percent of white Americans believe that racism is still a significant problem. And this view is based, at least in part, on widespread misperceptions: a startling 65 percent of white Americans believe that there is little difference between the economic and social conditions of whites and blacks in our society; 58 percent of white Americans even contend that blacks have jobs that are either "equal" (46 percent), "a little better" (6 percent), or "a lot better" (6 percent) than those held by whites.[5]

Significantly, we ignore the problematic and still festering genesis of Rocker's comments: Rocker said what he thought because, to him, there was nothing wrong with saying it—after all, he was likely reflecting the types of comments that he had probably heard in private throughout his life. Unfortunately, instead of recognizing that the real problems are the racist segments of society that made John Rocker comfortable enough to say what he said, people quickly labeled Rocker as a bad guy, an anomaly, a deviant in the new America.

The judiciary has wholeheartedly embraced such a response. While discrimination based explicitly on race is subjected to strict scrutiny by the courts—usually resulting in the striking of a law—discrimination based on language or culture has received relaxed rational basis review—usually resulting in the upholding of a law. In the *Hernandez v. Texas* decision, issued on the eve of *Brown v. Board of Education*, the Supreme Court found that the systematic exclusion of Mexican Americans from juries constituted race discrimination in violation of the Constitution's Equal Protection Clause. But in the *Hernandez v. New York* decision, rendered some thirty-seven years later, the Court found that the systematic striking of Latinos from a jury on the basis of language raised no such constitutional concerns.[6] As the Court reasoned, the exclusion of Latinos in the later case could be rationalized on the "race neutral" basis that Spanish speakers might not accept a translator's version of trial testimony, whereas the exclusion in the earlier case was explicitly predicted on race. In practice, the resulting outcome—the removal of Hispanics from the jury pool—is the same. As Ariela Gross contends, the race/culture/language distinction is nothing more than a red herring: "race is produced by practices of subordination, and . . . racial discrimination can be disguised as discrimination on the basis of culture or language."[7] By technically deracializing discrimination, policies of exclusion have received immunity from equal protection scrutiny.

The increasing immunity granted to policies of exclusion stems in part from the public discourse that almost uniformly designates systemic racism as a decidedly historical phenomenon. Justice Sandra Day O'Connor's 2003 majority opinion in *Grutter v. Bollinger* perfectly captures this myth, exalting with irrational exuberance that there should be no need for affirmative action within a generation: "We expect that 25 years from now, the use of racial preferences will no longer be necessary to further the interest approved today."[8] Besides the arbitrariness of this time limit and its unwarranted optimism that centuries of pervasive institutional racism can be undone with a few decades of carefully circumscribed government intervention of dubious efficacy,[9] O'Connor's declaration is troublesome for another reason. O'Connor argues that limited, remedial race-based policies may still be needed to attack the vestiges of past discrimination, but she assumes that racism does not exist in the present and is unlikely to spur further inequities in the future. Polls have repeatedly shown that the vast majority of Americans of European descent view discrimination as a mere relic and even feel that African Americans are treated the same as whites in their communities.[10] The public discourse on race now focuses on the days of Rosa Parks, the standoff at Central High in Little Rock, and Governor Wallace of Alabama as an ugly page from our *history*, an embarrassing heirloom from our *past*. We smugly point to the gradual progress of society as a whole in advancing civil rights as evidence of this.

On the issue of the civil rights movement and the standoff at Central High in Little Rock, a brief personal anecdote illustrates the powerful endurance of racism in our society. Several years ago, I found myself in Little Rock, Arkansas. I was in the wedding party for an old law-school friend who had fallen for an Arkansan during his judicial clerkship. It was my first trip to the old Dixie, and I arrived, naturally, with a jaundiced eye, looking for something different, some sign of the old Confederacy, the segregationist South. After all, as much as I loved Lynyrd Skynyrd and belting out my own rendition of "Sweet Home Alabama" on the guitar, that line about Birmingham loving its governor (and the attendant images of George Wallace that it inevitably conjured) always made me uneasy.

At first, though, I felt as if I were in Anytown, USA. Sure, the first exit on the freeway as I left the airport was "Confederate Blvd." There were the southern accents, the signs for BBQ, biscuits and gravy, turnip greens, fried okra, and chicken fried steak. But the topography seemed to differ little from the northeastern woodlands, the humidity was surprisingly not quite as bad as Washington, D.C., and the highway signs were the familiar shade of green you would see anywhere in our country. And everyone was so friendly. The white construction worker I saw at the Shell food-mart seemed so chatty with the Indian checkout clerk. The two blue-collar Arkansans flying into Little Rock with me were thoroughly jovial as we commiserated about our flight delays. Maybe what they said about a New South really was true: the War of Northern Aggression was a part of the past, as was the legacy of slavery, but the gentility still remained. Maybe I could even see myself living here. Before I got a chance to grab a relocation guide, however, my most cynical thoughts about the South were rekindled.

She was a Little Rock native—born, raised, and college-educated there—and a dedicated liberal Clintonite. Yet that did not stop her from speaking with shocking racist candor in front of us:

"You should get some Southern food while you're here," she suggested.

"What—like soul food? You know where we can get some soul food?" one of my friends eagerly questioned.

"No, Southern food is different than soul food. Soul food is what black people eat. You know, like chitlins."

"What are chitlins?"

"Pork intestines, or something like that. That's what *they* eat. White people don't eat that kind of stuff," she said with a sickened expression.

The next day, she was kind enough to show us around town—along with racism, clearly the fabled Southern hospitality was still in tact. We asked if she could take us to Central High, the site of the infamous segregation standoff in 1957, and she acquiesced after a brief protest: "Why would you want to go *there*?" she quizzically asked. But as we approached the school, it was clear that she had some additional thoughts about our choice of tourist destination. "I'm not sure what *your* blacks in the North are like. But *our* blacks, they make you prejudiced real quick—the way they act, the way they live, the things they eat." Her use of the possessive indicated that the idea of humans as property was apparently still alive and well in certain circles in the Old South.

Unfortunately, as much as I would like to dismiss my Southern tour guide as a radical outlier, facts suggest otherwise. On November 7, 2000, the voters of Alabama eliminated a provision in their state constitution that dictated that "the legislature shall never pass any law to authorize or legalize any marriage between any white person and a Negro, or descendant of a Negro."[11] It is shocking that it took until 2000 for such a provision to be removed from the state constitution. This fact might be mitigated by an argument that the Supreme Court's decision in *Loving v. Virginia*,[12] which held that prohibitions on miscegenation violated the Equal Protection and Due Process Clauses of the Fourteenth Amendment, had rendered Alabama's constitutional provision moot and void. But another fact is all but impossible to mitigate: a startling 40 percent of the Alabama electorate actually voted *against* the removal of the hateful prohibition from the state constitution.

Racism, both conscious and unconscious, still exists. And we must not underestimate its powerful effect on our daily lives.

The Civil Rights Movement Inchoate:
The Rising Tide of Hate against Middle Eastern Americans

Despite the continued existence of racism, civil rights have generally improved in recent decades. By and large, women, African Americans, Native Americans, Asian Americans, Latinos, and sexual minorities enjoy greater protection of their civil rights today than at virtually any other point in American history. By sharp contrast, Middle Eastern Americans do not. If anything, they now suffer from more systemic racism than ever before, a fact that makes them unique among America's ethnic and racial groups. For example, a 2007 Zogby poll of Arab Americans found that, among older Arab Americans (those aged sixty-five or older), only 31 percent reported ever having personally experienced discrimination based on their ethnicity. By sharp contrast, 76 percent of younger Arab Americans (those aged eighteen to twenty-nine) expressed having personally experienced discrimination because of their ethnic background.[13] These statistics point to a troubling and notable shortcoming in the otherwise successful history of the civil rights movement.

Two examples—one played out publicly in recent months, the other privately over the course of a generation—highlight this point. The first example involves the furor over the potential transfer of the operations of several American ports to DP World, a company owned by the government of the United Arab Emirates (UAE)—a controversy that exemplifies the prevailing vision of Middle Easterners as "the other." Despite the UAE's ostensible role as an ally in the war on terrorism, the fact that port security would remain in U.S. government hands (via the Coast Guard and the Customs and Border Control Agency), and the financial incentive that any port-management company would naturally have in opposing attacks against its ports,[14] the outcry among the American public reached a frenzied level not witnessed in years.[15] Democrats such as Senators Hillary Clinton and Chuck Schumer and House Minority Leader Nancy Pelosi jumped at the opportunity to appear tougher than Republicans on a national-security issue.[16] In the biting words of the *Economist*, seizure of the ports issue gave Democrats "a soundbite—'Arab hands off our ports'— that even the dimmest voter can understand. (Such soundbites have traditionally been a Republican strong point.) It allows them to pander to racist voters with plausible deniability. (Again, this is usually Republican turf.)."[17] Meanwhile, leading members of President Bush's own party, including Senate Majority Leader Bill Frist, House Speaker Dennis Hastert, and House Majority Leader John Boehner, expressed severe misgivings about the deal, which the Bush administration saw no reason to oppose.[18] Many observers, including congressional aides, remarked that they had never received such overwhelmingly one-sided emails, letters, and phone calls to their offices on a political issue. There was near unanimous opposition coming from both sides of the aisle against the president.[19]

Foreign companies and contractors have long managed operations of American ports—in fact, DP World's immediate predecessor was a foreign entity.[20] The issue was plainly not one of foreign control—a practice that had gone unnoticed until the specter of Arab-run port operations arose. The port incident highlighted the way that rampant racism had caused Americans to harbor such misgivings about Middle Easterners, though not any other group of individuals, from having some control over our infrastructure. Sadly, the incident seemed to suggest that one of the few things that both the populist left and right can agree on is their distaste for Arabs and people from the Middle East.

The second example is a personal anecdote. My dad, who grew up in Eisenhower's America, often reminisces at how enthralled people used to be with his ethnic background. From the snowy mountains of New Hampshire, where my dad attended college at Dartmouth, to the plains of Wyoming, where he visited his college roommates during the Christmas holidays, being Persian in the 1950s was perceived as exotic and exciting. Harems and sheiks, Persian carpets, and camels, oases, and deserts constituted the predominant images of the Middle East in the American mindset. No one associated the Middle East with fundamentalism and terrorism back then. In fact, at a time when old bastions of East Coast elitism—Ivy League fraternities—closed their doors to all but the whitest of Americans, my dad was welcomed into one of Dartmouth's most (in) famous old boys' club—Sigma Phi Epsilon.[21]

Contrast the image of the Middle East in the 1950s with the image that formed during the Arab oil embargo in the 1970s, only to grow worse with the Iranian hostage crisis and the Iranian Revolution led by the Ayatollah Khomeini. A generation later, the average Iranian American faces a very different inquiry about his or her ethnic heritage. One Iranian American woman I know endured such constant pestering over her ethnic background during her school years that, in a classic case of covering, she changed her Iranian surname to something more ethnically ambiguous. Although she is extremely proud of her ethnic heritage and readily acknowledges it, "Middle Eastern" is no longer the first thought people have when reading her name or meeting her. Instead, they cannot classify her, and that is the way she prefers it. Unfortunately, in the post-9/11 world, the negative associations with and hostility toward Americans of Middle Eastern descent have only gotten worse.

The War on Terrorism, the War on Race: Profiling, Special Registration, and Government Targeting of Middle Easterners

The promulgation of government policies targeting Americans of Middle Eastern descent and the racialization of Middle Easterners is not a new phenomenon.[22] In the wake of the Munich attacks on Israeli athletes at the 1972 Olympic Games, President Nixon set up a special cabinet committee to address the issue of terrorism in the United States. The committee enacted a series of now-forgotten (but eerily familiar) policies, ominously dubbed the "Special Measures." As a result, the government placed limitations on Arab immigration into the United States (including access to permanent resident status), increased FBI surveillance of individuals of Arab origin regardless of their immigration status,[23] and facilitated the accumulation of data on individuals of Arab origin who were "potential terrorists" or likely to assist terrorists.[24]

Only a few years later, the Iranian hostage crisis precipitated a wave of state action targeting Iranian individuals residing in the United States. In Mississippi, the legislature passed an appropriations bill that raised tuition solely for those students whose home government did not have diplomatic relations with the United States and against which the United States had economic sanctions.[25] Despite its potential to affect Cuban, Vietnamese, Cambodian, Albanian, Iraqi, and Yemeni students, the bill clearly targeted Iranian students attending state schools, as it was passed in response to the hostage crisis.[26] The policy was ultimately struck down as unconstitutional.[27] Meanwhile, New Mexico completely barred Iranians from attending its state university.[28] A federal district court rejected as pretextual the ostensible paternalistic justification for the measure—the protection of Iranians out of fear for their safety—and held that the policy violated the Equal Protection Clause.[29] The courts, however, upheld other discriminatory actions in the wake of the hostage crisis, including special registration requirements for all Iranian students.[30]

Suspicions about individuals of Middle Eastern descent continued to fester throughout the 1980s and '90s. A 1991 ABC News poll conducted during the first Gulf War found that 59 percent of Americans associated Arabs with terrorism; 58 percent, with violence; and 56 percent, with religious fanaticism.[31] In a 1993 Gallup poll, 67 percent of Americans thought that there were too many Arab immigrants in our country.[32]

The continuing crises in the Middle East and our military efforts over the past few decades have, unfortunately, contributed to a growing dehumanization of individuals from the region. Historian David Prochaska has argued that the first Gulf War in the early 1990s exacerbated the deteriorating view of Middle Easterners.[33] Wars often thrive on the dehumanization of one's opponent, and the Gulf War was no different. Prochaska refers to a defining moment when, at a press conference, the leader of the Allied Forces, General H. Norman Schwarzkopf, responded to a report of alleged Iraqi atrocities by stating, "They're not part of the same human race, the people who did that, as the rest of us are."[34] With a tone of profound disappointment, Prochaska observes that no one protested Schwarzkopf's characterization. As writer Anton Shammas urges, we must "ponder how a sentence such as 'they're not part of the same human race' . . . could have served first as a moral go-ahead to order the massacre of thousands of retreating Iraqi soldiers and other nonhumans then as a license to *whitewash* their image from the American memory."[35]

In the wake of 9/11, the rising tide of hate against Americans of Middle Eastern descent has become particularly pronounced. Despite the very real need to combat militant extremism in all forms, the war on terrorism has unnecessarily exhibited severe racial undertones. As Kevin Johnson has noted, "Many Arab Americans generally feel that the 'war on terrorism' during the 1990s in fact has been a war on them."[36] This sentiment has reverberated with greater vigor in the wake of 9/11. For example, the American-Arab Anti-Discrimination Committee (ADC) has reported a fourfold increase in hate crimes and incidents of discrimination against Americans of Middle Eastern descent since 9/11.[37]

This surge of hate is not just the product of extremist groups operating at the margins; it also emanates from the very mainstream of American society and even government itself. Indeed, complaints of workplace discrimination against Middle Easterners have risen exponentially in recent years.[38] A search of the Lexis federal and state case-law database for use of the epithet "sand nigger" reveals fifty results—all of them from cases decided since 1987. A substantial majority (66 percent) of these cases was decided in the short time since 9/11.[39] A similar search for use of the pejorative term "camel jockey" produces sixty-three results—all of them from cases decided since 1985.[40] Again, a majority (52 percent) of these cases was decided in the brief period since 9/11.

Most disturbingly, the government's own policies have both reflected and spurred on the wave of hate. Legislation specifically targeting the rights of Middle Easterners continues to be proposed with alarming regularity. A recent bill in California, for instance, sought to deprive noncitizens from selected Middle Eastern countries of the right to obtain a driver's license.[41] Besides the obvious and troublesome racial animus underlying this proposal, the bill was not particularly well reasoned. The presumptive fear that a Middle Eastern individual would rent a truck, drive to a prominent California target, and detonate an explosive device is hardly dissuaded by the state's refusal to grant driver's licenses to such individuals. After all, a suicide bomber is not going to let the absence of a driver's license stop him from carrying out an act of terror. More likely, the bill simply would have deprived hard-working, legal immigrants from the Middle East from enjoying the basic rights to travel and to earn a living—rights freely enjoyed by individuals of other backgrounds.

One of the most troubling manifestations of the war on terrorism is the government-supported racial profiling of Americans of Middle Eastern descent. As David Cole reminds us, prior to 9/11, state legislatures, local police departments, and even the president of the United States and his attorney general, John Ashcroft, had decried the practice. The U.S. Customs Service had promulgated new measures to counter racial profiling at the borders. Even a federal law against the practice seemed likely.[42] These official postures reflected an emerging and widespread consensus condemning the practice. In late 1999, a Gallup poll found that fewer than 20 percent of Americans considered racial profiling an acceptable practice.[43]

After 9/11, views changed radically, and support for racial profiling suddenly tripled. Seemingly overnight, 60 percent of Americans now favored racial profiling, including more-intensive airport scrutiny—insomuch as it was directed against Arabs and Muslims.[44] In fact, in a poll taken immediately after 9/11, over 30 percent of Americans supported "special measures" for Americans of Arab descent, including special identification and even *internment*.[45] Numerous noted legal and political commentators, including Charles Krauthammer, Peter Schuck, and James Q. Wilson, began to advocate racial profiling as an instrumental tool in the fight against terrorism.[46] Seeking to capitalize on the zeitgeist, one spectacularly insensitive congressman, Representative John Cooksey of Louisiana, even declared that anyone with "a diaper on his head and a fan belt around that diaper" ought to be stopped and questioned by the authorities.[47] Support for racial profiling of Arabs and Muslims has even come from the African American community, the group that has historically suffered the most from the practice.[48] A Gallup poll conducted shortly after 9/11 found that African Americans were actually *more* likely than any other ethnic group to support racial profiling and tighter security checks at airports for Americans of Middle Eastern descent.[49] A whopping 71 percent of blacks (compared to 57 percent of whites) said that they would favor subjecting Middle Easterners to extra security at airports. Like the Irish, who attained their white status and American bona fides through their embrace of the rhetoric of racial supremacy and hatred of African Americans,[50] other minority groups have consolidated their standing as good Americans through support for the targeting of Middle Easterners. As Leti Volpp argues, "Other people of color have become 'American' through the process of endorsing racial profiling. Whites, African Americans, East Asian Americans, and Latinas/os are now deemed safe and not required to prove their allegiance."[51]

In the months and years following the 9/11 attacks, the Bush administration approved a series of homeland-security measures, including fingerprinting and deportation orders, that singled out Arab immigrants—even those with no connection to terrorism. In early 2002, the Department of Justice launched Absconder Apprehension Initiative, or Operation Absconder, a program seeking to locate, apprehend, and deport individuals subject to removal orders from the U.S. government. Ostensibly a neutral enforcement of immigration laws, the program has drawn fire for its targeting of individuals of Middle Eastern descent. Although over 314,000 "absconders" exist in the United States,[52] the initiative focused its efforts on over 6,000 young men from Middle Eastern countries.[53] As Susan Akram and Maritza Karmely note, Operation Absconder has been attacked as a veritable witch hunt on Arabs and Muslim.[54] Most significantly, not a single individual detained in the program was charged with a terrorist crime.[55]

On June 6, 2002, the attorney general formally announced the National Security Entry-Exit Registration System (NSEERS), which subjected visitors to the United States from certain countries—predominantly Arab or Muslim—to increased scrutiny, including fingerprinting, periodic registration, and exit controls.[56] In November 2002, NSEERS was amended to include special "call-in" registration. Known as "Special Registration," the policy singled out a limited class of noncitizens—male, nonimmigrant visa holders over the age of sixteen who are from one of twenty-five Muslim and Middle Eastern countries—for special registration requirements with the government that further exacerbated the sense of inquest within the Middle Eastern community.[57]

There is deep irony in these policies. The Bush administration has opposed affirmative action as an outmoded government program that unnecessarily preserves racial differentiation in the colorblind New America.[58] Yet it ensures the perpetuation of invidious racial discrimination through its support of profiling practices. Apparently, to the administration and others, remedial programs meant to offset centuries of racial oppression constitute unacceptable violations of the Equal Protection Clause, but the targeting of racial minorities in the dubious name of national security is perfectly sound. If nothing else, the continued vitality (and even legality) of racial profiling undermines a key assumption of opponents of affirmative action: that we live in a society free of most prejudice and discrimination, save affirmative action itself. If the government continues to engage in the practice of racial profiling on the grounds that it is an effective tool in protecting our national security, then the government must necessarily admit that we do not live in the race-blind society imagined by opponents of affirmative action.

Admittedly, as we all know and have been told time and time again, each one of the 9/11 perpetrators was a man of Middle Eastern descent. Yet even this seemingly simple, factually ascertainable narrative of 9/11 is a product of a biased lens. In an alternative world, using the same set of facts, the interpretive narrative could have been constructed quite differently. The attacks could have been anthologized as the work of a group of anti-Americans, of frustrated young men, of the disenfranchised and socioeconomically disadvantaged,[59] of Saudi Arabians, or of Islamic radicals (with no specific racialized elements). Thus, our collective epistemological summation of the perpetrators could have reduced them to any number of other identity signifiers, including shared ideology, ages, socioeconomic status, gender, religion, or nationality. But it did not. The terrorists were, above all, racialized. Not only is the impact of such a bent dangerous from the point of view of protecting basic civil liberties and preventing the war on terrorism from becoming a war on a race, but its misguided reductionism is also bad public policy.

Supporters of policies targeting Middle Eastern individuals have defended such practices as rational responses to a legitimate threat to the United States. A mass email that has floated about cyberspace over the past several years captures this prevalent mindset. Encapsulating the prevailing zeitgeist and providing a powerful testament, through its repeated forwarding, to its resonance with the public, the email purports to represent a transcript of a speech entitled "America WAKE UP!" and given by Navy Captain Dan Ouimette before the Pensacola Civilian Club, a service organization in Florida. The speech views the events of 9/11 as part of a continuing chain of events that began with the American hostage crisis in November 1979. "Most Americans think [9/11] was the first attack against US soil or in America. How wrong they are. America has been under constant attack since 1979 and we chose to hit the snooze alarm and roll over and go back to sleep."[60] Billed with the subject line "When WWIII Started—1979," the email specifically posits that events during the past quarter century form a systematic campaign of Middle Eastern terrorism against the United States. Understood in a vacuum and as a purely factual and unbiased history lesson, the analysis appears imminently well reasoned, making it virtually impossible for any rational reader not to conclude that there is a monumental race war at hand, pitting two distinct civilizations against each other. Analyzed more carefully and in a fuller context, however, the pedantic chronology exemplifies the sophomoric reductionism that has unfortunately framed perceptions of the Middle East.

Indeed, the selective list of events highlighted—the Iranian hostage crisis in 1979; the attacks on American embassies in Beirut and Kuwait in 1983; the bombings of TWA flight 840 over Argos, Greece, in 1986 and Pan Am flight 103 over Lockerbie, Scotland, in 1988; the attacks on American embassies in Kenya and Tanzania in 1988; the World Trade Center bombing in 1993; the bombing of the USS *Cole* in 2000 in Aden, Yemen; and the horrific attacks of September 11, 2001—is but one oversimplified narrative of a history of recent mass violence involving much more than Middle Eastern terrorism. As uniformly tragic and inexcusable as each of these vicious and barbarous acts was, they were not alone. Indeed, one could construct a similar narrative involving the Oklahoma City bombings, the Columbine massacre, the Waco conflagration, the standoffs with militiamen in Idaho, and various abortion-clinic bombings and conclude that we are facing a systematic threat to our basic freedoms and way of life from Anglo-Saxon conservative Christian evangelicals. Such racist reductionism, however, is unwarranted. Unfortunately for the purveyors of the "America WAKE UP" vision, reality is much more nuanced and complex than the myth of the Middle Eastern peril allows.

It is instructive to compare our collective response to the "America WAKE UP" trope to a possible narrative involving the terrorist threat from Anglo-Saxon conservative Christian evangelicals. Take our national reaction to the largest terrorist attack on American soil prior to 9/11: the Oklahoma City bombing. Although the mainstream media and the American public initially speculated that the attack was the product of Middle Eastern terrorism,[61] investigations proved otherwise. Some observers have noted that law enforcement's focus on Middle Eastern suspects in the wake of the attack even allowed Timothy McVeigh to evade the authorities initially.[62] As we now know, the perpetrators of the Oklahoma City bombing were a cell of crew-cut-sporting Americans of European descent. Interestingly, the response to the Oklahoma City bombing and the problem of "domestic" terrorism never took on a racialist bent. "Timothy McVeigh did not produce a discourse about good whites and bad whites, because we think of him as an individual deviant, a bad actor,"[63] notes Leti Volpp. "We do not think of his actions as representative of an entire racial group. This is part and parcel of how racial subordination functions, to understand nonwhites as directed by group-based determinism but whites as individuals."[64] For example, antiabortion bombers are not identified on the basis of their race (often white) or their religion (often evangelical Christian), and they are certainly not billed as terrorists. When a Christian individual of European descent commits a barbaric act against civilians, he is simply an outlier, a crazed lone gunman. By contrast, when a Muslim of Middle Eastern descent commits a barbaric act against civilians, his acts of terrorism are imputed to all members of his race and religion.

Of course, Middle Easterners are not alone in facing this conundrum. As legal scholar Steven Bender notes, "Anglos tend to be judged by their individual merits—few Anglos viewed Timothy McVeigh or teenage school gunman Kip Kinkel as suggesting Anglos are inclined as a group towards terrorism or mass murder. By contrast, Latinas/os often are regarded in group terms, so that the depiction of a Latino as a murderous, soulless drug dealer is taken to represent all Latinas/os, and the reputation of individual Latinas/os is affected by each such image."[65] That feeling of collective dread that emanates from the bad actions of a member of one's race afflicts many minority groups. Shortly after the Virginia Tech massacre, a friend was expressing to me how affected he was by the tragedy. I thought his focus was on the victims, but it turned out to be on the perpetrator of the crime. An individual of South Korean descent, my friend felt personally humiliated, ashamed, and scared about the fact that the killer shared his ancestry. This internalization of group-based determinism becomes almost second nature to any member of a minority community. When an act of terrorism occurs, Middle Easterners throughout the United States wince in pain. Other than the obvious sadness over the tragic loss of human life, they also have a more selfish motive. They cringe at the possibility that the perpetrator will be Middle Eastern, a fact that will only further ignite hatred and suspicion against them. Holding their collective breaths, they pray that the mug shots on the news are not of men named Mohammed or Amir.

Throughout my childhood and teenage years, I repeatedly was called on by my classmates to respond to any unpleasant event in the Middle East or act of terrorism. I can vividly remember the day during tenth grade when a fellow student waylaid me between classes and confronted me with a belligerent cross-examination about whether my family had ties to the Ayatollah Khomeini and if we thought of the United States as the Great Satan. What my classmate did not realize is that the Ayatollah did more harm to my life, and the lives of other Iranian Americans, than he did to most Westerners. But it did not matter to my classmate that I was an American citizen; it made no difference that it was nonsensical to accuse my family of supporting Khomeini since, as he well knew, we, like so many others, left Iran precisely because of our disgust over Khomeini;

it made no difference to him that I was Catholic, not Muslim. There was nothing that I could do to escape the association, and my classmate's artless bigotry reflected a prevailing misperception that I felt utterly powerless to change.

Of course, many individuals continue to insist that the only rational response to the terror threat is the continued targeting of Middle Eastern Americans. To be sure, there is an understandable temptation to respond to public pressure, if for nothing else than the placebo effect. Take as an example the fascinating case of New York City's crosswalk push buttons. The city houses 3,250 of these push-button boxes, which, in the words of the *New York Times*, offer "harried walkers a rare promise of control over their pedestrian lives."[66] Yet a 2004 investigation revealed that 2,500 of them do not work—and by design. Over the years, they have been intentionally deactivated by city officials because they actually interfered with the coordination of the computer programming of lights that the city uses to better regulate traffic flow. But the buttons continue to provide pedestrians with the illusion of control, and though many pedestrians now realize the buttons no longer function, they still push the buttons when waiting to cross. In our modern interdependent global society, we are all vulnerable to terrorism, and truthfully, there is only so much that a government can actually do to protect its citizenry. Racial profiling takes its place alongside the screening of all shoes through x-ray scanners as efforts to at least make us *feel* that the government is actively doing something. But in promulgating policies targeting individuals on the basis of their race, we are sacrificing fealty to our most precious democratic principles. As David Cole reminds us, "The argument that we cannot afford to rely on something other than racial or ethnic proxies for suspicion, after all, is precisely the rationale used to intern 110,000 persons of Japanese ancestry during World War II."[67]

In this regard, Middle Eastern Americans are asked to—or, more accurately, told that they need to—take one for the team. Take an incident at the University of California at Los Angeles in November 2006, when an Iranian American student, Mostafa Tabatabainejad, was repeatedly Tasered after failing to show identification to campus police at the library. The brutal episode, captured on film by an eyewitness,[68] presents a scene almost as disturbing and difficult to watch as the Rodney King beating some fifteen years earlier. After the first round of Tasering, Tabatabainejad lay incapacitated on the ground. Yet the police repeatedly commanded him to get up. When he was unable to do so, the police callously Tasered him again and again as he screamed in pain. They continued to Taser him even as he was handcuffed, and as the police dragged him through the room, he wailed, "I'm not fighting you" and "I said I would leave."[69] But, unlike the Rodney King beating, the event did not make national headlines, nor did it trigger a debate about law enforcement's treatment of Middle Easterners or even receive widespread condemnation.

Although Internet discussion forums do not exactly constitute bastions of reasoned and erudite discourse, they do reveal popular perceptions and prejudices. A brief exchange from an Internet forum dedicated to discussions about the Tasering incident captures the prevailing sentiment that a failure to profile would represent a colossal lapse in judgment. "When terrorists start having blonde hair and blue eyes," noted one commentator, "I will agree that ID should be checked on blonde haired blue eyed woman rather than arabic [sic] looking young men. It is foolish and irresponsible to refuse to profile. If Mostafa doesn't like that then he should expect to get tazed."[70] The folly of the commentator's viewpoint becomes readily apparent with a simple examination of the most realized terrorist threats against the United States since 9/11, as the face of terrorism does not even reflect the prevailing Middle Eastern racial profile. Richard Reid is the notorious shoe bomber convicted on charges of terrorism for attempting to blow up an American Airlines flight on December 22, 2001. While en route from Paris to Miami, he attempted to light a match to detonate plastic explosives hidden in his shoes. Reid is a British citizen of English and Jamaican descent. Jose Padilla, the American citizen convicted for aiding extremists in a dirty-bomb plot, was born in Brooklyn and is of Puerto Rican descent. More recently, on June 22, 2006, the FBI arrested seven individuals in connection with their alleged terrorist plot against such buildings as Chicago's Sears Tower and sites in Miami. Of the seven, five were American citizens, and the other two were Haitian nationals. All seven were of African descent.[71] Moreover, the group had no apparent ties to Al-Qaeda or other foreign terrorist organizations. Similarly, on May 7, 2007, the federal government arrested six individuals with a domestic plot to attack Fort Dix. Two of the individuals were from Jordan and Turkey, but the remaining four, including a group of three brothers, were born in Yugoslavia and were of Yugoslavian descent.[72] On June 2, 2007, the government arrested four individuals involved in planning a deadly terrorist attack at JFK Airport; none of them hailed from the Middle East.[73]

Most of the recent terrorist acts on American soil have also had no Middle Eastern connection. The deadliest shooting in American history took place on the morning of April 16, 2007, at Virginia Tech and resulted in the death of thirty-three people, including the perpetrator, Seung-Hui Cho. Cho was an American of South Korean descent. The second-deadliest shooting on American soil occurred at the University of Texas some four decades earlier. On August 1, 1966, Charles Whitman, a blond-haired, blue-eyed ex-Marine and former altar boy, an American citizen of European descent, went on a killing spree at the university's clock tower, killing fifteen people and wounding an additional thirty-one. Finally, the third-deadliest massacre—and perhaps the most vivid in the minds of Americans—took place at Columbine High School in Colorado. On April 20, 1999, Eric Harris and Dylan Klebold took their own lives as well as those of thirteen of their classmates and teachers. Harris, a native Kansan of European descent, was raised as a Catholic. Klebold, a native Colora-dan also of European descent, was raised as a Lutheran.

Indeed, recent years have witnessed an alarming increase in acts of do-mestic terrorism. In a single week span, dating from August 24 through October 2, 2006, four separate deadly acts of terrorism took place in our nation's schools: a fatal shooting of a teacher followed by the suicide of the perpetrator, Christopher Williams, an African American, on August 24 at Essex Elementary School in Vermont; the fatal shooting of a hostage following the sexual assault of six school girls by Duane Roger Morrison, a fifty-three-year-old American of European descent, at Platte Canyon High School in Bailey, Colorado, on September 27; the fatal shooting of a school principal by Eric Hainstock, a fifteen-year-old student of European descent, at Weston High School in Cazenovia, Wisconsin, on September 29; and finally, the deadly shooting of five Amish girls at a schoolhouse in Nickel Mines, Pennsylvania, on October 2, by Charles Carl Roberts IV, an American milk-truck driver of European descent.

In another Internet discussion forum in which one commentator had supported the UCLA police's decision to Taser the Iranian American stu-dent, a respondent struck back, "ok racist, your wish is our command— Killings at US schools have never been conducted by Muslim terrorists. Not at the Quaker school this year, not from the University of Texas's clocktower and not from the halls and lunchrooms at Columbine. Those were all carried out by Caucasians. Infact [sic] using your dipshit logic, ONLY whites should have their IDs checked in school libraries since they are the ones who kill people in American schools."[74]

Profiling has also threatened to relegate Americans of Middle Eastern descent to the status of second-class citizens and cement their position as perpetual foreigners who can never quite become American. In short, the practice betrays our most basic and cherished values of inclusiveness and equality. Witness the case of Cyrus Kar, a former Navy SEAL, staunch supporter of the war in Iraq, and American citizen of Iranian descent and Zoroastrian faith. In 2005, Kar found himself in the midst of a Kafkaesque ordeal. As a filmmaker working on a documentary about his namesake, King Cyrus the Great of Persia, Kar had visited England, Germany, Iran, Turkey, Afghanistan, and Tajikistan to conduct interviews and shoot footage for his movie. He then obtained specific permission from the U.S. government to visit Iraq in order to film archeological sites around ancient Babylon. Several days after his entry into the country, he and his cameraman hired a cab driver to take them to the city of Balad. At a checkpoint, police discovered two plastic bags with washing-machine timers in the trunk of the car. Kar was summarily arrested and handed over to American military officials, who subsequently detained him. The FBI quickly cleared Kar of any wrongdoing, concluding, as Kar had claimed all along, that the timers belonged to the cab driver and that Kar had had no knowledge or involvement with any terrorist or insurgent activities. Nevertheless, the military continued to hold him without charges and in solitary confinement for approximately seven weeks. As Kar's attorney later observed, "Saddam Hussein [was given] more due process than Cyrus Kar."[75]

Eventually, concerned relatives in the United States learned of Kar's whereabouts and filed a habeas corpus petition on Kar's behalf. It was only then—after more than fifty days in custody—that the government released Kar. While Kar was in captivity, the government denied him his fundamental right to counsel. The military, for its part, remained unapologetic: "This case highlights the effectiveness of our detainee review process," noted Brigadier General Don Alston, a Coalition Forces spokesperson. "We followed well-established procedures and Mr. Kar has now been properly released." Understood literally, Alston's comments strangely suggest that depriving Americans of the right to counsel and the ability to know the charges facing them are now well-established procedures. Understood in context, however, the comments appear to communicate a more specific idea: that well-established procedures now involve depriving Americans *of Middle Eastern descent* of basic civil rights whenever the remotest specter of national security is raised.

The effectiveness of racial profiling is also problematic, even if one wishes to target on the basis of apparent Arab ancestry. Criminologist Albert Alschuler has noted that the defensibility of racial profiling rests on the ability of law enforcement to distinguish members of different racial groups.[76] Courts have already questioned the ability to identify Latinos by their appearance,[77] and one can make the same critique of efforts to profile Arabs. As Akram and Karmely posit, "Arabs are even less racially or ethnically homogeneous than Mexicans or Hispanics—those fitting stereotypical 'Arab-appearance' will most likely be profiled and stopped, while many Arabs will not be."[78] Thus, even if there is a meaningful correlation between Arab or Muslim background and terror risk, the policy is both wildly over- and underinclusive—a fact with which I am intimately familiar. I am frequently perceived as an Arab Muslim. I am neither Arab nor Muslim.

Our racial-profiling practices are not only bad policy, however. They also fail to pass muster under the Constitution, which requires any government policy implicating race to be narrowly tailored to further a compelling government interest. Although our national security undoubtedly constitutes a compelling government interest, the racial profiling of Middle Easterners as a part of the war on terrorism is not a narrowly tailored policy under existing Supreme Court jurisprudence.

In *Craig v. Boren*,[79] the Supreme Court addressed an equal protection challenge to a government policy based on gender classifications—a type of discrimination traditionally subject to lesser scrutiny by the courts than racial categorizations. Law-enforcement statistics have long confirmed that young men, especially those between the ages of eighteen and twenty-one, are far more likely than young women of the same age to engage in drunk driving. Drawing on this fact, the State of Oklahoma set two different minimum drinking ages: eighteen for females, twenty-one for males. When the policy was challenged by two underage men and a female beer vendor, the Supreme Court struck the law on the grounds that it violated the Constitution's Equal Protection Clause. As the Court readily admitted, the fact that only 0.18 percent of females yet 2 percent of males between the ages of eighteen and twenty had engaged in drunk driving represented a "disparity [that] is not trivial in a statistical sense."[80] Yet, as the Court concluded, such a disparity "hardly can form the basis for employment of a gender line as a classifying device. Certainly if maleness is to serve as a proxy for drinking and driving, a correlation of 2% must be considered an unduly tenuous 'fit.'"[81] As legal scholar David Cole reminds us, "the vast majority of persons who appear Arab or Muslim—probably well over 99.9 percent—have no involvement with terrorism."[82] As such, the percentage of drunk drivers among college-age men is undoubtedly far greater than the percentage of terrorists among men of Middle Eastern appearance. If a classification based on gender is impermissible under the former fact, then surely classification based on race is manifestly unconstitutional under the latter fact.[83]

As the facts reveal, *terrorism knows no creed or color*. By thinking otherwise, not only do we sacrifice our true national security, but we also threaten to make the war on terrorism into a race war. By abandoning the rule of law, we betray the principles of equality and nondiscrimination that form the bedrocks of our democracy. The tale of John Walker Lindh, the American Taliban, is revealing on several levels. First, Lindh demonstrates that the terror threat can come from socioeconomically advantaged American males of European descent. More importantly, it reveals the impending danger that the war on terrorism will indeed degenerate into a war on a particular race.

After his capture while fighting for Al-Qaeda in the hills of Afghanistan, Lindh was tried for his treasonous actions in a federal court, where, among other things, he enjoyed full due-process protection, the requirement of a unanimous jury for conviction, strict admissibility rules for evidence used against him, and perhaps most significantly, a top-notch legal defense team composed of attorneys from one of the most reputable law firms in the country. At the same time, 158 nonwhites captured for their alleged activities against the United States (including some individuals who were fighting alongside Lindh) were held in cages at a U.S. military base in Guantánamo Bay, Cuba, conveniently located outside the United States proper to avoid complications with constitutional protections. These individuals were held indefinitely without charges, and the government refused to accord them the basic protections of the Geneva Conventions. The government also denied them individualized hearings to determine the lawfulness of their detainment. When asked why Lindh enjoyed the benefits of civil justice while others were relegated to a regime of military justice with substantially fewer protections for the accused, the Bush administration claimed that Lindh was an American, whereas the others were foreign nationals.[84] But that distinction held no weight. Not long after proffering this rationalization, the administration discovered that Yasser Hamdi, one of the individuals held at Guantánamo Bay, had been born in Louisiana and was, therefore, an American citizen. Yet Hamdi did not receive the rights enjoyed by Lindh. Although our government eventually transferred Hamdi from Guantánamo Bay to the continental United States, it "continued to assert authority over him under the same conditions as the foreign nationals held in Guantánamo Bay: indefinitely, without charges, without trial, without access to a lawyer, and, for all practical purposes, incommunicado."[85] Ultimately, the Supreme Court rejected the constitutionality of the administration's treatment of Hamdi. In a 6–3 decision, the Court sustained the government's right to hold American citizens as enemy combatants without criminal charges if they were engaged in hostilities against the United States. But, in a repudiation of the Bush administration's position, the Court found that Hamdi had a right to petition civil courts with the assistance of effective counsel to challenge his status as an enemy combatant.[86]

One further note on Hamdi bears mentioning. Instead of pushing forward with the proceedings following the Supreme Court's ruling, the government released and deported Hamdi to Saudi Arabia on October 9, 2004. In return, Hamdi simply agreed to renounce his American citizenship and comply with strict travel restrictions going forward. Hamdi's release represents a shocking turn of events involving a supposedly grave threat to our national security. If Hamdi were really as dangerous as the government repeatedly asserted, his release is a stunning abdication of the government's duty to protect us from terrorism. If he is not as dangerous as claimed, his treatment deserves scrutiny and demands, at the very least, a compelling justification.

Whether rightly or wrongly, our constitutional jurisprudence draws a sharp divide between the rights to which citizens are entitled and the rights afforded to noncitizens. But the stark contrast in treatment between Lindh and Hamdi suggests that civil rights entitlements are even more fractured than that. Specifically, we appear to have two distinct classes of citizenship: the white and the Other. The prevalent discourse surrounding the Lindh affair epitomized this double standard. Lindh was repeatedly portrayed as just a lost, confused teenager experimenting with alternative ways of life. Indeed, no less than George W. Bush referred to Lindh as merely "some misguided Marin County hot-tubber."[87] Our president's word choice is emblematic of our problematic approach to the war on terrorism. The white American of European descent who fights for Al-Qaeda is just "misguided." The brown guy who fights for Al-Qaeda is a terrorist and an embodiment of the anti-American hostility ubiquitous throughout the Middle East.

The Problem with Plenary Power: Immigration Authority, the Lessons of History, and the Middle Eastern Question

The promulgation of such racially suspect policies as the disparate treatment among Lindh, Hamdi, and the Guantánamo Bay detainees has been particularly facile given the cognitive dissonance between our mythic embrace of a race-blind society and the realities of our equal protection jurisprudence. On one hand, we have a domestic set of rules that dictates equal protection for all, regardless of race, ethnicity, or national origin. Thus, any government policy that accounts for race—even in remediation of past or present discrimination—must survive strict scrutiny. On the other hand, through the plenary power doctrine, which grants the legislative and executive branches broad authority on immigration issues, the Supreme Court has virtually exempted government action in the immigration arena from equal protection analysis and exacting constitutional scrutiny.[88] As a result, we have legitimized an external set of rules in which the admission and deportation of noncitizens are intricately intertwined with notions of race, ethnicity, and national origin.[89] Since many Middle Easterners in our country are immigrants, efforts to target them are frequently immunized from significant judicial scrutiny.

The historical treatment of both Latinos and Asian Americans at the hands of the plenary power doctrine is critical to understanding the ominous implications of post-9/11 government policies. Under the plenary power doctrine, courts have granted the federal government unilateral authority to exclude specific populations from immigration to the United States. This principal was firmly established in *Chae Chan Ping v. United States*, the Chinese Exclusion case.[90] In 1882, on the heels of massive American sinophobia, Congress passed the Chinese Exclusion Act, which banned all Chinese immigration to the United States. Six years later, Chae Chan Ping, a longtime legal resident of California, attempted to return to the United States following a trip to China. Port officials in San Francisco refused to permit his entry on the grounds that the 1882 act, as amended, had excluded all Chinese nationals from admittance into the United States. Ping fought the decision all the way to the Supreme Court, challenging the constitutionality of the Chinese Exclusion Act. The Court, however, affirmed the decision of the port officials, holding that "[t]he power of exclusion of foreigners being an incident of sovereignty belonging to the government of the United States as a part of those sovereign powers delegated by the constitution, the right to its exercise at any time when, in the judgment of the government, the interests of the country require it, cannot be granted away or restrained on behalf of any one."[91]

The Chinese Exclusion case firmly established the wide latitude that Congress possessed in making nationality based determinations on immigrant fitness. As the Court freely admitted, the Chinese Exclusion Act was inspired by the prevailing belief that Chinese immigrants "had a baneful effect upon the material interests of the state, and upon public morals; that their immigration was in numbers approaching the character of an Oriental invasion, and was a menace to our civilization; that the discontent from this cause was not confined to any political party, or to any class or nationality, but was well nigh universal; [and] that they retained the habits and customs of their own country . . . , without any interest in our country or its institutions."[92] When these sentiments obtained the imprimatur of the federal government, the fate of Chinese immigrants was sealed. Other ethnic groups from the Far East followed in the footsteps of the Chinese. When their inassimilability was established in the public imagination, they found themselves similarly excluded. By 1907, the government successfully tapped off the flow of Japanese immigration to the United States. And by 1924, the government banned all immigration from the Asian continent.

The racialization of these ethnic groups was intricately related to the assimilability debate. As Deenesh Sohoni has documented, although various ethnic groups from the Far East were originally treated as legally distinct, they were eventually fused into an "Asian" collective. This social category was a response to congressional legislation and judicial rulings that envisioned these distinct groups as outsiders, not entitled to the benefits of naturalization and incapable of fully performing whiteness.[93] The Chinese, Japanese, and Filipino became Asian precisely because of their shared status as the inassimilable, and always foreign, Other.

Images of the Chinese contagion in the 1880s were therefore readily transferred to fuel anti-Japanese sentiment, providing support for the "Gentleman's Agreement" of 1907 that similarly restricted Japanese immigration to the United States and the Alien Land Laws of the western states that limited Japanese property ownership in California and elsewhere.[94] In the words of Keith Aoki, laws such as the Chinese Exclusion Act and the Alien Land Laws "created a category of persons existing at sufferance of their white neighbors—as well as the state attorney general and county district attorneys—a 'caste' of less-than-worthy persons occupying land at the pleasure of white 'owners.' This symbolic dispossession and material deprivation laid the ideological, legal and cultural foundation for the mass physical dispossession, evacuation and internment of Japanese and Japanese Americans on the West Coast in 1942."[95] Regulation and stereotype therefore fed on each other, ultimately and ominously laying the groundwork for Executive Order 9066, which authorized the internment of Japanese Americans during World War II.[96]

As race theorist Neil Gotanda reminds us, tragic abuses such as the internment do not simply emerge from a vacuum.[97] They are often the logical product of a growing assault on civil rights that institutionalizes racism through the course of many decades. What began as a seemingly constitutional exercise in plenary authority over immigration issues degenerated into the wholesale assault on the civil rights of Asian Americans. The events leading up to the Japanese American internment convey, in the words of Aoki, an "inescapable lesson . . . that the denial of basic rights such as due process and property ownership of noncitizens may be a step toward the cavalier denial of civil rights to citizens."[98] We face a similar danger in today's environment.

Unfortunately courts have ignored this lesson, glibly ignoring the risks inherent in condoning immigration policies that create a disfavored, or enemy, alien. A war against enemy aliens from a particular country or region can rapidly degenerate into a declaration of war against an enemy race. David Cole has demonstrated how quickly American policy during World War II devolved from singling out the enemy aliens to persecuting an entire enemy race. During that era, demands to protect the nation from subversive activities by Japanese nationals residing in the United States devolved into the wholesale targeting of all individuals of Japanese ancestry.[99] In the words of Lieutenant General John L. DeWitt, the driving force behind the Japanese internment, "A Jap's a Jap. It makes no difference whether he is an American citizen or not."[100] Thus, with the blessing of the Supreme Court,[101] the government rounded up over 110,000 individuals of Japanese ancestry, the majority of whom were American citizens, and threw them into internment camps in the name of national security. The war against a nation became a war against a particular ethnicity.

The contemporary Middle Eastern question has antecedents in the experiences of Latinos. Race scholar Kevin Johnson has drawn instructive parallels[102] between the war on terrorism and the often-forgotten "repatriation" of almost one million individuals of Mexican descent—60 percent of whom were U.S. citizens—during the 1930s.[103] In a study of this virtual ethnic-cleansing campaign that took place at the height of the Great Depression, economist Leo Grebler notes that "local agencies, saddled with mounting relief and unemployment problems, used a variety of methods to rid themselves of 'Mexicans': persuasion, coaxing, incentive, and unauthorized coercion. Special railroad trains were made available, with fare at least to the Mexican border prepaid; and people were often rounded up by local agencies to fill carloads of human cargo. In an atmosphere of pressing emergency, little if any time was spent on determining whether the methods infringed upon the rights of citizens."[104] The roundups recall the Special Registration and Extraordinary Rendition programs of the U.S. government in conducting the war on terrorism.

The Chinese, Japanese, and Mexican American experiences therefore serve as cautionary tales for our troublesome handling of the Middle Eastern question and the war on terrorism. In a comprehensive study, Susan Akram and Maritza Karmely have documented the ominous evolution of post-9/11 policies into a broader inquest on Middle Eastern Americans.[105] In the immediate aftermath of 9/11, the government targeted predominantly Arab and Muslim *noncitizens*. With policies such as the Special Registration and Operation Absconder, the government used visa violations and deportation orders as a pretext to conduct further investigation of potential persons of interest. These initial policies, however, soon gave way to broader programs that implicated Arab and Muslim citizens and noncitizens alike, including the expansive use of surveillance authority permitted under the USA Patriot Act, racial profiling at the airports, and growing rates of job discrimination and hate crime to which the government has not sufficiently responded.

Existing jurisprudence does not help matters, as courts have become prey to the same conflation of nationality and ethnicity. The Supreme Court's tragic *Korematsu* decision, which affirmed the constitutionality of the internment of Japanese Americans during World War II, is an obvious example. But, more subtly, consider how easily the available Supreme Court precedent on profiling meanders between policies governed by alienage to law enforcement based on race. In *United States v. Brignoni-Ponce*,[106] the Supreme Court considered whether an immigration stop by border officials predicated solely on the "apparent Mexican ancestry" of a vehicle's occupants violated the Fourth Amendment. Although the Court held that singular reliance on apparent Mexican ancestry violated the reasonableness standard of the Search and Seizure Clause, the Court blessed the explicit use of racial factors in the enforcement of immigration laws, confidently stating that "the likelihood that any given person of Mexican ancestry is an alien is high enough to make Mexican appearance a relevant factor."[107] The targeting of aliens of a particular nationality (in this case, Mexican) easily led the Court to condone the singling out of both citizens and noncitizens of particular ethnicities (in this case, "Mexican looking") by law enforcement. Despite the rhetoric of colorblindness that permeates recent Supreme Court jurisprudence, one cannot help but wonder whether the Court would respond similarly in situations involving Middle Eastern Americans and national security.

All told, the plenary power doctrine has subjected groups on the precipice of whiteness to be singled out during times of national crisis, enabling these "perpetual foreigners" to be targeted as scapegoats. Whether it was economic security at play during the Great Depression (as in the case of Mexican Americans) or military security at play during World War II (as in the case of Japanese Americans), the plenary power doctrine paved the way for the war on a particular nation to transcend alienage and transform itself into a war on a particular race. In the post-9/11 era, we are in danger of repeating this ugly mistake.

Consider the results of 2006's *Turkmen* case,[108] which emphasizes the minimal legal protection granted Middle Eastern immigrants facing discriminatory conduct from state actors. In the suit, which challenged a variety of government actions in the wake of 9/11, a federal district court in New York largely immunized the government from liability, despite a record replete with proof of vile racial and religious animus. The facts of the case are simple and troubling. A group of eight male noncitizen Muslim immigrants from the Middle East (with the exception of one Hindu from India) sued the federal government for a series of roundups after 9/11 in which they were detained indefinitely, without bond or criminal charges, pending investigation by the government of their possible ties to terrorist organization. Broadly speaking, the plaintiffs charged that the government arrests impermissibly targeted them on the basis of their perceived race, religion, ethnicity, and national origin in violation of the Equal Protection Clause. They also argued that the conditions of their extended confinement violated their basic constitutional rights.

Although the Court allowed their challenge to certain specific terms of their confinement to proceed, their equal protection challenge to their general arrest and detention failed and was dismissed. The Court found no constitutional violation in the imposition of a blanket "no bond" policy and the virtually indefinite detention of the plaintiffs. In short, the Court's summary dismissal of many of the plaintiffs' constitutional claims granted the government a veritable carte blanche in the treatment of noncitizens, thereby blessing the creation of equal-protection-free zones at the whim of the executive. Fears David Cole, "What this decision says is the next time there is a terror attack, the government is free to round up every Muslim immigrant in the U.S., based solely on their ethnic and religious identity, and hold them on immigration pretexts for as long as it desires."[109]

As the stories of the six men held at the Metropolitan Detention Center in Brooklyn, New York, reveal, the plight of each of the *Turkmen* plaintiffs was all too similar. Two consistent themes emerge: the systematic hatred that animated the treatment they received and the dehumanizing consequences. At the end of their ordeal, most of the *Turkmen* plaintiffs were summarily removed from the county and their money and personal papers never returned. They were simply rendered nonpersons at the direct hands of the state.

Shakir Baloch, a medical doctor, Pakistani Muslim, and citizen of Canada since 1994, had entered the United States in order to find work. He was rounded up after September 11 and detained on suspicion of terrorist links. Among other things, he suffered a beating from five guards who called him a "fucking Muslim terrorist" and asserted, "You did this to us. We're going to kill you."[110] After more than six months of detention, and absent any proof of terrorist ties, he was summarily deported from the county: he was placed on a plane with a one-way ticket to Toronto without money or identification.

Yasser Ebrahim, who had been married to an American citizen for several years, was a web designer and Egyptian Muslim. Hany Ibrahim, his brother, worked at a delicatessen. They too were gathered following 9/11 and held on suspicion of terrorist links. In detention, they were repeatedly called "fucking Muslims" and "terrorists" while being physically beaten.[111] The racial and religious hostility animating official actions manifested itself on numerous occasions during their confinement. One guard warned them, "If you open your mouth, I will crush you under the elevator, just like at the World Trade Center."[112] When they pleaded for respect of their basic civil rights, they were told, "Forget about human rights. Three thousand people died in the World Trade Center. You have no rights."[113] When they asked for a pen, a guard asked them, "Are you going to write to Osama bin Laden?"[114]

Yasser and Hany received clearance for deportation within three months of arriving at the detention center. Yet they remained there for an additional six months. Ultimately, after a total of nine months in custody, they were summarily deported. Unable to substantiate any terrorist link, the government deposited them on a plane with a one-way ticket to Cairo without money or any of the personal belongings confiscated from them upon arrest.[115]

Ashraf Ali Ibrahim, a citizen of Egypt and a Muslim, had lived in the United States for over a decade and owned a bottled-water distribution business. Detained two weeks after 9/11, he remained in custody without any criminal charges or proper access to counsel for a period of six months. During this time, he suffered numerous beatings, denial of access to medical treatment for his injuries, and repeated excessive strip searches that involved, inter alia, abuse of his genitalia. Although his deportation cleared in December, he spent an additional four months in detention before being shipped off to Cairo in March 2002 without any property or money.[116]

Syed Amjad Ali Jaffri, a Canadian resident and Muslim native of Pakistan, was detained by the FBI and INS. For the first two months of his detention, officials denied him a bar of soap. He received two squares of toilet paper per day and was served meals without any utensils. At one point, a detention-center guard slammed his head into a wall and injured his teeth. He was denied proper medical attention for the incident, and when he finally did see a dentist, he was diagnosed with advanced bone loss and periodontal disease, forcing him to have numerous teeth extracted. On December 20, 2001, an immigration judge ordered him deported for having an expired visa. But the government continued to detain him, without explanation, for an additional three months. When he was finally placed on a plane leaving the country, officials did not return his money or personal papers.[117]

Asif Ur-Rehman Saffi, a citizen of France and a Muslim native of Pakistan, held a master's degree in political science and was a Microsoft Certified Professional doing computer-related work in the United States. He was initially denied all reading material during his detention. Eventually, he was given a Bible. Denied free exercise of his religion, he faced repeated rejections to his request for Halal food and told that the detention center was "a jail, not a hotel, and that [he] should ask Allah for food."[118] Though he was eventually cleared of any link to any terrorist organization, he spent half a year in detention.[119] Ultimately, the U.S. government deported him, placing him on a plane to France without money or identification cards.[120]

Admittedly, all the *Turkmen* plaintiffs had expired visas. That fact, though, did not warrant the abusive treatment they received in blatant violation of their due process rights. Not a single criminal charge was ever filed against any of the *Turkmen* plaintiffs, yet they endured many months in detention, including significant time after immigration judges had ordered them deported. Even if our national-security concerns absolutely demanded prolonged detention, there is no reason to immunize the government's treatment of them from constitutional scrutiny.

In June 2003, the Office of the Inspector General (OIG) of the U.S. Department of Justice released a 198-page report entitled *A Review of the Treatment of Aliens Held on Immigration Charges in Connection with the Investigation of the September 11 Attacks* ("OIG Report"). Six months later, the OIG issued its *Supplemental Report on September 11 Detainees' Allegations of Abuse at the Metropolitan Detention Center in Brooklyn, New York*. These two reports independently substantiated many of the plaintiffs' claims and demonstrated that countless other individuals of Middle Eastern descent had suffered similar abuse.

Despite these troubling facts, the court repudiated the viability of many of the plaintiffs' claims. Right from the outset, the troubling logic of the court manifests itself. The opinion's introduction reduces the plaintiffs' claims to a simple, and ultimately spurious, analogy: the case of a routine traffic stop. Reasoned Judge Gleeson, "An officer who wants to search a suspect's car for a handgun can pull him over (a Fourth Amendment 'seizure') for changing lanes without using his blinker (a traffic violation), even if the officer has no interest in enforcing the laws requiring drivers to signal a lane change. . . . Similarly, the government may use its authority to detain illegal aliens pending deportation even if its real interest is building criminal cases against them."[121] This disturbingly flippant analogy fails on numerous levels. The slight inconvenience of a traffic stop hardly compares to the massive deprivation of freedom from the prolonged detention that the *Turkmen* plaintiffs faced, even discounting the abusive treatment. Moreover, in the end, there was no criminal case, or even any criminal charges pressed, against any of the *Turkmen* plaintiffs, let alone probable cause. Finally, the court conveniently omits the fact that, under basic equal protection jurisprudence, a police officer cannot solely target individuals of one ethnic group for traffic stops, no matter how minor the predicate violations.

Yet the "traffic stops" occurring after 9/11 indisputably and facially targeted individuals on the basis of race and religion, a fact that the government made no attempt to obfuscate and a tack that the court ultimately upheld: "There is thus nothing outrageous about the plaintiffs' claim of national-origin discrimination in this context; the executive is free to single out 'nationals of a particular country' and 'focus[]' enforcement efforts on them. . . . In the immediate aftermath of [9/11], when the government had only the barest of information about the hijackers to aid its efforts to prevent further terrorist attacks, it determined to subject to greater scrutiny aliens who shared characteristics with the hijackers, such as violating their visas and national origin and/or religion."[122] As the court concludes, "As a tool fashioned by the executive branch to ferret out information to prevent additional terrorist attacks, this approach may have been crude, but it was not so irrational or outrageous as to warrant judicial intrusion into an area in which courts have little experience and less expertise."[123]

Although the court admits that the government's methods were crude, it finds nothing irrational or outrageous about them. But the methods of the government were far more than crude and, arguably, were irrational. Although most (but not all) of the *Turkmen* plaintiffs shared a religion with the hijackers, strangely enough, they did not share the same national origin. Fifteen of the nineteen perpetrators of the 9/11 attack hailed from one country: Saudi Arabia. Of the remaining four, two came from the United Arab Emirates, one from Egypt, and one from Lebanon. By sharp contrast, not a single *Turkmen* plaintiff came from Saudi Arabia. The eight named plaintiffs were Muslims from Pakistan, Egypt, and Turkey and a Hindu born in India. Clearly, the court's discussion of national origin is nothing more than a red herring, attempting to ground the government's policies within its power to regulate immigration from various countries. The court fails to call the roundup what it really was: a government policy dominated by *perceptions* of racial affiliation and religious identification. The lack of a match between the hijackers and the *Turkmen* plaintiffs on national origin betrays the religious and racial targeting at the heart of the government's decision-making calculus. Indeed, the logic of the policy, and the blessing it received from the court, is not far removed from the infamous *Korematsu* decision upholding the internment of Japanese Americans during World War II. After all, to the Supreme Court, the roundup of Japanese Americans seemed a crude but reasonable response to the hysteria about the possibility of a Japanese invasion on American soil.

The didactic flow of the court's decision bears disturbing similarity to antecedent cases in which our judiciary has turned a blind eye toward constitutional violations. For example, an analysis of the first reported American decision on the issue of segregation follows a strikingly similar logical train. Although the following analysis does not aim to equate the horrors of segregation with post-9/11 measures taken against "persons of interest," it does illuminate the shared jurisprudential rationalizations that enable manifest injustices to continue unabated, in brazen circumvention of our constitutional values.

The first case to address the constitutionality of segregation, *Roberts v. City of Boston*,[124] came nearly half a century before the Supreme Court's infamous separate-but-equal decision in *Plessy v. Ferguson*. In 1850, Sarah C. Roberts, through her father, Benjamin, contested her exclusion from a Boston public school on the grounds of her race. As an African American, she could not attend schools segregated by the city's school committee. Roberts challenged the segregation policy, arguing that it violated the Constitution and laws of the state of Massachusetts by depriving African Americans of equal protection under the law. The court ultimately rejected her plea. For our purposes, the court's methodology is particularly salient. The narrative arc of the decision forms an all too common trope embraced by courts when they shirk their obligations and refuse to undo policies that clearly violate the Constitution's spirit and tenor.

First, in a classic move, the court waxes eloquent in flowery language about the high-minded principles of our constitutional democracy, even paying homage to the plaintiff's position: "The great principle, advanced by the learned and eloquent advocate of the plaintiff, is, that by the constitution and laws of Massachusetts, all persons without distinction of age or sex, birth or color, origin or condition, are equal before the law. This, as a broad general principle, such as ought to appear in a declaration of rights, is perfectly sound; it is not only, expressed in terms, but pervades and animates the whole spirit of our constitution of free government."[125] Second, in a resounding shift, the court notes, almost with seeming reluctance, that critical exceptions to these high-minded principles are needed in order to allow government to respond to particular circumstances or exigencies. Wrote the Massachusetts Supreme Court,

> But, when this great principle comes to be applied to the actual and various conditions of persons in society, it will not warrant the assertion, that men and women are legally clothed with the same civil and political powers, and that children and adults are legally to have the same functions and be subject to the same treatment; but only that the rights of all, as

they are settled and regulated by law, are equally entitled to the paternal consideration and protection of the law, for their maintenance and security. What those rights are, to which individuals, in the infinite variety of circumstances by which they are surrounded in society, are entitled, must depend on laws adapted to their respective relations and conditions.[126]

Based on these exigencies, the court proceeds to defer to the government's judgment, granting plenary authority in the particular area at issue in the suit. In *Roberts*, this meant deferring to the city's school committee to decide what was best for the educational needs of children: "The power of general superintendence vests a plenary authority in the committee to arrange, classify, and distribute pupils, in such a manner as they think best adapted to their general proficiency and welfare."[127]

Finally, the court blesses this grant of deference with a frequently unscrutinized assertion that the policy question is well within the reasonable judgment of the governing authority. Rationalized the *Roberts* court, "The committee, *apparently upon great deliberation*, have come to the conclusion, that the good of both classes of schools will be best promoted, by maintaining the separate primary schools for colored and for white children and we can perceive no ground to doubt, that this is the honest result of their experience and judgment."[128]

This four-part process—disingenuous lip service to principle, followed by an exception that swallows the rule, a grant of plenary authority, and the use of only the most superficial judicial scrutiny of the government policy in question—is particularly powerful because it has the power to render the most vile and unconstitutional of policies seemingly reasonable. Upon cursory examination, the *Roberts* opinion sounds entirely acceptable and judicious—until one stops to scrutinize carefully the logic and understand the context. And therein lies its precise danger. This pattern has replicated itself at various times in American jurisprudence. Most significantly, one can see the same logic come to bear in the post-9/11 cases.

Indeed, the narrative arc of the *Turkmen* decision bears a haunting resemblance to that of the *Roberts* decision rendered a century and a half earlier. The *Turkmen* court begins by acknowledging the high-minded principle that discrimination on the basis of race, religion, and national origin is generally impermissible under the Constitution. Then, the court provides the exception to that rule: "This is, of course, an extraordinarily rough and overbroad sort of distinction of which, if applied to citizens, our courts would be highly suspicious. Yet the Supreme Court has repeatedly held that the political branches, '[i]n the exercise of [their] broad power over naturalization and immigration . . . regularly make[] rules that would be unacceptable if applied to citizens.'"[129] Akin to the *Roberts* court, the *Turkmen* court upholds the broad latitude of the federal government under immigration laws to enforce policies with disparate treatment according to religion, race, and national origin by appealing to the need to allow government to respond to exigencies. This gaping hole in the Constitution's guarantee of equal protection under the law, however, eviscerates the universalism of our respect for rights and undermines our democratic values.

The rationalizing principle for the exception to basic equal protection norms is none other than the plenary power granted to the executive in the areas of immigration, foreign policy, and national security. One of the frequent criticisms of equal protection and antidiscrimination jurisprudence is the animus requirement. Discriminatory impact on a particular class of individuals is not enough to call a government policy into question on equal protection grounds. Instead, a plaintiff must also demonstrate actual animus behind the policy. For example, in *McClesky v. Kemp*,[130] an African American death-row inmate in Georgia charged with murdering a white police officer challenged the administration of the death penalty in the state, arguing that it violated the Constitution's Equal Protection Clause. Statistics demonstrated that a defendant who killed a white victim was 4.3 times more likely to receive the death penalty than a defendant who killed a black victim. Consequently, the administration of the death penalty in Georgia involved disparate treatment among defendants depending on the race of their victim. Inmate McClesky nevertheless could not establish that disparate treatment resulted from actual animus or discriminatory intent by lawmakers and those implementing the penalty. As such, the Supreme Court denied McClesky's petition. In the immigration and foreign-policy contexts, the standard is even more heavily weighed in favor of the government: even with a showing of animus, you cannot make out an equal protection violation since the courts simply will not scrutinize the purpose behind the government's actions.

Indeed, the *Turkmen* court refuses to subject the government's actions to any kind of meaningful scrutiny. In the spirit of the *Roberts* court some 150 years earlier, the court pleads the importance of deference. True to form, the *Turkmen* decision is riddled with language opining how ill equipped courts would be to scrutinize decisions by the executive on foreign-policy or immigration issues. "The Executive should not have to disclose its 'real' reasons for deeming nationals of a particular country a special threat—or indeed for simply wishing to antagonize a particular foreign country by focusing on that country's nationals—and even if it did disclose them a court would be ill equipped to determine their authenticity and utterly unable to assess their adequacy."[131] The court's conclusion is one of deference. At another juncture, the court reasons that although the approach taken by the government may have been crude, it was not actionable. But these bald assertions beg a simple question: Why not? Why shouldn't the courts scrutinize such government activities?

The reasoning of the court is deterministic and specious on several levels. First, courts make judgments about myriad aspects of human life about which they possess little expertise. In my own field of intellectual property, judges have no problem making aesthetically bound judgments as to what constitutes transformative artistic use for the purposes of copyright's fair-use test. Judges regularly decide cases involving complex patents in the absence of any scientific background. In the area of constitutional law, judges virtually determine questions as profound and ill suited for their range of expertise as when life itself begins.[132] It is somewhat perplexing, then, for a court to assert that judges somehow cannot understand national-security issues and their attendant confidentiality concerns. The purported concern over judicial intrusion smacks a bit disingenuous, especially given the fact that the lack of experience by the judiciary in the arena of foreign affairs is brought on by the courts' repeated deference to the executive in these matters in the first place. If security and confidentiality is a question, in camera review is a possibility. For example, over the course of the past three decades, the U.S. Foreign Intelligence Surveillance Court (FISC)—established in 1978 with the passage of the Foreign Intelligence Surveillance Act—has conducted reviews of government wiretap requests in foreign-intelligence investigations. Never once has the FISC court suffered from a leak, and all its hearings and decisions are conducted in complete secrecy. Thus, with its hollow lip service to constitutional values, its use of the plenary power heuristic, and its ruse of deference and inexperience, the court allows even the most brazen violations of our "race-blind"[133] Constitution to escape judicial scrutiny.[134]

Several observations highlight the dangers of the government's post-9/11 policies and the court's ruling in *Turkmen*. Our government's promulgation of the policies at issue in *Turkmen* undermines the weight of our diplomatic rhetoric promoting the rule of law and civil rights abroad. Additionally, and more directly, the executive's policies and the judiciary's blessing thereof emasculate any credible claim that we live under a race-blind government. If anything, the government's policies, which may grant certain ethnic groups (e.g., those of Middle Eastern descent) fewer rights than others, actively promotes a message of not just difference but a badge of inferiority. "Separate," wrote the Supreme Court in *Brown v. Board of Education*, is "inherently unequal."[135] Yet we fail to heed that decision's important lesson. Indeed, continued support for government policies that specifically target individuals on the basis of their ethnicity or religion for indefinite suspension of their most basic civil rights blatantly flies in the face of the Bush administration's embrace of a race-blind Constitution when opposing such ostensibly outmoded policies as affirmative action. Evidently, we do not live in a race-blind society, and, in part, the government is responsible for that by continuing to promulgate policies that indisputably target particular ethnic groups.

Finally, the court's ruling was particularly significant in light of the serious abuses raised by the government's detention policies—abuses confirmed by the Justice Department's own Inspector General, who issued a report criticizing the government's policies for their cavalier implementation and failure to carefully distinguish between potential terrorism suspects and immigrants with minor visa violations. *Turkmen* brought to light a litany of concerning violations: excessive detention terms to secure removal from the United States; inhumane detention conditions; unusually harsh treatment based on race, religion, and national origin; violation of the right to counsel and consular communication; unreasonable and excessive strip searches; communication blackouts; sleep deprivation; denial of religious freedom and interference with religious practices; and vicious beatings and verbal abuse. In short, it raised a list of civil rights violations that we more commonly associate with a despotic Third World regime rather than the world's most powerful democracy.

Unfortunately, the events recounted in the *Turkmen* case represent only the tip of the iceberg. The full extent of our government's activities in Guantánamo Bay remains unknown. Just as disturbingly, details have only recently come to light about the government's remarkable Extraordinary Rendition program, which functions as a form of veritable torture outsourcing. Under the program, the U.S. government operates interrogation centers in countries where, in the euphemistic words of one court, "legal safeguards do not constrain efforts to interrogate suspected terrorists."[136]

Take the case of German citizen Khaled el-Masri, who was abducted in Macedonia, turned over to the CIA, held for twenty-three days, severely beaten, drugged, and, oddly enough, given an enema. He was then taken, dressed in a diaper and jumpsuit, to Afghanistan, where he was held at the notorious "Salt Pit" prison and subjected to repeated rounds of torture. Five months later, he was chained to the seat of a plane and unceremoniously deposited on a desolate road in Albania without apology, money, or personal effects. The government admitted that there was no evidence tying him to terrorism. It appears that his "detainment" was the result of a confusion stemming from the similar spelling of his last name with that of suspected terrorist Khalid al-Masri, an alleged mentor to Al-Qaeda's Hamburg cell.

Following his experience, el-Masri sued the U.S. government, charging the CIA with infringement of his basic due process rights and violation of the Alien Torts Statute. The suit was dismissed when the government raised the state-secrets privilege in its defense. The government maintained that adjudication of the case would invariably lead to the disclosure of state secrets, and therefore the case should not proceed. In response, the court initially warned that judges "must not blindly accept the Executive Branch's assertion [of the state-secrets privilege], but must instead independently and carefully determine whether, in the circumstances, the claimed secrets deserve the protection of the privilege."[137] In blatant disregard of this caveat, however, the court dispatched with the suit. The Fourth Circuit ultimately affirmed this decision, and the Supreme Court denied certiorari.[138]

The courts' handling of state-secrets claims reveals a problematic absence of meaningful judicial scrutiny. To avoid a suit allegedly involving state secrets from continuing, the government need merely show a "reasonable danger that compulsion of the evidence will expose military matters which, in the interest of national security, should not be divulged."[139] Moreover, the privilege is absolute and is not balanced against any other interests.[140] Thus, under the state-secrets privilege, the executive's powers remain wholly unchecked—a resounding abdication of the separation-of-powers doctrine that has historically informed our constitutional superstructure. The *El-Masri* court rejected even the possibility of in camera review,[141] a perplexing tack considering the government's acknowledgment of the Extraordinary Rendition program's existence, the profound civil rights issues at stake, and the experience of courts in competently dealing with review of sensitive information.

The problematic abuse of civil rights and the perpetuation of discriminatory immigration-related policies that escape judicial review is not just a product of 9/11. The Extraordinary Rendition program at issue in the *El-Masri* case actually came into effect during the Clinton administration. Although justified under the banner of the "extraordinary factual context that gave rise to the plaintiffs' detention,"[142] numerous aspects of the government's treatment of the *Turkmen* plaintiffs actually predate 9/11. For example, the *Turkmen* plaintiffs charged the government with obstructing their ability to carry out their religious practices, placing minor visa violators in detention with hardened criminals in disregard for their safety, and abusive treatment based on anti-Islamic and anti–Middle Eastern sentiment. Although such treatment is more prevalent after 9/11, it is nothing new. The case of Salah Abbod Saleh Al Salami, which took place largely before 9/11 and the present Iraq war, is particularly instructive. It is also one with which I am intimately familiar; I had the privilege of serving as Al Salami's legal counsel. The story, all too common, reveals a fundamental disconnect between our constitutional values and the government's frequent mistreatment of individuals of Middle Eastern descent.

Al Salami was born and raised as a Shi'a Muslim in Iraq. Throughout his formative years, endemic poverty, political conflict, and religious discord were a part of everyday life. With Saddam Hussein's ascension to power in 1979, however, the political and economic situation in Iraq rapidly devolved into something much more dire. Large-scale political repression, mass hunger, and overt religious strife grew quotidian, and life became particularly trying for those groups identified as enemies of the state. As a Shi'a Muslim, Al Salami fell within this targeted class, and he was constantly under suspicion for subversive activities against Saddam Hussein—a Sunni Muslim—and his Baath Party.

Shortly after the failed uprisings against Hussein following the first Gulf War in the early 1990s, Al Salami's cousins were assassinated by Hussein's security forces. Al Salami and his brother were arrested and, on a theory of guilt by association, brutally tortured and beaten. After enduring multiple rounds of electroshock torture, Al Salami's brother was permanently rendered into a catatonic state. Al Salami was only slightly luckier. Among other things, he suffered repeated physical abuse as he was tied down to a chair and whipped, and he had his teeth forcibly removed by pliers. In the end, he managed to survive and was released. But Hussein had made sure that he could not return to his existing job, and for the next few years, he was periodically arrested and brutally tortured at random. Finally, in 1999, when an opportunity arose to escape the country, Al Salami made the difficult decision to leave his friends and family behind in order to flee the intolerable conditions in Iraq and to seek a better life in the United States. His departure proved difficult, however. From Iraq, Al Salami traveled to Syria by boat, and then from Syria to Thailand, which took two months. He left Thailand and flew to China, where he remained for three days. From China, he flew to the United States, where his journey finally ended at Los Angeles International Airport.

Unfortunately, Al Salami's arrival in the United States on November 18, 1999, did not bring the freedom he had envisioned. Upon arrival, he approached an immigration official at Los Angeles International Airport and requested political asylum. He told the official that if forced to return to Iraq, he would be executed. He was immediately detained by the Immigration and Naturalization Service (INS) and transported to the Mira Loma Detention Center in Lancaster, California. After eighty-four days in detention, on February 9, 2000, a credible-fear interview was finally conducted. The asylum officer who conducted the interview determined that Al Salami demonstrated a credible fear of persecution along with a "significant possibility that [he] could establish eligibility for asylum."[143] Following the credible-fear interview, Al Salami was ordered to appear before an Immigration Judge (IJ) to formally show cause as to why he should not be sent back to Iraq.

On May 18, 2000, Al Salami made his appearance in Immigration Court. Despite the fact that Al Salami was initially found to have had a credible fear of persecution, the IJ ordered him removed to Iraq. The IJ based his denial of relief entirely on an adverse credibility finding, while inexplicably stating that his determination was not based on Al Salami's demeanor. While Al Salami appealed the decision, he remained in detention, where he suffered from severe Post-Traumatic Stress Disorder (PTSD) caused by his numerous arrests and constant torture in Iraq. Additionally, he was unable to eat or sleep. Despite no proof that he presented a danger to the community, the INS refused to release him. Even worse, following a request from counsel for a written denial of release, the INS transferred him from an immigration detention center to the Bakersfield County Jail. No written response to the request was ever issued.

Al Salami's experiences at the INS detention center in Lancaster left him feeling depressed, hopeless, confused, and fearful. The transfer to Bakersfield County Jail only worsened his mental and physical state and severely exacerbated his PTSD. Additionally, Al Salami's constitutional rights were blatantly violated when he was repeatedly offered only a daily pork diet, despite his protests that this infringed on his religious beliefs. This pork diet was continuously served during an especially important time in the Muslim year—the holy season of Ramadan, which lasted from November 27, 2000, through December 26, 2000. Ultimately, Al Salami lost thirty-two pounds. He was also in constant anguish because of the damage to his gums from the beatings in Iraq. The pain in his lower back was so severe that he spent five days in the jail hospital.

After 265 days in jail, Al Salami was a broken man. He insisted that his appeal be withdrawn so that he might obtain release from jail. In return for dropping his appeal, the INS granted him release from incarceration, but he had no assurance of asylum in the United States. At a moment's notice, the INS still had the authority to round him up and deport him back to Iraq, where he would face immediate death. But Al Salami believed that he would die if he remained incarcerated, and he hoped that withdrawal of the appeal might lead to his release—even if it ultimately led to his deportation back to Iraq, where he would surely face death. As Al Salami described it, "I was sad. I felt hopeless. I felt I had no future. I felt I was going to die there. Bakersfield was terrible. I will die in [Bakersfield]."[144] The appeal was withdrawn from the Board of Immigration Appeals (BIA) on August 24, 2000. The order of removal went into effect, but because of international treaty obligations, the United States could not deport him back to Iraq immediately.

Though his appeal was withdrawn, Al Salami remained in detention and subjected to severe, degrading, and abusive treatment. So that he might be released from these conditions, a petition for writ of habeas corpus was filed in federal district court on his behalf on December 28, 2000. The petition argued that Al Salami's detention exceeded the scope of a lawful detention, that his procedural due process rights were violated, and that the district director abused his discretion by failing to consider Al Salami's individual circumstances in determining whether he was a flight risk. On January 31, 2001, and before a decision on the petition was issued, the INS finally released him.

Yet his release hardly constituted a victory. Al Salami found himself in legal limbo: he was not entitled to legally remain in our country and faced the continual threat of imminent deportation. He was a man without a country, and his circumstances rendered him unable to hold a steady job. At regular intervals, he had to meet INS officials, who at any moment could carry out his deportation.

Free at least from the confines of detention, Al Salami was able to gather further evidence to substantiate his asylum claim. As such, on July 18, 2001, he filed a motion to reopen proceedings based on three new evidentiary bases: the issuance by the Iraqi regime of a death warrant in Al Salami's name, detailed postrelease psychological and physical evaluations, and published reports from human-rights organizations documenting deteriorating conditions in Iraq.

The warrant, issued by and bearing the seal of the Iraqi Central Intelligence Agency and dated October 10, 1999, called for Al Salami's arrest for "opposing the authority, attacking the political leadership, and causing trouble."[145] Al Salami's family bribed an Iraqi official at great expense in order to acquire the arrest order. Since it was too dangerous to mail the warrant directly out of Iraq, they smuggled it out of Iraq to a Jordanian friend, who then mailed it to Al Salami. Based on the regime's prior treatment of Al Salami and persons similarly situated, the arrest warrant was, in reality, tantamount to a death warrant.

New evidence obtained from dental examinations of Al Salami was also offered to support the motion to reopen. From May 18, 2001, to June 28, 2001, Al Salami received dental treatment that confirmed that his upper front teeth were broken during a torture session and that his teeth were later removed with pliers. Dental notes indicated that bone chips were found, along with a cracked root and nerve damage. These dental notes and the surgery confirmed Al Salami's claims of torture.

An evaluation of Al Salami, conducted by a licensed psychotherapist who specialized in the assessment and treatment of trauma, documented how, during a recounting of his brother's torture, Al Salami "appeared deeply affected, angry, and saddened by much of the traumatic material that he shared."[146] The report also assayed Al Salami's sleeping difficulties, appetite loss, sadness, fear, and lack of interest in activities that he once enjoyed, noting his frequent spells of terror, marked by panic, crying, and disabling headaches. The psychotherapist diagnosed Al Salami with PTSD, caused by the traumatic violence he experienced in Iraq and exacerbated by prolonged detention in the United States. Additionally, the psychotherapist assessed Al Salami's credibility. He reported that several factors contributed to his belief that Al Salami testified accurately about the traumatic events in Iraq. First, Al Salami demonstrated significant emotional effects of the trauma during the evaluation sessions. Second, Al Salami described his problems in a manner consistent with one who had experienced such trauma. Third, in support of his motion to reopen, Al Salami also presented reports by various human-rights organizations documenting recent deteriorating changes in the conditions in Iraq. As all the reports noted, although human-rights abuses had long existed in Iraq, conditions had deteriorated significantly. Amnesty International reported that Hussein's regime had found new and even more inhumane ways of torturing alleged enemies of the Iraqi regime; people who spoke out in opposition to the government now faced tongue amputation. Even those who merely made slanderous or abusive remarks about Saddam Hussein or his family received such punishment. Even more appalling, the Iraqi government had added beheading to its repertoire of terror. These new facts demonstrated that any fear that Al Salami had about returning to Iraq was legitimate and well founded. Deportation would only have made him another statistic in Iraq's long line of human-rights violations.

Despite the introduction of the aforementioned evidence, on September 1, 2001, the IJ denied the motion to reopen. Al Salami appealed, arguing that he had made a sufficient demonstration of changed circumstances, new evidence, and extraordinary conditions to warrant reopening. The BIA issued a one-line summary affirmation of the IJ's flat denial of the motion to reopen.

At this point, Peter Afrasiabi (my friend and fellow attorney) and I heard about Al Salami's case and the manifest injustice he had suffered. With the support of our law firm at the time, O'Melveny & Myers, we obtained from the Ninth Circuit a stay on his deportation and proceeded to prepare his appeal. In our appeal, we challenged the failure of the BIA and IJ to reopen the case, the unconstitutional treatment that Al Salami had endured in detention, and the constitutionality of the BIA's summary affirmance mechanism, which denied Al Salami's claim for political asylum. As we argued, the mechanism, which enables the BIA to affirm an immigration judge's findings without any opinion or analysis, violated Al Salami's right to a meaningful appeal and deprived him of his constitutional right to due process. Though the summary affirmance mechanism had been in place for quite some time, its use dramatically increased with the blessing of Attorney General John Ashcroft in the wake of 9/11.

After reviewing our arguments, the Department of Justice agreed to waive its right to challenge the appeal and consented to remand the case to the BIA to properly consider Al Salami's claims on their merits. Subsequently, we returned to the BIA. On July 31, 2003, the board unanimously overturned the refusal of the IJ to reopen Al Salami's case. Finally, in

2004, Al Salami returned to the IJ with a renewed opportunity to have his case adjudicated from the very beginning, on its merits. With the trial, we were finally able to obtain political asylum for Al Salami. He now possesses a green card and resides in California.

Our victory in the case affirmed the basic notion that the constitutional right to due process and meaningful appellate review extends to everyone, including Middle Eastern immigrants seeking political asylum in our country. Al Salami came to the United States to flee the brutal dictatorship of Saddam Hussein. The victory acknowledged not only Al Salami's rights but the fundamental differences between a country such as ours—one that operates on the basis of the rule of law and the extension of basic rights to all individuals, citizens and noncitizens alike—and the autocracy from which Al Salami fled.

Unfortunately, our government's initial treatment of Al Salami highlights the fundamental inconsistencies between our democratic values and egalitarian principles, on one hand, and the realities of our equal protection jurisprudence and our targeted policies against immigrants of Middle Eastern descent, on the other hand.[147] Al Salami had fled his homeland after being brutally tortured solely as a result of his religious affiliation and his purported political activities in opposing the totalitarian regime of Saddam Hussein. Al Salami's cousins had already been assassinated by Hussein, and deportation back to Iraq would have assured him of the same fate. Al Salami had anticipated freedom when he arrived on our shores. Instead, he was immediately detained, waited eighty-four days before a credible-fear interview was even conducted by the INS, and spent 265 days incarcerated with hardened criminals, where he suffered verbal and physical abuse and violations of his rights. Ultimately, he was arbitrarily denied his request for political asylum and ordered deported back to Iraq. There was never a single charge against Al Salami, not a scintilla of evidence suggesting he threatened our national security, and no accusation that he had even the remotest link to a terrorist organization. Yet at virtually every step of the administrative process, his plea for asylum was rebuffed. It was not until his case came before the U.S. Court of Appeals for the Ninth Circuit that the abuses of the government came undone. Al Salami now enjoys a life far removed from the incomparable brutality and horror of the Hussein regime, and there is much to praise about our county's ability and willingness to provide him with this new start. But Al Salami's story also suggests that we need to do a better job of safeguarding the rights of immigrants, including those of Middle Eastern descent.

Unfortunately, since 9/11, the treatment of Middle Eastern immigrants has only gotten worse.

Justice Denied: The Judiciary and the Middle Eastern Subject

Executive, administrative, and judicial bodies have failed to adequately protect the civil rights of Americans of Middle Eastern descent, a situation exacerbated by those bodies' own procedural machinations. For example, in an eerie recasting of the naturalization cases of the early twentieth century, some courts have continued to play pernicious racial-determination games that threaten the ability of Middle Easterners to seek legal redress for the violation of their rights.

In 1978, Majid Ghaidan Al-Khazraji, an Arab American professor, was denied tenure by his employer, St. Francis College. When his efforts to appeal the decision internally failed, he sought redress in the American justice system by filing a section 1981 action against the school, claiming a violation of his civil rights on the grounds of race.[148] Originating from the Civil Rights Act of 1866,[149] § 1981 dictates that

> [a]ll persons within the jurisdiction of the United States shall have the same right in every State and Territory to make and enforce contracts, to sue, be parties, give evidence, and to the full and equal benefit of all laws and proceedings for the security of persons and property as is enjoyed by white citizens.[150]

As the Supreme Court held in *Runyon v. McCrary*,[151] the section applies to all racial discrimination in both private and public contracts.[152] Al-Khazraji claimed that the college's denial of tenure deprived him of the contractual rights enjoyed by similarly positioned white citizens. In response, the college contended that Al-Khazraji, as an Arab, was Caucasian and therefore not a member of a race different from that of his supervisors. As such, he was "not a protected person under Section 1981 when he is presumably claiming other Caucasians or whites were improperly favored over him,"[153] and therefore he had no standing to sue under § 1981. A federal district court in Pennsylvania agreed, granting summary judgment to the college and holding that a claim of discrimination on the basis of being an Arab was not cognizable under § 1981.[154] Ultimately, the Third Circuit reversed,[155] and the Supreme Court agreed.[156] The issue, however, occupied the federal court system for almost a decade, forcing both the Third

Circuit and Supreme Court to consider an absurd and seemingly facile question: whether Arabs could ever be the victims of racial prejudice.

Despite the Supreme Court's holding in *Al-Khazraji*, the problematization of whiteness reemerged a few years later. In 1991, Dale Sandhu, an Indian male from Punjab, sued his employer of eight years, Lockheed Missiles and Space Company. According to Sandhu, race discrimination had resulted in his 1990 termination from the company.[157] Initially, a California court quickly dispensed with the case, dismissing the suit on the grounds that Sandhu was technically a Caucasian and that he could therefore not sue his employers for race discrimination.[158] Wrote the court, "by definition, [Sandhu] is Caucasian, . . . [and] a person who is in fact Caucasian may not complain of race [discrimination]."[159] Besides the troublesome assumption that Caucasians cannot seek relief for race discrimination, the trial court's decision was ironic in light of the Supreme Court precedent of *United States v. Thind*,[160] in which the Court held that Indians were not white for the purposes of qualifying for naturalization.[161] The California Court of Appeals ultimately reversed the *Sandhu* decision. But both the *Al-Khazraji* and *Sandhu* cases reflect the continuing antinomy of whiteness and the tangible problems that result from it. When it was a matter of denying naturalization rights, courts frequently found individuals of Middle Eastern and Indian descent not white; but when it was a matter of denying relief for discrimination, courts have found the same individuals white. The results echo the Catch-22 illustrated at the outset of this book.

The failure to learn from the past and acknowledge the extent to which race is a social construct almost led to a similarly problematic result in *Shaare Tefila Congregation v. Cobb*.[162] In that case, a federal district court in Maryland dismissed charges against eight private defendants for violations of federal law arising from the defendants' alleged desecration of a congregation's synagogue. One of the key issues in the case centered on whether the defendants' alleged acts constituted racial discrimination in violation of 42 U.S.C. § 1982, for the defendants admittedly perceived Jews as a racially distinct group. Section 1982 provides that "[a]ll citizens of the United States shall have the same right, in every State and Territory, as is enjoyed by white citizens thereof to inherit, purchase, lease, sell, hold, and convey real and personal property."[163] The congregation averred that desecration of the synagogue stemmed from racial prejudice and deprived them of the right to hold real and personal property.[164] As both the district court and the Fourth Circuit (in affirming the lower court) held, § 1982 was not meant to attach to "situations in which a plaintiff is not a member of a racially distinct group but is merely perceived to be so by defendants."[165] As Jewish individuals did not constitute a racially distinct group, the court had to sustain the defendants' dismissal motion.

In their rulings, the two courts failed to recognize race as a social construction, rather than as a scientific fact or an inherent element of human existence. "Although we sympathize with appellant's position," the court noted, "we conclude that it cannot support a claim of racial discrimination solely on the basis of defendants' perception of Jews as being members of a racially distinct group. To allow otherwise would permit charges of racial discrimination to arise out of nothing more than the subjective, irrational perceptions of defendants."[166] Strangely, the court did not acknowledge that *all* discrimination suits arise from these senseless misperceptions; as the racial-prerequisite cases have taught us, racial categories themselves are arbitrary constructs of the human mind. Judge Wilkinson's partial concurrence eloquently captures this critique of the majority view: "All racial prejudice is the result of subjective, irrational perceptions, which drain individuals of their dignity because of their perceived equivalence as members of a racial group."[167]

Although the Supreme Court eventually reversed the Fourth Circuit, its resolution of the case remained problematic: the Supreme Court itself failed to establish an unambiguous test for § 1982 violations and chose instead to ignore the lower courts' definition of race.[168] Writing for the majority, Justice White suggested that § 1982 did protect plaintiffs from intentional discrimination solely because of their "ancestry or ethnic characteristics."[169] But his opinion never explained how this phrase could apply to Jews, who arguably constitute neither a distinct race nor an ethnic group.[170] Furthermore, the Court made no mention of Judge Wilkinson's subjective-perception test, which acknowledges race as a social construction. Adoption of such a test—which reflects the reality of racial categories—would "avoid[] the problem of defining ancestry or ethnicity by expanding the scope of racial discrimination to include subjective perceptions of groups as race. Jews would qualify under this test regardless of their status as a religious group because Jewish people are perceived as a race."[171] Instead, the Supreme Court stubbornly refused to acknowledge race as a social construct.[172] In so doing, the Court left the door open for it to continue to engage in games of racial determination that can only place excessive discretion in the hands of judges and lead to perversions of justice. It makes no sense, for example, to declare Indians nonwhite for the purpose of denying them citizenship but then to declare them white for the purpose of denying them § 1982 relief when they face discrimination.

The use of inconsistent racial machinations to systematically deny rights is nothing new. Take, for example, the pliable definition of blackness. On one hand, courts have accepted a broad definition of blackness to uphold social sanctions such as segregation against African Americans. The petitioner in *Plessy v. Ferguson* was, without question by the Court, subject to segregation and treated as black even though he possessed only "one-eighth African blood."[173] Yet in the rare instances when black racial identity conferred a privilege under the law, its definition was read narrowly. In the *Cruz* case in 1938,[174] an individual with three-quarters Native American ancestry and one-quarter African ancestry petitioned for naturalization on the grounds that he was of African descent. The federal district court that heard his case firmly rejected his plea, arguing that one-quarter ancestry did not make someone of African descent. Notably, the court ignored the fact that, by the early 1900s, several states, including Georgia, Virginia, Alabama, and Oklahoma had adopted one-drop rules, thereby making any individual with the slightest quantum of African blood subject to segregation.[175]

Similarly, courts have strategically exploited the contested whiteness of Latinos to facilitate the deprivation of rights. In the 1940s, when civil rights litigators began to challenge the segregation of Mexican Americans, state courts would "dismiss claims by covering Mexican Americans with the Caucasian cloak" and would "chastise civil rights litigators for presenting their 'white' clients as victims of racial discrimination."[176] Concludes Ariela Gross, "while at times, Mexican American activists and litigators were able to use legal whiteness as a tool in their civil rights struggles, especially in the effort to desegregate schools, whiteness was used against them more often than on their behalf."[177] In sum, racial-determination games produce results that undermine faith in the judicial system and convince Middle Easterners (perhaps, quite rightfully) that the odds are stacked against them in modern America.

Besides occasionally delving into racial-determination games that yield absurd results, courts have been similarly unsympathetic to many recent efforts by Middle Easterners to vindicate their civil rights. In 2005, a federal jury held that Abdul Azimi, a Muslim immigrant from Afghanistan, had suffered racial, religious, and ethnic harassment at his prior workplace, a meat market in Maine.[178] The uncontroverted evidence presented at trial demonstrated that Azimi had endured, among other things, years of racial and ethnic invective and abuse at the hands of his co-workers. At one point, Azimi received an anonymous note in his work locker that read, "Hey MotherFucker Why don't you GO BACK to your Own Country. You don't bE long HERE you Fucking musselum [*sic*][.] You PIECE of Shit WE HATE YOU."[179] The note, which included a swastika, concluded, "YOUR [*sic*] NOTHing but a Fucking NIGGER."[180] At another point, one of his co-workers railed, "Nigger, Sudan [*sic*] Hussein is waiting for you."[181] Azimi's co-workers also once placed a photograph of Osama bin Laden in his locker with the words "Your Dad need [*sic*] Help"[182] scribbled on it.

The hatred even grew physical. In one incident, co-workers forced pork into Azimi's mouth as they shouted "fuck you and fuck your God; fuck your religion."[183] Co-workers frequently filled Azimi's pockets with ham, destroyed his work equipment and placed his shoes in the toilet. In short, Azimi was verbally and physically assailed, humiliated, and threatened repeatedly on the grounds of his race and religion. Left with no other options, he sought relief from the government, filing a human-rights complaint with the appropriate authorities. Shortly after filing his complaint and just a few weeks after the attacks of 9/11, Azimi was summarily fired.

Despite this overwhelming evidence of brutal hostility and hatred aimed at Azimi's race and religion, the jury found that he had not endured any harm for which he could receive compensatory, punitive, or even nominal damages. The jury declined to award Azimi even a single dollar for the discrimination it wholeheartedly admitted that he had suffered. Although the special verdict acknowledged that Azimi's employer "knew or should have known of the offensive hostile work environment and failed to take adequate and effective remedial measures," the jury shockingly found that the employer's unlawful harassment had not caused Azimi "to be damaged by emotional distress, pain, suffering, emotional anguish, loss of enjoyment of life and/or inconvenience."[184]

Azimi appealed the verdict. Argued Zachary Heiden, a staff attorney with the Maine Civil Liberties Union, who filed an amicus brief on Azimi's behalf, "If our country's civil rights laws are to mean anything, there must be some real penalty associated with severe racial, ethnic or religious harassment."[185] The U.S. Court of Appeals for the First Circuit, however, disagreed, affirming in its entirety the jury verdict and denial of relief to Azimi. The court's opinion touted the need for deference: "Although a reasonable jury could have awarded damages based on the evidence presented, there is no plausible argument that on these facts a reasonable jury was *compelled* to give a compensatory damages award."[186]

The stunning verdict, and the published appellate opinion affirming it, provided a virtual carte blanche for the targeting of Middle Easterners in the workplace and threatened to send a profoundly disturbing message that the courthouse door could be effectively shut for Middle Easterners seeking redress for the brazen violation of their most basic civil rights. In short, the *Azimi* case provides ample support for the view that it is open season on Middle Easterners.

Shockingly, as far as civil rights suits involving Middle Easterners go, the *Azimi* case was a relative success for the plaintiff. In 2007, the year of the *Azimi* decision, courts reported decisions on sixty-nine employment-discrimination cases involving claims by Muslims. The *Azimi* case, notes the *New York Times*, was the only "victory, if you can call it that."[187]

Indeed, matters appear to be getting worse, as courts have begun to bless explicitly the racial profiling on airlines of individuals bearing Middle Eastern appearances. Supreme Court Chief Justice Roberts's plurality opinion in *Parents Involved in Community Schools v. Seattle School District No. 1* famously announced that "[t]he way to stop discrimination on the basis of race is to stop discriminating on the basis of race."[188] Yet that edict apparently gave the First Circuit no pause when it declared that "[r]ace or ethnic origin of a passenger may, depending on context, be relevant information in the total mix of information raising concerns that transport of a passenger 'might be' inimical to safety."[189] On this basis, the First Circuit took the remarkable step of reversing a jury verdict finding in favor of an individual allegedly racially profiled and forcibly deplaned because of his Middle Eastern looks.

Not only have Middle Easterners seen efforts at justice spurned by the courts; they have also experienced injustice at the hands of the judiciary, a particularly disturbing fact in light of the judicial system's traditional role in serving as the last bastion for the protection of civil rights. Although the evidence is largely anecdotal, the principle of equality before the law is being undermined by the specter of hatred against Middle Easterners. In 2003, a Lebanese American woman appeared in a Tarrytown, New York, court for a parking violation. The judge promptly asked her if she was a terrorist. Stunned, she did not answer. Later, according to the woman, the judge castigated her: "You don't want to pay a ticket, but you have money to support terrorists."[190] The woman collapsed. The judge later resigned, admitting to the first, but not second, statement.[191]

More recently, in Alexandria, Virginia, Ali Al-Timimi—an Arab American, Muslim, biologist, religious scholar, and lecturer on Islamic studies—faced federal criminal charges for his exhortations to a group of followers.[192] His lectures, argued the government, incited listeners to join the Taliban. In closing arguments, Assistant United States Attorney Gordon Kromberg instructed the jury that Al-Timimi would lie to the jury because the jurors were "kafir"—nonbelievers: "If you're a kafir, Timimi believes in time of war he's supposed to lie to you. Don't fall for it. Find him—find Sheik Ali Timimi—guilty as charged."[193] The jury convicted Al-Timimi, and he now faces the possibility of lifetime imprisonment. Whether Al-Timimi's speaking activities constituted unprotected imminent incitements to violence is one question; drawing on the religious and racial prejudices of jury members in order to assure conviction of a defendant is quite another. As the Al-Timimi and Tarrytown cases reflect, even the judiciary has threatened to make the civil rights of Middle Easterners yet another casualty of 9/11.

At the same time, the war on terrorism has heightened intolerance not only toward Arabs, Muslims, and individuals perceived to be either but also "toward all immigrants and racial minorities."[194] As a result, minority groups that have previously endured challenges to their loyalty are once again being targeted for additional scrutiny. In the area of immigration, for example, national-security concerns posed by the war on terrorism have increasingly dominated public discourse and influenced the body politic. An immigration monism, as Kevin Johnson and Bernard Trujillo dub it,[195] has emerged triumphant in the post-9/11 era and has rendered border control synonymous with the preservation of national security and unity, broadly defined.[196] Perversely, this singular focus has resulted in targeted policies with a racialist bent that have only alienated immigrant groups and important potential allies in the war on terrorism. Additionally, stricter immigration laws have resulted. Thus, the war on terrorism has had a profound collateral effect on Latinos. Some Latinos have suffered because they may look Middle Eastern. More significantly, the concern about border security precipitated by the events of 9/11 has led to increased scrutiny of immigration policies and consideration of ethnic assimilability. The resulting immigration debate has occasionally degenerated into outright xenophobia and racism that has targeted Latinos, especially Mexican Americans.[197] The increased scrutiny of Arab and Muslim immigrants in the wake of 9/11 has expanded into a broader debate over security, assimilability, race, and loyalty that touches everyone whose whiteness is in question.

All told, despite its many successes, the modern civil rights movement has fundamentally failed Americans of Middle Eastern descent. And that failure now threatens the many advances we have made in civil rights for all groups. Although troubling, however, the situation is not without hope. Chapter 6 explores some of the steps that we can take in order to extend the fruits of the civil rights movement to America's Middle Eastern minority and reaffirm our country's proud and remarkable history of inclusion and equality.

6

Lifting the Veil
Thinking about Reform

We now turn our attention to the issue of reform and how we might ensure better protection for the civil rights of Middle Eastern Americans. As we have seen, the antinomy of Middle Eastern racial classification has stifled the identification and resolution of issues facing the Middle Eastern American population. Although the ultimate cure to the ongoing assault on Middle Eastern civil rights may take years to achieve, several relatively simple steps can help initiate meaningful reform.

The various chapters of this book have flagged numerous areas where concrete changes are needed. We must

- reform media portrayals of the Middle East and Middle Easterners;
- encourage greater political action in the Middle Eastern community itself through grassroots initiatives;
- tackle the airline industry's problematic treatment of individuals of Middle Eastern descent;
- reevaluate the plenary power doctrine and the immunization of immigration law from equal protection jurisprudence;
- consider outlawing the practice of racial profiling;
- recognize Middle Easterners in a separate category to help promote their contribution to diversity in education and the workplace and to prevent the absurd racial-determination games that have threatened to undermine efforts to vindicate their civil rights;
- step up enforcement efforts against both public and private discrimination against Middle Eastern Americans; and
- raise public consciousness about issues of concern to the Middle Eastern community and dismantle stereotypes about individuals of Middle Eastern descent.

In this chapter, I examine a few of these proposals in greater detail. First, I argue that the government should consider relieving Americans of Middle Eastern descent from compulsory whiteness and granting them a distinct demographic category. In a bureaucratic age, the only thing worse than being reduced to a statistic is not being reduced to one. Without their own category, Middle Eastern Americans remain relatively invisible, and the issues specific to them are whitewashed from the public and political discourse. Second, I advance the view that Middle Easterners contribute as meaningfully as any minority group to racial and cultural diversity in both the educational and workplace environment. To this effect, I emphasize the need to expand the Middle Eastern presence in elite American legal circles, including the academy, judiciary, and upper echelons of private practice, as a vehicle to advance recognition of issues related to the Middle Eastern population. Finally, I urge academics, both legal and nonlegal, policymakers, and the public at large to engage in a dialogue regarding the pressing issues facing Middle Eastern Americans. It is time to lift the metaphorical veil hanging over our Middle Eastern minority.

Quantifying Discrimination against Middle Eastern Americans

One of the largest problems facing the Middle Eastern population in the United States is that of invisibility. Specifically, the Middle Eastern population remains unorganized and unrecognized, a fact spurred on by the government's approach to categorizing them. As noted earlier, there is little doubt that in the wake of 9/11, Middle Eastern individuals have become a key target of racial profiling by police and security officers. However, the magnitude of this practice is impossible to quantify when there is no accurate government measurement of it. And without data to measure its existence, the problem is underappreciated, and potential remedies cannot be effectively assessed.

Of course, the collection of data raises immediate concerns. For example, it recently came to light that the U.S. Census Bureau provided, upon request, detailed information about the Arab American population—including population size, specific ancestry, and national origin by zipcode—to the U.S. Customs Service and the Bureau of Customs and Border Protection at the Department of Homeland Security (DHS).[1] When asked to comment, DHS claimed that the information was needed to create language-specific signage for outbound airport operations.[2] Besides the disingenuous explanation proffered by DHS, the leak becomes particularly troubling when one considers that a similar information-exchange campaign enabled the internment of Japanese Americans during World War II.[3] Data collection certainly makes racial profiling and the targeting of Middle Easterners easier for the government. And, as this example makes clear, Middle Eastern Americans are not being categorized as white within the national-security apparatus—a step that should be taken in other areas of government, where disaggregated data could benefit, rather than harm, the Middle Eastern community.

A recent example from Chicago demonstrates the problematic categorization of Middle Easterners as white in government data. In a misguided, but well-meaning, attempt to combat racism, Illinois law now requires police officers to identify the race of individuals they stop. But, in so doing, police officers may choose only from the following list of racial categories: "Caucasian, African-American, Hispanic, Asian/Pacific Islander, and Native American/Alaskan Native."[4] When questions arose as to how the Chicago police should classify individuals of Middle Eastern descent, they initially checked the "Asian/Pacific Islander" box.[5] Higher authorities then instructed them to check the "Caucasian" box.[6] Confusion abounded, obfuscating the data and undermining analysts' ability to parse its meaning. As Rouhy Shalabi, the president of the Arab American Bar Association, has argued, "You can't tell whether Arab-Americans are being profiled if we're counted with whites. Ideally, there should be another box . . . to be more specific."[7]

In fact, prior to 9/11, a series of high-profile studies by social scientists sought to analyze the problem of racial profiling. Remarkably, none of these studies gave Middle Easterners their own category. Instead, the racial profiling of a Middle Easterner counted simply as the racial profiling of a white person—a flagrant shortcoming even at the time of the studies.[8]

Surprisingly, this problem continues even after 9/11. In 2007, the U.S. Department of Justice issued a comprehensive empirical report of contact between the police and the public.[9] Among other things, the study concluded that although they faced traffic stops at a similar rate as whites, blacks and Hispanics were more than twice as likely to be searched. Yet the study's use of racial categories was inherently flawed, as it divided individuals into one of four basic racial categories: white, black, Hispanic, and other (American Indians, Alaska Natives, Asians, and Native Hawaiians and other Pacific Islanders). Individuals of Middle Eastern descent were once again dissolved into the white category, as dictated by the Office of Management and Budget (OMB) racial and ethnicity guidelines introduced for demographic surveys.

Prior efforts to change this classification have failed. For example, in 1993, the Arab American Institute and the American-Arab Anti-Discrimination Committee lobbied Congress to create a separate "Middle Eastern" or "Arab American" category, arguing that, by moving Arabs from the "Caucasian" category, they would obtain eligibility for certain remedial programs and better protection under antidiscrimination laws.[10] As a consequence, from 1994 through 1997, the OMB solicited comments from the public and conducted a review to determine whether to create a separate racial category for individuals of Middle Eastern descent. Ultimately, though, the federal government decided against adopting the new category.[11] In its report, the OMB first acknowledged the arguments in favor of a separate Middle Eastern category, noting that it would (1) reduce difficulties in detecting and assessing discrimination against Middle Easterners; (2) alleviate rampant confusion facing Middle Easterners when responding to race questions; (3) aid the administration of certain state and local programs; (4) support the principle of self-identification; and (5) provide a more complete picture of American society.[12] But it rejected the proposal on several grounds, many of which do not withstand careful scrutiny.

First and foremost, the study noted the difficulty in defining a Middle Eastern race. Although this is entirely true, it is no more arduous and riddled with ambiguity than any other racial classification, including, as our analysis has clearly demonstrated, such categories as white or Hispanic. Furthermore, the study concluded that "[g]iven the small size and geographic concentration of this population, the analytical power gained by a separate identification at the national level would be minimal compared to the costs."[13] This is a bizarre statement given the separate categories that actually did make it on the 2000 census with their own check boxes: Asian Indian (which represents only 0.675 percent of the U.S. population),[14] Chinese (0.97 percent), Filipino (0.84 percent), Japanese (0.41 percent), Korean (0.44 percent), Vietnamese (0.44 percent), Native Hawaiian (0.14 percent), Guamanian or Chamorro (0.03 percent), and Samoan (0.04 percent). By contrast, individuals of Middle Eastern descent represent *at least* 0.58 percent of the U.S. population based on figures garnered by the 2000 census from *write-in* entries alone.[15]

In prior years, Mexicans were also undercounted by the census, diminishing their social and political voice. The first effort to count Mexican Americans in the United States came in 1930, when Mexican Americans were captured in the "other" category. The 1940 census then defined Mexicans as white unless "definitely Indian or of other non-white race." It was not until 1980 that the census introduced the general term *Hispanic*. It is not a coincidence that the power and visibility of the Latino electorate has grown dramatically since then. The term *Hispanic* has been utilized as "a way for ethnic political leaders to draw diverse groups together around a liberal political agenda while avoiding divisive questions of cultural heritage."[16]

Individuals descending from the Indian subcontinent have faced a similar plight. Now categorized as Asians or South Asians, their classification has changed in almost every census taken from 1910 through 2000.[17] In 1910 and 1920, for example, South Asians were classified as "other." Specifically, in 1910, they were asked to check the "Non-white Asiatic/Hindu" subcategory. Then, in 1920, religion and race became explicitly conflated, and South Asians were placed in a "Hindu" subcategory. In 1930 and 1940, an actual "Hindu" category appeared on the census. In 1950 and 1960, though, South Asians made their way back to the "other" category, using either the "Non-white/Asiatic Indian" (1950) or "Non-white/Hindu" (1960) subcategories. Mysteriously, on the 1970 census form, South Asians suddenly were designated as "white." As Vinay Harpalani argues, this radical change was particularly puzzling in light of the explicit "non-white" designation used in the prior census and the Supreme Court's ruling in *Thind*, which squarely declared South Asians nonwhite.[18] The new white categorization then served to deny South Asians the benefits of recent civil rights legislation, including affirmative action, which only protected persons with minority status. The South Asian community eventually rallied against the bizarre contradiction between their white status at law and their nonwhite status on the street, leading to the creation of a separate "Asian Indian" category in 1980. The year 1990 saw further change, as South Asians were fused into the broader "Asian or Pacific Islander/ Asian Indian" designation. In 2000, the census returned the "Asian Indian" classification. It is no accident that the past two decades have witnessed a significant rise in the collective political power of South Asians. For example, although South Asians represent just 0.675 percent of the U.S. population,[19] there have been several prominent politicians of South Asian descent, including Congressman Bobby Jindal (R-Louisiana) and Kamela Harris, the elected district attorney of San Francisco.

A failure to recognize Middle Easterners as a separate racial group leads to their relative anonymity as a collective social force. In turn, the Middle Eastern American community lacks the ability and resolve to address issues of diversity and discrimination related to them. In a bureaucratic society, invisibility is the worst of punishments, and nothing enhances invisibility more than not being counted. An example from the early years of Middle Eastern migration to the United States captures the problematic consequences of whitewashing. Historian Sarah Gualtieri begins her essay *Strange Fruit? Syrian Immigrants, Extralegal Violence and Racial Formation in the Jim Crow South* by recounting the sad tale of Nicholas and Fanny Romey, a Syrian couple lynched in Lake City, Florida, on May 17, 1929. The crime, committed by an angry mob, occurred after police officers had asked Romey to cease the display of vegetables outside his grocery store, an apparent violation of local ordinance. An emblematic report of the crime appeared in the *New York Evening World News*, whose evening headline read "Mob in Florida Lynches White Man; Wife Slain." The article went on to identify the victim as simply "N.G. Romey, white, a grocer." On the surface, therefore, the incident appeared to be an anomalous resort to mob violence. But Romey was no ordinary "white" man living in the South—he was a Syrian immigrant. And as Gualtieri notes, "early in the morning of 17 May 1929 he became the victim of the state's well-established tradition of extralegal violence."[20] Understood as a crime against a white man, the act of violence seems random and suggests no systemic basis. Understood as a crime against an Arab, however, Romey's "death be[comes] part of a larger story of the frequency with which . . . [justice was inflicted] on the bodies of the powerless."[21] Yet the *New York Evening World News*'s report was, under prevailing standards of the time, wholly accurate. As he would be today, Romey was classified as a foreign-born white man.[22]

The subjugation of Middle Eastern Americans by lynching belies their ostensible classification as white and as a part of the mainstream majority. Indeed, just as with other lynchings involving racial minorities, government officials turned a blind eye to such extrajudicial reigns of terror. Efforts to rouse the governor of Florida to investigate the incident failed for "lack of public support."[23] The Romey incident was no isolated event. In 1923, for example, terrorists with apparent links to the Ku Klux Klan dynamited the house of a Syrian family in Marietta, Georgia.[24] Understood simply as indiscriminate acts of violence, the racial dimensions of these incidents becomes, as the title of this book suggests, *whitewashed*.

The classification of Middle Eastern Americans as white also renders redress of their legal rights problematic. Attorney Meenoo Chahbazi, for example, has documented the host of problems facing individuals of Middle Eastern descent in discrimination litigation.[25] Besides the issues identified in our earlier discussion of *Al-Khazraji* and related cases, in which whiteness has been used against Middle Eastern Americans to deprive them of an opportunity to vindicate their civil rights, many Middle Easterners themselves mistakenly assume that their classification as white under federal law precludes them from protection of laws against racial discrimination.[26]

Diversity and the Shortcomings of Critical Theory

One significant consequence of the current classification regime is its perverse role in encouraging educational institutions, employers, and other entities to ignore the potential impact that Middle Eastern Americans may have in advancing school and workplace diversity. Take for example the racial data form used at the University of California at Los Angeles for faculty recruitment. Each time the university conducts a faculty search, hiring departments complete the document, dubbed the "Academic Recruitment—Selection Data and Compliance Form," in order to ensure that the school is recruiting from a diverse pool of job applicants. Ultimately, however, the form reveals less about diversity and more about the intimate link between political power and racial construction. The form recognizes twelve major ethnic categories: (1) Black; (2) Japanese/Japanese-American; (3) American Indian/Alaskan Native; (4) Mexican/Mexican-American; (5) White; (6) Filipino; (7) Pakistani/East Indian; (8) Unknown/Unidentified; (9) Other Spanish/Spanish-American; (10) Other Asian; (11) Chinese/Chinese-American; (12) and Latino/Latin-American. Hiring departments are then asked to fill out data on the Recruitment Pool and Selection Pool from which they ultimately selected their employee. This information is reported in broader racial categories (Black, Asian, Native American, Hispanic, White, and Unidentified) and divided between women and men.[27]

The careful parsing out of the Asian category—into Japanese, Filipino, Chinese, East Indian, and other Asian subcategories—reflects both the size of California's various Asian populations as well as their increasingly successful efforts to obtain recognition and exert influence. Surprisingly, despite the fact that California is home to the largest Middle Eastern population anywhere in the world, outside the Middle East itself, there is nary a mention of them on the documents. White is defined as "not of Hispanic Origin. Persons having origins in any of the original peoples of Europe, North Africa or Middle East." Middle Easterners are therefore lumped into the white category—a particularly curious identification given how carefully the form subdivides both Asian and Latin heritage.

The creation of a separate racial category for Middle Eastern individuals would greatly aid recognition of the way Middle Eastern Americans might contribute to diversity. Widespread efforts to quantify minority representation in education and industry have brought attention to systemic discrimination and problems of underrepresentation. These efforts, in turn, have fueled attempts by such institutions to improve minority recruitment. Unfortunately, minority numbers reported by schools and employers simply do not count individuals of Middle Eastern descent as anything but white. As a consequence, it is impossible to measure the degree to which individuals of Middle Eastern descent suffer from discrimination or underrepresentation. Middle Easterners contribute to diversity as much as any other minority group. To the extent that diversity is considered a factor in the educational-admission or job-hiring processes, Middle Eastern extraction should be considered as relevant as African American, Hispanic, Native American, Pacific Islander, or Asian descent.

Indeed, under the factors enunciated in the Supreme Court's *Grutter* decision on race-based preferences, Middle Eastern descent should qualify as a diversity category, even though it does not: greater representation of Middle Easterners both in the academy and elsewhere promotes cross-racial understanding, enervates invidious racial stereotypes, and enlivens classroom discussion.[28] Quoting Justice Powell's opinion in *University of California v. Bakke*,[29] the *Grutter* Court found that the "nation's future depends upon leaders trained through wide exposure to the ideas and mores of students as diverse as this Nation."[30] Strategically, a focus on increased Middle Eastern representation in American society would also advance key foreign-policy interests by diluting the belief—most prevalent abroad— that the war on terrorism is tantamount to a war against an entire race and religion. By ensuring the fluidity and openness of our society, especially for those most in fear of stigmatization, we prevent critiques of our domestic hypocrisies that might threaten our efforts to bring democracy to the Middle East and achieve international cooperation in the war on terrorism.

An examination of the legal academy illustrates the way that the quandary of Middle Eastern classification adversely affects the place of Middle Easterners in American society. For example, although law schools have, in recent years, taken large strides with concerted efforts to hire more minorities, none of these efforts has focused on hiring individuals of Middle Eastern descent. On the basis of government classifications, a Middle Eastern presence at a law school is not even considered a plus in the diversity column.

This situation is particularly problematic in light of the significant size of the Middle Eastern population in the United States and the wide range of legal issues that face individuals of Middle Eastern descent. As far as I can tell, there are only a handful of other full-time law professors of Arab, Turkish, Iranian, Armenian, or other Middle Eastern lineage. I cannot be sure, however, since Middle Easterners count as white in all official data. Thus, while we have very specific counts for law professors of African, Asian, Pacific Island, Latino, and Native American descent,[31] the numbers are conspicuously missing for professors of Middle Eastern descent.

For example, a recent newsletter for the American Bar Association (ABA) touted and celebrated significant increases in minority hiring on law-school faculties. As the article noted, from 2000 to 2004, minorities increased their share of full-time faculty positions from 13.9 percent to 16.0 percent.[32] As the newsletter proudly concluded, the data demonstrated "meaningful progress in diversifying the law school community."[33] Nevertheless, like almost all data on diversity, no attention was paid to identifying strides toward (or failures in) increasing Middle Eastern representation on faculties. The tacit, but utterly untenable, assumption is that Middle Easterners do not contribute meaningfully toward racial diversity in the law-school community. And as the anecdote at the outset of this book indicates, this view is reified through the continued notation of a Middle Eastern hire as a white hire.

State bar associations are similarly guilty of this shortcoming. A recent article in the *California Bar Journal,* the official publication of the State Bar of California, examined the racial composition of the bar and bench in California. Despite the sizable Middle Eastern population in the state, the journal examined the racial "diversification" of the bar and bench by counting only Asians, African Americans, and Latinos.[34]

The consequences of this situation are far-reaching, and not merely limited to the life of law schools or the legal community. In his influential commentary *The Imperial Scholar,* published two decades ago, Richard Delgado noted that much of the most cited and widely discussed literature on civil rights law was the product of "an inner circle of about a dozen white, male writers who comment on, take polite issue with, extol, criticize, and expand on each other's ideas."[35] Delgado then discussed the importance of having legal scholars of African, Latin, Asian, and Native American descent addressing civil rights issues.[36] Ironically, despite his passionate and groundbreaking scholarship and his status as one of the founding members of the critical race theory movement,[37] Delgado entirely and inexplicably omitted the Middle Eastern category from his argument. Delgado is not alone in this shortcoming. This oversight is pervasive in the academy and in American society, and it is repeated among critical race scholars, a group one hopes would recognize otherwise. Other leading scholars in the field have discussed the problems facing African, Asian, Latin, and Native Americans, with no mention of individuals of Middle Eastern descent.[38] Sumi Cho and Robert Westley's comprehensive examination of law-faculty hiring[39] is emblematic of this rampant oversight. Their article discusses strides made in hiring individuals of African, Asian, Latino, and Native American descent and even contemplates the importance of gender and sexual-orientation diversity on law-school campuses.[40] Remarkably, there is not a single mention of Middle Easterners.

Since Delgado's plea, the academy has made significant strides in addressing his concerns, and there is now a flood of critical race theory literature in law reviews focusing on African, Latin, Asian, and Native American issues—much of it authored by law professors of African, Latin, Asian, or Native American descent. Critical race theory itself emerged from the presence and activism of students of color at several major law schools.[41] Save the recent rash of articles on the issue of racial profiling in the wake of 9/11, however, there is no such corresponding literature addressing the legal issues facing the Middle Eastern population. Given the relative dearth of Middle Easterners being granted the privilege of entering the legal academy, this is not surprising.[42]

As Devon Carbado and Mitu Gulati have argued, the debate over affirmative action and race-based preferences has consistently overlooked a critical question of first principles: the meaning of diversity.[43] Under the taxonomy advanced by Carbado and Gulati, diversity serves seven overlapping and interconnected areas: inclusion, social meaning, racially cooperative citizenship, belonging, colorblindness, speech, and institutional culture.[44] Increasing the Middle Eastern presence in the law-school student body and faculty serves each of these interests recognized under the Carbado/Gulati heuristic. In so arguing, I do not intend to provide an indiscriminate, blanket endorsement of affirmative action. Affirmative action is, at best, a highly imperfect social policy, and there are strong arguments both for and against its practice. But if it is going to exist and be rationalized on diversity grounds, there is little reason for its wholesale exclusion of individuals of Middle Eastern descent.

First, increased student and faculty recruiting advances inclusion by facilitating the entrance of Middle Easterners into the leading institutions of power in American society—the law school, the bar, and the bench. The Middle Eastern population suffers from a surprisingly low profile in the nation's political and legal life, a fact that is especially unusual given the community's relatively high levels of educational and economic attainment.[45] Alexis de Tocqueville's admonishment about power in the United States, made over a century and a half ago, still rings true today: "If I were asked where I place the American aristocracy, I should reply, without hesitation, that it is not among the rich, who are united by no common tie, but that it occupies the judicial bench and the bar."[46] The gateway to the bar and the bench is the American university or, more specifically, the American law school. As Carbado and Gulati argue, "Universities and colleges define American democracy and serve as gateways to its benefits. To the extent that certain groups are excluded from universities and colleges, a democratic process failure has occurred."[47] Given the vital role of the law in American social structure, we must focus on expanding the opportunities for Middle Easterners with the same vigor with which we seek to advance the African American, Native American, Pacific Islander, Hispanic, and Asian American presence on both the bench and the bar.

Second, by recruiting more individuals of Middle Eastern descent both to the student body and faculties, law schools would achieve a central aim of diversity programs: subversion of stereotypes through exposure. Presently, the only time law schools appear to make an effort to recruit a scholar of Middle Eastern descent is when they seek to fill an adjunct position for the requisite biennial courses on Islamic law that most law schools offer. A simple look at many law-school faculty roster illustrates this point: the only individuals of Middle Eastern descent that you are likely to see are those teaching the Shari'a. Imagine if law schools only recruited African Americans to teach courses on slavery, Latinos to teach immigration, or Asian Americans to teach critical race theory. This practice—unconscious though it may be—both results from and reinforces a central stereotype that colors American perceptions of Middle Easterners: the inextricable association of the Middle East with Islam, especially its more radical elements.

In reality, the vast majority of the world's Muslims are located outside the Middle East. Indeed, only 12 percent of the world's Muslims are Arab.[48] Moreover, the Middle East is rife with religious diversity. Take the Iranian population, for example. With images of the Ayatollahs in mind, the link between Iran and Islam has been inextricably forged into the mind of mainstream America. However, sizable portions of the Iranian American population are not Muslim. In Los Angeles County alone, there are thirty-five thousand Iranian Americans of Jewish faith.[49] Yet the specter of Islamic fundamentalism is so intertwined with our perceptions of Iran that the existence of an Iranian Jew (let alone their existence in vast numbers) is frequently a shock to the average American. Iran is actually home to one of the world's oldest continuous Jewish settlements outside Israel, dating from 722 BCE to the present day.[50] Large pockets of Iranians of Bahá'í and Zoroastrian faith also live in the United States, as do Armenian-Iranians, who are Christian (Armenia was, of course, the first nation in the world to adopt Christianity as the state religion).[51] As far too few Americans recognize, the Middle East is a place of tremendous religious diversity, and many Middle Eastern Americans, myself included, are not Muslim.

Third, improving the Middle Eastern presence at law schools advances racially cooperative citizenship by providing students and faculty alike with greater opportunities to mediate and contemplate social, political, and legal issues relevant to both the classroom and scholarship. Middle Eastern legal theorists would be indispensable to negotiating the tensions between American law and non-Christian traditions including, but not limited to, Islam; they can provide critical guidance to emerging democracies in the Middle Eastern world as they grapple with the delicate and intricate task of constitution drafting; and they can play a valuable role in cross-cultural liaising.[52]

Fourth, by counting Middle Eastern individuals as a plus in the diversity column, we would be sending a message of belonging. This message can temper the daily headlines replete with messages of ostracism and otherness—headlines that inform Middle Easterners that we, as a country, do not want their hands on our ports and that we do not want them immigrating into our country. Such integration would facilitate the view that we do not, as a society, reduce Middle Easterner individuals into a monolithic enemy of the West.

Fifth, advancing Middle Eastern diversity on campuses ultimately serves the goal of colorblindness. When there is only a single voice coming from a race, people will be forced to "gather the insight and experience of an entire race from one person."[53] To that end, the instigation for this book is instructive. So long as the vast problems discussed herein continue to go unaddressed in law-review literature, I feel a nagging urge to speak up on behalf of the "race" to which I am categorized, even though the general focus of my own research, writing, and teaching is intellectual-property, entertainment, and constitutional law. I therefore become (self-?) racialized because there are so few others of Middle Eastern descent on American law faculties. In short, the stunning absence of legal scholarship on the pressing issues facing individuals of Middle Eastern descent compelled me to write this book. I raise my voice in the hope that, ultimately, all the categories of race will eventually dissolve and become irrelevant.

Finally, a Middle Eastern presence in the legal academy advances the richness and range of perspectives brought to the law-school classroom and law-review literature,[54] thereby broadening institutional activities to cover issues of concern to this significant segment of American society. As Richard Delgado has argued, although backgrounds do not inextricably determine perspectives, they may affect viewpoints and the types of questions asked in legal research. Thus, an absence of diversity can adversely affect the quality and breadth of legal scholarship, since a "uniformity of life experiences of the inner circle of writers may color not only the way they conceptualize and frame problems of race, but also the solutions or remedies they devise."[55] To illustrate this point, Delgado points to civil rights literature, circa 1983, which was largely the product of a small inner circle of upper-middle-class white male attorneys. As sympathetic as members of this inner circle may have been to the general advance of civil rights, their backgrounds sometimes appeared to limit their remedial perspectives. For example, Delgado argues, these men often advanced such programs as affirmative action, which ended up "pit[ting] minorities against each other and against low-income whites. [Such] programs generate hostility among these groups, while exempting from such unpleasantness the high-achieving white product of a private prep school and Ivy League college, who can remain aloof from these battles."[56] By contrast, notes Delgado, minority commentators who entered the fray sometimes advanced a fundamentally different type of solution to issues of privilege in higher education: "an overhaul of the admissions process and a rethinking of the criteria that make a person a deserving law student and future lawyer."[57]

Members of a minority group are not necessarily going to bring different perspectives to their writing, and members of a majority group are not necessarily going to be unable to understand fully and relate to the minority experience. Nevertheless, diversity of perspective does help. Without being overly deterministic, I can safely assert that the issues raised in this book are the direct product of my own background. More- over, these issues may have remained unexplored in the literature because of a lack of a sufficient number of Middle Eastern legal academics.

A Middle Eastern American Moment?

In 1991, Jerome Culp boldly declared the beginning of an African Amer- ican Moment in the legal academy, where "different and blacker voices will speak new words and remake old legal doctrines. Black scholars will demand justice with equality and nonblack scholars will understand."[58] In 1993, Robert S. Chang referenced Culp in decreeing an Asian Ameri- can Moment in the legal academy, "marked by the increasing presence of Asian Americans in the legal academy who are beginning to raise their voices to 'speak new words and remake old legal doctrines.'"[59] Both Culp and Chang had good reasons for optimism. Significant strides had been made in the prior two decades toward increasing the numbers of both African and Asian American law students and faculty members. In fact, by 1993, two journals dedicated exclusively to Asian American issues were in circulation.[60]

Unlike Jerome Culp and Robert Chang, I cannot optimistically an- nounce a Middle Eastern Moment in the legal academy. There are simply too few Middle Easterners in the legal academy to effectuate such a mo- ment. It is unknown how many law students of Middle Eastern descent there are in the United States because no one bothers to count. Middle Easterners, unlike African, Latin, Asian, and Native Americans, are not actively recruited by law schools, and they are not seen as contributors to diversity on campus. In effect, they are given no voice, and they are not seen as having a voice.

But as the events in recent years have made plain, increased attention must be given to the particular legal issues facing individuals of Middle Eastern descent in the United States. Like its predecessors, a Middle Eastern legal scholarship will recognize that Middle Easterners are "dif- ferently situated historically with respect to other disempowered groups. But it will also acknowledge that, in spite of these historical differences, the commonality found in shared oppression can bring different disem- powered groups together to participate in each others' struggles."[61] The almost complete absence of a Middle Eastern voice in the legal academy renders all but impossible the achievement of such a goal. The purpose of this book is, therefore, rather modest. I hope it plays a role, no matter how small, in leading us toward a day when we can finally contemplate a Middle Eastern Moment in legal scholarship.

A Word of Caution: The Risk of Essentialization

The position I advocate in this chapter does run certain risks. First, I am advancing the creation of a broad category of "Middle Eastern" even though such as category does not necessarily exist in the minds of those whom it would include. Second, by collapsing individuals of Arab, Turkish, Persian, and other descents (such as Armenian) into a racial category dubbed "Middle Eastern," we run the risk of essentializing racial identity. Such a categorization inevitably downplays the diversity within the group and might simply serve popular perceptions of a monolithic Middle Easterner, rather than attacking the stereotyping that plagues our society. However, I believe the potential benefits of such a tack outweigh the risks of essentialization.

Some people might object that Middle Easterners think of themselves not necessarily as Middle Eastern but, rather, as members of a particular ethnicity (e.g., Persian) or as part of the "white" race. Iranians, for example, do not think of Arabs and Turks as belonging to the same "race" as they do. As writer Gelareh Asayesh notes, Iranians see themselves as Aryans, and "this tenuous link to the global ruling class permits Iranians to look down on the other people of the Middle East, most notably the Arabs, who had the temerity to defeat the faltering Persian Empire in the seventh century."[62] To outsiders, the notion of Arab-Persian tension is surprising since they frequently think that Persians *are* Arabs. But a significant strain of Persian discourse views Arab race and culture as a foreign element that has insidiously penetrated Iranian society. It is not uncommon to hear an Iranian American bemoan the Arab invasion of Persia several centuries ago as the death knell of the learned traditions of the Persians—"they burned our books, they raped our women, they imposed their religion upon us" goes a common strain of thought. The typical Iranian will quickly demur at any suggestion that he or she is an Arab and will remind you that the Persian language is Indo-European, not Semitic, that Persians come from a different, Aryan racial stock, and that Persian civilization has had a rich and independent tradition. Many Iranians—especially, but not only, non-Islamic ones—continue to view

Islam as a foreign pariah, an imposition on Persia by the Arabs that has overwhelmed "true" Persian culture.

Thus, the creation of a Middle Eastern category risks lumping together groups that, in many cases, may not want to be associated with one another. As a social construct, however, race is all about perceptions. The notion of a Middle Eastern race has already been constructed from without, and whether or not individuals who fall within its parameters like it, it is here to stay. As attested by the myriad examples detailed in this book, the term is already being used as an oppressive force. Individuals of Arab, Turkish, Armenian, and Persian descent will be deemed "Middle Eastern" by society when it inures to their disadvantage: at the border, in security lines at the airport, at traffic stops, and by prosecutors and jurors. Though the transparent wings of the government count Middle Easterners as white in official, released statistics, you can bet that the Transportation Security Administration does not lump Middle Easterners into the category of white when profiling individuals at airports and that the FBI does not call Middle Easterners white when trailing "persons of interest."

Since the term *Middle Eastern* has been used instrumentally to regulate and marginalize individuals who fall within its definition, some people may denounce its use as an official racial category. But this is not a reason to shirk from use of the term. As Robert Chang has observed with respect to the term *Asian American,*

> I hesitate to define "Asian American" further because this term is malleable and is often used by the dominant group to confer and deny benefits. . . .
>
> . . . [L]ike its predecessor, "Oriental," . . . [it] was created in the West from the need to make racial categorizations in a racially divided or, at least, a racially diverse society.
>
> Regardless of its origins, however, "Asian American" can serve as a unifying identity based on the common experiences of Asian Americans because of the inability of most non-Asian Americans to distinguish between different Asian groups.[63]

Most important, the risk of essentialization is tempered by the vast benefits that would accrue from wresting the term *Middle Eastern* as one imposed from without to one embraced from within. As Kenji Yoshino has eloquently stated, the risk of essentialization ought not to be understood in a vacuum, but rather relative to the risks of alternative regimes. It is the risk of essentialization that facially lends such credibility to formalistic regimes that denude identities of any content, such as color-blindness, sex-blindness, and orientation-blindness. Yet while the risk of essentialization is a serious one, I believe that the costs of such formalistic regimes are greater.[64]

Admittedly, forcing individuals from widely varied linguistic, religious, and cultural traditions into one category is an act rife with danger. For example, the use of the designator "Asian" to capture such diverse ethnicities as the Japanese, Chinese, Korean, Vietnamese, Indians, Thai, Indonesians, Malaysians, and Filipinos has sometimes obfuscated the true impact of social policies on these constituent and discrete populations. Witness the effect of Resolution SP-1[65] and Proposition 209[66] on the student population at University of California (UC) law schools. With the repeal of affirmative action in the UC system, the percentage of Asian law students matriculating at UCLA, Boalt Hall, UC Hastings, and UC Davis changed only negligibly. As a result, many observers concluded that the policy change did no harm to the Asian community, benefited white law-school candidates, and harmed Latino, African, and Native Americans.[67] A more nuanced examination of the data, however, suggests otherwise.[68] Although those of Chinese, Japanese, and Korean ancestry may, on average, possess higher incomes and higher degrees of formal education than whites, this is not true of many other Asian populations within the United States, including those of Filipino, Vietnamese, Laotian, and Cambodian descent. As it turns out, the end of affirmative action in the UC system resulted in a precipitous decline in enrollment of law students of Filipino and Southeast Asian descent, matched by a commensurate rise in enrollment by students of Japanese, Chinese, and Korean descent.[69] The categorization of such diverse ethnicities as Arabs, Turks, and Persians under the banner of "Middle Eastern" runs similar risks.

But the limitations of broad racial categories do not render such terms meaningless. In the words of Angela Harris, racial categories can be used by the categorized groups themselves as "strategic identity" to organize a voice for common interests and issues,[70] especially when members of the category possess a shared experience of subordination.[71] Indeed, Latino, Asian American, and even African American identities "reflect the political organization of distinct ethnicities and nationalities"[72] to serve instrumental goals on behalf of their "membership," including redress of common histories of discrimination. Thus, even if the term *Middle East-ern* is imposed on us from without and if it is subject to imprecision and inaccuracies, there is tremendous value in strategically adopting the term to give a voice to individuals who presently have little political and legal capital.

Finally, to avoid essentialization, one must be prepared eventually to deconstruct a racial identity and disassemble it. As Robert Chang has argued, once a racial categorization has been used as an effective organizing tool to counterbalance years of oppression by a dominant group, we must be prepared to deconstruct it.[73] In the end, therefore, poststructural narratives eventually dismantle the notion of race, and people become free to choose their own individual identities: "Only when we are free of [racial categories] can we be free to give ourselves our own identity. Only in this way can we be free to embrace our identity rather than having our identity thrust upon us from the outside."[74] It is my hope that we will someday do away with the entire notion of race and that all Americans, including those of Middle Eastern descent, will then enjoy the right to determine their identities individually.

Conclusion

Our country possesses an unparalleled tradition of respect for civil rights and the rule of law. For generations, immigrant groups have sought, and received, a better life upon arrival on American shores. The Middle Eastern immigrant experience has generally been no different. Middle Eastern Americans enjoy economic, political, and legal rights and freedoms that almost uniformly surpass those that they received in their ancestral homelands. And there is little doubt that they have shared in the American dream.

By many leading indicators, Middle Eastern Americans have thrived in the United States. For example, data from the 2000 census found that Iranian, Turkish, and Arab Americans outearn the general population by 39.6 percent, 27.6 percent, and 11.5 percent, respectively, on a per capita basis.[1] Similarly, 57.2 percent of Iranian Americans and more than 40 percent of Arab Americans over the age of twenty-five have earned a bachelor's degree, compared to 24.4 percent of the general population.[2] In fact, the percentage of Iranian Americans with a graduate degree (27 percent) exceeds the percentage of all other Americans with bachelor's degrees.[3] Nevertheless, educational achievement and wealth accumulation do not tell the full story. As this book has documented, there is also a darker side to the Middle Eastern American experience—one that is fundamentally inconsistent with the promise of our constitutional values—as Middle Easterners have suffered from growing rates of job discrimination, hate crime, racial profiling, and explicitly targeted infringements of their civil rights.

In the span of a generation, Middle Easterners have become the quintessential Other in American society. The problematization of Middle Eastern classification has, of course, afflicted our racial hierarchy for years. Through the course of our analysis, we have traced the race-making process and the construction of whiteness over time, witnessing the precarious position of Middle Easterners within the category. With the performance of whiteness driving racial heuristics, in a bygone era Middle Easterners were viewed more as friendly strangers, inextricably tied to the cultural and philosophical roots of the West, and as having an ambiguous, but likely white, status. As the associations with Islam and terrorism have strengthened in recent years and cast further doubt on their assimilability, Middle Easterners have grown considerably less white in the American imagination. Reconceptualized, they have gone from friendly foreigner to enemy alien and from enemy alien to enemy race. As the subject of increasing levels of both government-condoned discrimination and prejudice in the private sector, Middle Easterners now represent one of the most demonized minorities in the United States. Meanwhile, the law has not caught up with these harsh realities, as the government continues to insist on categorizing Middle Easterners as white.

The government's policy is not surprising when one considers that many Middle Easterners themselves insist on a white designation. Responding to the rising tide of discrimination, many Middle Eastern Americans have embraced whiteness and assimilation through the strategic implementation of covering tactics involving association, appearance, affiliation, and activism that downplay their ethnicity or race. In the short term, they have benefited from such strategies, which enable them to opt out of the less favored racial category and all its accompanying hardships. Yet this tactic has also left Middle Eastern Americans at the margins of the civil rights movement and with little collective social or political force. All the while, the process of selective racialization—through which Middle Easterners who conform to our values are reified as white while Middle Easterners who transgress are reified as the Other—further perpetuates invidious stereotyping by creating a vicious feedback loop that constantly reaffirms the most negative associations with the group.

This book has called attention to the invisibility of America's Middle Eastern minority and proposed how we might lift the veil shrouding the community, with the goal of ultimately rendering Middle Eastern Americans full and equal members of the American body politic. By focusing on the intimate relationship between the law, racial dramaturgy, and the realities of daily life for Middle Eastern Americans, this book takes a first step in addressing a topic that has received far too little attention in academic, legal, and policy circles. Ideally, it represents only the beginning of a broader public discussion on the subject.

Notes

NOTES TO THE INTRODUCTION

1. Anita Famili, *What About Middle Eastern American Ethnic Studies?* Undergraduate Research Opportunities Programs symposium, May 17, 1997, available online at http://www.urop.uci.edu/symposium/past_symposia/1997/ablist3.html.

2. EDWARD SAID, ORIENTALISM (1979).

3. STEVEN W. BENDER, GREASERS AND GRINGOS: LATINOS, LAW, AND THE AMERICAN IMAGINATION (2005).

4. ROBERT S. CHANG, DISORIENTED: ASIAN AMERICANS, LAW, AND THE NATION-STATE (2000).

5. Richard Delgado, *The Imperial Scholar: Reflections on a Review of Civil Rights Literature*, 132 U. PA. L. REV. 561 (1984).

6. KENJI YOSHINO, COVERING: THE HIDDEN ASSAULT ON OUR CIVIL RIGHTS (2006).

7. JAMES BALDWIN, THE PRICE OF THE TICKET: COLLECTED NONFICTION 1948–1985, 55 (1985) ("Our dehumanization of the Negro then is indivisible from the dehumanization of ourselves: the loss of our own identity is the price we pay for the annulment of his.")

8. Robert S. Chang, *Toward an Asian American Legal Scholarship: Critical Race Theory, Post-Structuralism, and Narrative Space*, 81 CAL. L. REV. 1241, 1244–45 (1993).

9. Delgado, *supra*, at 561.

10. Richard Bausch, *Letter to a Young Writer*, in NATIONAL ENDOWMENT FOR THE ARTS, NATIONAL INITIATIVES: OPERATION HOMECOMING, ESSAYS ON WRITING, available online at http://www.nea.gov/national/homecoming/essays/bausch.html.

NOTES TO CHAPTER 1

1. HERMAN MELVILLE, MOBY-DICK 234–36 (Constable & Co. 1922) (1850).

2. As I argue later in the book, the conception of race was eventually problematized into a hermeneutics of color.

3. Gerald M. Rosberg, *Aliens and Equal Protection: Why Not the Right to Vote?* 75 MICH. L. REV 1092 (1977).

4. Kiyoko Kamio Knapp, *The Rhetoric of Exclusion: The Art of Drawing a Line between Aliens and Citizens,* 10 GEO. IMMIGR. L.J. 401, 405–06 (1996).

5. A number of observers have questioned the decision to deny resident aliens the right to vote. Gerald Neuman, for example, highlights the fact that we continue to permit American citizens who reside in foreign countries to vote while denying that right to lawful permanent residents—individuals who pay taxes, contribute to the local economy, and actually have a physical presence within U.S. borders. *See* GERALD L. NEUMAN, STRANGERS TO THE CONSTITUTION: IMMIGRANTS, BORDERS, AND FUNDAMENTAL LAW 63, 70–71 (1996). Gerald Rosberg also wonders whether there is any compelling justification to deny this fundamental right to aliens. Rosberg, *supra,* at 1092–93. And, as David Cole has noted, the absence of a direct alien voice in American politics has limited the ability of aliens to challenge numerous policies of dubious constitutionality that target them. David Cole, *Enemy Aliens,* 54 STAN. L. REV. 953, 959 (2002).

6. James B. Raskin, *Legal Aliens, Local Citizens: The Historical, Constitutional and Theoretical Meanings of Alien Suffrage,* 141 U. PA. L. REV. 1391, 1397 (1993).

7. Jayanth K. Krishnan, *Mobilizing Immigrants,* 11 GEO. MASON L. REV. 695, 703 (2003).

8. Cheryl I. Harris, *Whiteness as Property,* 106 HARV. L. REV. 1709, 1716 (1993).

9. Alien Property Initiative Act (Alien Land Law) of 1920, 1 Cal. Gen. Laws, Act 261 (Deering 1944 & Supp. 1949).

10. *See* Porterfield v. Webb, 263 U.S. 225 (1923) (finding that the California Alien Land Law's differential treatment of naturalization-eligible and naturalization-ineligible aliens was not arbitrary and unreasonable and therefore did not violate the Equal Protection Clause); *see also* Morrison v. California, 291 U.S. 82 (1934) (upholding the California Alien Land Law's burden on defendants to prove citizenship once the government provides proof of race as not an impairment of immunities secured by the Constitution); Cockrill v. California, 268 U.S. 258 (1925) (finding that the California Alien Land Law and its prima facie presumptions did not violate the Constitution or the treaty obligations of the United States); Webb v. O'Brien, 263 U.S. 313 (1923) (finding it within the power of states to deny to ineligible aliens the privilege to use agricultural lands within its borders); Terrace v. Thompson, 263 U.S. 197 (1923) (finding the plaintiffs had no Fourteenth Amendment right to lease their land to aliens lawfully forbidden to take such a lease under the Washington Alien Land Law).

11. *See* Takahashi v. Fish & Game Comm'n, 334 U.S. 410 (1948) (upholding as constitutional a California statute barring the issuance of a commercial fishing license to any person ineligible for citizenship).

12. *See* United States v. Pandit, 15 F.2d 285 (9th Cir. 1926) (upholding the removal of a law license from an attorney when it was learned that he had "illegally procured" citizenship since he was of Indian descent and therefore ineligible for naturalization).

13. *Saturday Night Live* (NBC television broadcast, Oct. 22, 1988), available at http://snltranscripts.jt.org/88/88cbush3.html.

14. *Id.*

15. *Id.*

16. *Id.*

17. *Id.*

18. *Id.*

19. Dukakis famously enjoyed a seventeen-point lead in the polls following the candidates' respective party conventions.

20. Quoted in Martin Schram, *The Making of Willie Horton*, NEW REPUBLIC, May 28, 1990, at 17.

21. *Election '88, Race to the Finish: Waving the Bloody Shirt*, NEWSWEEK, Nov. 21, 1988, at 116.

22. Joni Hersch, *Profiling the New Immigrant Worker: The Effects of Skin Color and Height*, Vanderbilt Law and Economics Working Paper No. 07-02, Jan. 19, 2007, available online at http://ssrn.com/abstract=927038.

23. NBC News, *Study: Immigrants' Skin Tone Affects Earnings*, MSNBC.COM, Jan. 26, 2007, http://www.msnbc.msn.com/id/16831909/.

24. Arthur H. Goldsmith, Darrick Hamilton, and William Darity, Jr., *Shades of Discrimination: Skin Tone and Wages*, 96 AM. ECON. REV. 242, 242–45 (2006).

25. Joseph Price and Justin Wolfers, *Race Discrimination among NBA Referees* 1, Nat'l Bureau of Econ. Research Working Paper No. 13206 (2007), available online at http://graphics.nytimes.com/packages/pdf/sports/20070501-wolfers-NBA-race-study.pdf.

26. BBC News, *Blondes "to Die Out in 200 Years"* (BBC television broadcast, Sept. 27, 2002), available online at http://news.bbc.co.uk/2/hi/health/2284783.stm.

27. *Id.*

28. Jo Casamento, *Disclosure*, SUNDAY TELEGRAPH, Aug. 3, 2003, at 87.

29. XENOPHON, AGESILAUS: AN ENCOMIUM (H.G. Dakyns trans., Kessinger 2004).

30. THEODORE W. ALLEN, THE INVENTION OF THE WHITE RACE (1994).

31. *Id.* at back cover.

32. Act XVI, *Laws of Virginia*, April 1691 (*Hening's Statutes at Large*, 3: 87). The law in question banned miscegenation and remained in force for almost three hundred years. It was ultimately struck down as unconstitutional with the Supreme Court's decision in *Loving v. Virginia*, 388 U.S. 1 (1967).

33. JOHANN FRIEDRICH BLUMENBACH, ON THE NATURAL VARIETY OF MANKIND 98–99 (Thomas Bendyshe ed., Bergman 1969) (1775); *see also* Dow v. United States, 226 F. 145, 146 (4th Cir. 1915) (noting that Blumenbach's work "became known" and "generally accepted" in the United States upon its translation into English in 1807).

34. THOMAS HENRY HUXLEY, METHODS & RESULTS OF ETHNOLOGY (1868).

35. *In re* Najour, 174 F. 735, 735 (C.C. Ga. 1909); *In re* Kanaka Nian, 21 P. 993, 993 (Utah 1889).

36. Brewton Berry, *A Southerner Learns about Race*, COMMON GROUND 88, 90 (Spring 1942).

37. *See, e.g.*, DANIEL GARRISON BRINTON, RACES AND PEOPLES 171–72 (1890); LOUIS FIGUIER, LES RACES HUMAINES (1872); JOHN P. JEFFRIES, THE NATURAL HISTORY OF THE HUMAN RACES 12 (1869); A.H. KEANE, THE WORLD'S PEOPLES (1908); CHARLES PICKERING, THE RACES OF MAN li–liv (1851); and JAMES COWLES PRICHARD, THE NATURAL HISTORY OF MAN (1848).

38. Mark Perry, *Perceptions of Race in the Arab World* (2004) (unpublished paper), available online at http://inhouse.lau.edu.lb/bima/papers/Perry.pdf. Prior to the advent of whiteness, classifications were made by nationality (e.g., Frenchman, Irishman) or religion (e.g., Christian, "heathen"), which, as we shall see, was the original basis for distinguishing between the free and the enslaved.

39. MATTHEW FRYE JACOBSON, WHITENESS OF A DIFFERENT COLOR: EUROPEAN IMMIGRANTS AND THE ALCHEMY OF RACE 38 (1998).

40. *See, e.g.*, United States v. Thind, 261 U.S. 204, 213 (1923) (noting that the original framers of the Naturalization Act and their forebears had come from "the British Isles and Northwestern Europe").

41. *See generally* John Tehranian, *Performing Whiteness: Naturalization Litigation and the Construction of Racial Identity in America*, 109 YALE L.J. 817, 821–27 (2000).

42. For major works demonstrating the fundamental flaws of a scientific/ naturalistic view of race, see MICHAEL BANTON & JONATHAN HARWOOD, THE RACE CONCEPT 43–60 (1975); ASHLEY MONTAGU, STATEMENT ON RACE 46–50 (3rd ed. 1972); Frank B. Livingstone, *On the Nonexistence of Human Race*, in THE CONCEPT OF RACE 46, 46–59 (Ashley Montagu ed., 1964); and Henry P. Lundsgaarde, *Racial and Ethnic Classifications: An Appraisal of the Role of Anthropology in the Lawmaking Process*, 10 HOUS. L. REV. 641, 648–49 n.23 (1973).

43. Kevin R. Johnson, *The End of "Civil Rights" as We Know It? Immigration and Civil Rights in the New Millennium*, 49 UCLA L. REV. 1481, 1486–87 (2002).

44. *See* NOEL IGNATIEV, HOW THE IRISH BECAME WHITE 41 (1995).

45. *See, e.g.*, Herriott v. City of Seattle, 500 P.2d 101 (Wash. 1972) (noting the prevalence of such signs in Boston in prior eras).

46. Mays v. State, 96 S.W. 329 (Tex. Crim. Appl. 1906).

47. As late as 1942, a criminal prosecution in Nebraska drew contrast between the defendant, who was described as a "white girl," and her victim in the shooting, a "colored" man whom the court describes as having a father "of Irish descent" and a mother who "was a Creole." *See* Mantell v. State, 2 N.W.2d 586, 588 (Neb. 1942).

48. *The Commitments* (Beacon Communications 1991).

49. Benjamin Franklin, *Observations Concerning the Increase of Mankind* (1751), in Autobiography and Other Writings 259–60 (Oxford University Press 1993). *See also* Oscar Ronald Dathorne, In Europe's Image: The Need for American Multiculturalism 24 (1994); Winthrop D. Jordan, White over Black: American Attitudes towards the Negro, 1550–1812, 102, 143 (1968).

50. Meyer v. Nebraska, 262 U.S. 390 (1923); Bartels v. Iowa, 262 U.S. 404 (1923).

51. *See* Leonard Dinnerstein & David M. Reimers, Ethnic Americans: A History of Immigration and Assimilation 36 (1982), *quoted in* Mary C. Waters, Ethnic Options: Choosing Identities in America 2 (1990).

52. *See, e.g.,* Rollins v. State, 92 So. 35 (Ala. Ct. App. 1922).

53. Frank W. Sweet, *Jim Crow Triumph of the One-Drop Rule*, in Essays on the Color Line and the One-Drop Rule (2005), available online at http://backintyme.com/essay050501.htm. The procedural posture of the *Rollins* case is of particular salience. Southern courts in the early twentieth century were not renowned for their protection of the rights of criminal defendants, especially those of African descent. In part, Rollins and Labue were apparently well-respected members of their community, and it is believed that the court sought to exonerate them of the miscegenation charges in response to their favorable standing.

54. Westminster School Dist. of Orange County v. Mendez, 161 F.2d 774 (9th Cir. 1947) (Denman, J., concurring) (emphasis added); Lopez v. Seccombe, Mayor of the City of San Bernardino, California, 71 F. Supp. 769 (S.D. Cal. 1944).

55. Leonard Dinnerstein & David M. Reimers, Ethnic Americans: A History of Immigration and Assimilation 36 (1982).

56. *See, e.g.,* James Fenimore Cooper, The Pioneers 327 (Oxford University Press 1999) (1823) ("But damn the bit of manners has the fellow, any more than if he was one of the Guineas down in the kitchen there.").

57. Quoted by Dinnerstein & Reimers, *supra*, at 36.

58. *See* Thomas A. Gugliehno, *"No Color Barrier": Italians, Race, and Power in the United States*, in Are Italians White? 29–43 (Jennifer Gugliehno & Salvatore Salerno eds., 2003).

59. *See* Dinnerstein & Reimers, *supra*, at 36.

60. Quoted in Lawrence H. Larsen & Barbara J. Cottrell, The Gate City: A History of Omaha 164 (1997).

61. Macomber v. State, 291 N.W. 674, 678 (Neb. 1940).

62. Philip K. Hitti, The Syrians in America 89 (1924).

63. Jackson v. State, 129 So. 306 (Ala. App. 1930).

64. *See* Jacobson, *supra*, at 75–79.

65. Edward Alsworth Ross, The Old World in the New 291 (1914), *quoted in* Waters, *supra*, at 2 (emphasis added).

66. *See* Webster's Ninth New Collegiate Dictionary 1107 (1985) (linking both the words *Slav* and *slave* to the Medieval Latin word *sclavus*).

67. Quoted in Nancy Faires Conklin & Nora Faires, *"Colored" and Catholic: The Lebanese in Birmingham, Alabama,* in CROSSING THE WATERS: ARABIC-SPEAKING IMMIGRANTS TO THE UNITED STATES BEFORE 1940, 69, 76 (Eric J. Hooglund ed., 1987).

68. *Id.* at 76.

69. JOHN HINGHAM, STRANGERS IN THE LAND: PATTERNS OF AMERICAN NATIVISM 1860–1925, 164–65 (1971).

70. *See* JACOBSON, *supra,* 78–93.

71. KURT VONNEGUT, JR., MOTHER NIGHT vi (1961).

72. OPS is the sum of a player's on-base and slugging percentages and is widely recognized as a metric for a player's offensive value.

73. Richard Sandomir, *Who's a Latino Baseball Legend?* N.Y. TIMES, Aug. 26, 2005, at D1.

74. Gordon Edes, *Williams's Family Ties Complicated,* BOSTON GLOBE, July 7, 2002, at C1.

75. JEREMY RIFIN, BEYOND BEEF: THE RISE AND FALL OF THE CATTLE CULTURE 271 (1993); ERIC SCHLOSSER, FAST FOOD NATION: THE DARK SIDE OF THE ALL-AMERICAN MEAL 231 (2001).

76. RIFIN, *supra,* at 271.

77. *See, e.g.,* DERRICK BELL, RACE, RACISM AND AMERICAN LAW 6 (1st ed. 1973) (asserting that color-based racial categories were rigid and fixed during the colonial years); A. LEON HIGGINBOTHAM, JR., IN THE MATTER OF COLOR: RACE AND THE AMERICAN LEGAL PROCESS 19–22 (1978) (arguing that servitude and slavery moved from a nonracial to a racial basis during the colonial years but not recognizing that racial concepts themselves were constructed, moving from a basis in religious views to a basis in skin color).

78. Constructivist theorists of identity formation utilize the taxonomy of the Self and the Other to illustrate a common binary that results in hierarchical systems of differentiation. Typical dividing lines for the differentiation include ethnicity—*see* FREDERICK BARTH, ETHNIC GROUPS AND BOUNDARIES: THE SOCIAL ORGANIZATION OF CULTURE DIFFERENCE 9 (1969); Joane Nagel, *The Political Construction of Ethnicity,* in COMPETITIVE ETHNIC RELATIONS 93 (Susan Olzak & Joane Nagel eds., 1986)—and gender—*see* JACQUES LACAN, FEMININE SEXUALITY (Juliet Mitchell & Jacqueline Rose eds. & Jacqueline Rose trans., 1985) (arguing that men need to create the concept of "woman"—a dialectic "other" or a *petit objet à*—as a response to their existential emptiness, insecurity, and lack of psychological completion); *see also* SIMONE DE BEAUVOIR, THE SECOND SEX (H.M. Parshley ed. & trans., Bantam Books 1961) (1949); LUCE IRIGARAY, THIS SEX WHICH IS NOT ONE (Catherine Porter trans., 1985).

79. *See* DONALD L. HOROWITZ, ETHNIC GROUPS IN CONFLICT 43 (1985).

80. *See* Harris, *supra,* at 1717 n.20; *see also* Raymond T. Diamond & Robert J. Cottrol, *Codifying Caste: Louisiana's Racial Classification Scheme and the Fourteenth Amendment,* 29 LOY. L. REV. 255, 259 n.19 (1983).

81. 1 McIlwaine 479 (Va. Gen. Ct. 1630), *reprinted in* Higginbotham, *supra*, at 23.

82. *Id.*

83. Act XII, *Laws of Virginia,* December 1662 (*Hening's Statutes at Large,* 2: 170).

84. The Book of Mormon, 2 Nephi 30:6.

85. *Id.,* 3 Nephi 2:15–16.

86. *See, e.g.,* Edith R. Sanders, *The Hamitic Hypothesis: Its Origin and Functions in Time Perspective,* 10 J. African Hist. 521, 521–23 (1969).

87. *See* Higginbotham, *supra*, at 38.

88. Michel Foucault, *The Eye of Power,* in Power/Knowledge: Selected Interviews and Other Writings, 1972–1977, 146, 155 (Colin Gordon ed. & trans., 1980) (arguing that the Panopticon, with its heightened legibility, provides a remarkably effective and efficient means of exercising control over subjects, for "[t]here is no need for arms, physical violence, materials constraints. Just a gaze. An inspecting gaze, a gaze which each individual under its weight will end by interiorizing to the point that he is his own overseer, each individual exercising this surveillance over, and against, himself. A superb formula: power exercised continuously and for what turns out to be minimal costs."); James C. Scott, Seeing like a State: How Certain Schemes to Improve the Human Condition Have Failed (1998); James C. Scott, John Tehranian & Jeremy Mathias, *The Production of Legal Identities Proper to States: The Case of the Permanent Family Surname,* 44 Comparative Studies in History & Society 4, 6 (2002).

89. *See* Erving Goffman, Stigma: Notes on the Management of Spoiled Identity 48 (1963).

90. *See* F.G. Bailey, Politics and Social Change: Orissa in 1959, 126 (1963); F.G. Bailey, *Closed Social Stratification in Indian Society,* 4 Eur. J. Soc. 107, 113, 120 (1963).

91. *See, e.g.,* Higginbotham, *supra*, at 36–37 (emphasis added by Higginbotham).

92. *Id.* at 200.

93. *See* Jordan, *supra*, at 91–98.

94. Benedict Anderson, Imagined Communities 7 (1983).

95. *See* Kenneth M. Stampp, The Peculiar Institution: Slavery in the Ante-Bellum South 195–96 (1956); Ariela J. Gross, *Litigating Whiteness: Trials of Racial Determination in the Nineteenth-Century South,* 108 Yale L.J. 109 (1998).

96. *See* Gross, *supra*, at 156–76.

97. Johnson v. M'Intosh, 21 U.S. (8 Wheat.) 543 (1823).

98. *Id.* at 567.

99. *Id.* (emphasis added).

100. *Id.* at 590.

101. *Id.*

102. Quoted in Anderson, *supra,* 12–13.

103. *See* Korematsu v. United States, 323 U.S. 214, 236–40 (1944) (Murphy, J., dissenting). I want to thank Kenneth Stahl for pointing out the link to *Korematsu.*

104. *Id.* at 236–37.

105. *Id.* at 237 (citing Final Report, Japanese Evacuation from the West Coast, 1942, by Lt. Gen. J.L. De Witt (June 5, 1943)).

106. *Id.* (citing Final Report at 10–11). As Murphy sarcastically noted, "No sinister correlation between the emperor worshipping activities and disloyalty to America was shown." *Id.* at 237 n.5.

107. *See, e.g.,* Steven Bender, Greasers and Gringos (2003); David Gregory Gutierrez, The Columbia History of Latinos in the United States since 1960 (2004).

108. Hernandez v. Texas, 347 U.S. 475 (1954).

109. *Id.* at 478.

110. Soria v. Oxnard School Dist. Bd. of Trustees, 386 F. Supp. 539, 541 (C.D. Cal. 1974).

NOTES TO CHAPTER 2

1. Mark Twain, The Adventures of Tom Sawyer 16 (Penguin 2006) (1876).

2. *Id* at 27.

3. *Id* at 23.

4. *See, e.g.,* John Tehranian, *Performing Whiteness: Naturalization Litigation and the Construction of Racial Identity in America,* 109 Yale L.J. 817 (2000).

5. U.S. Equal Employment Opportunity Commission, *Introduction to Race and Ethnic (Hispanic Origin) Data for the Census 2000 Special EEO File,* Oct. 25, 2002, available online at http://www.eeoc.gov/stats/census/race_ethnic_data.html (accessed Aug. 24, 2006).

6. *Id.*

7. 28 C.F.R. § 42.402(e)(5) (2007).

8. U.S. Census Bureau, *Questions and Answers for Census 2000 Data on Race* (2001), available online at http://www.census.gov/Press-Release/www/2001/raceqandas.html; *see also* U.S. Office of Management and Budget, Directive No. 15: Race and Ethnic Standards or Federal Statistics and Administrative Reporting (1997), available online at http://wonder.cdc.gov/wonder/help/populations/bridged-race/Directive15.html (defining "white" as a person having origins in any of the countries of Europe, North Africa, or the Middle East).

9. U.S. Department of Defense, Directive No. 14401.1 (1987), available online at http://www.dtic.mil/whs/directives/corres/rtf/d14401x.rtf.

10. *Compare, e.g.,* U.S. Equal Employment Opportunity Commission, No. 915.003, Compliance Manual Section 15: Race & Color Discrimination 15-3 (2006), available online at http://www.eeoc.gov/policy/docs/race-color.pdf (designating five racial categories: "American Indian or Alaska Native; Asian; Black or African American; Native Hawaiian or Other Pacific Islander; and White; and one ethnicity category, "Hispanic or Latino") *with* West Virginia Equal Employment Office, *Race & Color Discrimination Definition,* available online at http://www.wvf.state.wv.us/eeo/Race.htm (accessed Nov. 30, 2006) (adopting the same categories).

11. UCLA Academic Recruitment—Selection Data and Compliance Form, available online at http://www.apo.ucla.edu/forms/aaform.pdf.

12. U.S. Census Bureau, *supra.*

13. George R. LaNoue & John C. Sullivan, *Presumptions for Preferences: The Small Business Administration's Decisions on Groups Entitled to Affirmative Action,* 6 J. Pol'y Hist. 439, 456 (1994); Sean A. Sabin, *Rethinking the Presumption of Social and Economic Disadvantage,* 33 Pub. Cont. L.J. 825, 828 (2004).

14. 15 U.S.C. § 637(d)(3)(C)(ii) (2000) (defining Black Americans, Hispanic Americans, Native Americans, and Asian-Pacific Americans as disadvantaged groups).

15. 13 C.F.R. § 124.103(b)(1) (2006) (designating "Black Americans; Hispanic Americans; Native Americans (American Indians, Eskimos, Aleuts, or Native Hawaiians); Asian Pacific Americans (persons with origins from Burma, Thailand, Malaysia, Indonesia, Singapore, Brunei, Japan, China (including Hong Kong), Taiwan, Laos, Cambodia (Kampuchea), Vietnam, Korea, The Philippines, U.S. Trust Territory of the Pacific Islands (Republic of Palau), Republic of the Marshall Islands, Federated States of Micronesia, the Commonwealth of the Northern Mariana Islands, Guam, Samoa, Macao, Fiji, Tonga, Kiribati, Tuvalu, or Nauru); Subcontinent Asian Americans (persons with origins from India, Pakistan, Bangladesh, Sri Lanka, Bhutan, the Maldives Islands or Nepal)" as socially disadvantaged groups).

16. Joan MacFarlane, *Egyptian Immigrant Fights for Black Classification,* CNN.com, July 18, 1997, http://edition.cnn.com/US/9707/16/racial.suit/.

17. Act of Mar. 26, 1790, ch. 3, 1 Stat. 103, *repealed by* Act of Jan. 29, 1795, ch. 20, 1 Stat. 414.

18. Dred Scott v. Sandford, 60 U.S. (19 How.) 393 (1856).

19. Act of July 14, 1870, ch. 255, § 7, 16 Stat. 254.

20. *See* Immigration and Nationality Act of 1952, ch. 2, § 311, 66 Stat. 239 (codified as amended at 8 U.S.C. § 1422 (1994)).

21. *See* Ozawa v. United States, 260 U.S. 178, 198 (1922).

22. *See* United States v. Thind, 261 U.S. 204, 215 (1923).

23. In one reported case, the petitioner sued for naturalization eligibility on the grounds of being black. *See In re* Cruz, 23 F. Supp. 774 (E.D.N.Y. 1938).

24. Ian F. Haney López, White by Law: The Legal Construction of Race (1996).

25. *See* Tehranian, *supra*, at 820 (citing Haney López, *supra*).

26. Haney López, *supra*, at 5.

27. *Id.*

28. *See id.* at 7–8, 107.

29. *Id.* at 19.

30. *See* Frank H. Wu, *From Black to White and Back Again*, 3 Asian L.J. 185, 186 (1996) (reviewing Haney López, *supra*).

31. Robert W. Gordon, *Critical Legal Histories*, 36 Stan. L. Rev. 57, 59 (1984).

32. *See* Alexander Saxton, The Rise and Fall of the White Republic (1990).

33. *See Ozawa*, 260 U.S. at 198.

34. *See id.*

35. *See Thind*, 261 U.S. at 206.

36. *See id.* at 208.

37. For the major scientific race treatises of the nineteenth and early twentieth centuries, see Daniel Garrison Brinton, Races and Peoples (1890); Louis Figuier, Les Races Humaines (1872); John P. Jeffries, The Natural History of the Human Races (1869); A.H. Keane, The World's Peoples (1908); Charles Pickering, The Races of Man (1851); and James Cowles Prichard, The Natural History of Man (1848), all of which are cited in Dow v. United States, 226 F. 145, 146 (4th Cir. 1915).

38. *Thind*, 261 U.S. at 209.

39. *See* Haney López, *supra*, at 107; Donald Braman, *Of Race and Immutability*, 46 UCLA L. Rev. 1375, 1410 (1999).

40. Braman, *supra*, at 1410.

41. *See* Ariela J. Gross, *Litigating Whiteness: Trials of Racial Determination in the Nineteenth-Century South*, 108 Yale L.J. 109, 117, 156–76 (1998).

42. *Id.*

43. Kenneth L. Karst, *Paths to Belonging: The Constitution and Cultural Identity*, 64 N.C. L. Rev. 303, 312 (1986).

44. *See id.* at 311–15.

45. *Cf.* Enid Trucios-Gaynes, *The Legacy of Racially Restrictive Immigration Laws and Policies and the Construction of the American National Identity*, 76 Or. L. Rev. 369, 371–72, 405–06 (1997) (demonstrating the power of assimilationist criteria in shaping immigration laws and policies throughout American history).

46. *Thind*, 261 U.S. at 215.

47. *Id.*

48. *See Ozawa*, 260 U.S. at 195–96.

49. *Thind*, 261 U.S. at 209 (citation omitted).

50. *Id.* at 210.

51. *In re* Hassan, 48 F. Supp. 843, 846 (E.D. Mich. 1942).

52. *Thind,* 261 U.S. at 213.

53. *Id.* at 213–14 (emphasis added).

54. 180 F. 694 (2d Cir. 1910). Incidentally, the *Balsara* court rejected the common-knowledge test in favor of the scientific-evidence inquiry. *See id.* at 695.

55. *Id.*

56. *Ozawa,* 260 U.S. at 197.

57. *Thind,* 261 U.S. at 210.

58. *But see* HANEY LÓPEZ, *supra,* at 107 (arguing that a popular, common-knowledge understanding of racial determination was endorsed by the Supreme Court); Braman, *supra,* at 1410 (arguing that, starting with *Ozawa* and *Thind,* the Supreme Court has progressively moved toward an understanding of racial determination as contextual and socially constructed).

59. *Ozawa,* 260 U.S. at 197.

60. 177 F. 101 (5th Cir. 1910).

61. *See* HANEY LÓPEZ, *supra,* at 206 n.c.

62. 1 THEODORE W. ALLEN, THE INVENTION OF THE WHITE RACE: RACIAL OPPRESSION AND SOCIAL CONTROL 28, 32 (1994).

63. I am indebted to Abner Cohen's brilliant study on the Creoles of Sierra Leone for inspiring the application of dramaturgy theory to law and social science research. *See* ABNER COHEN, THE POLITICS OF ELITE CULTURE: EXPLORATIONS IN THE DRAMATURGY OF POWER IN A MODERN AFRICAN SOCIETY (1981).

64. *See* JUDITH BUTLER, GENDER TROUBLE: FEMINISM AND THE SUBVERSION OF IDENTITY 25 (1990).

65. *Id.*

66. *See* JUDITH BUTLER, BODIES THAT MATTER ix–xi (1993), *cited in* Camille A. Gear, Note, *The Ideology of Domination: Barriers to Client Autonomy in Legal Ethics Scholarship,* 107 YALE L.J. 2473, 2484 (1998).

67. A number of legal scholars have drawn on Butler's performativity analysis. *See, e.g.,* Martha M. Ertman, *Contractual Purgatory for Sexual Marginorities: Not Heaven, but Not Hell Either,* 73 DENV. U. L. REV. 1107, 1166 (1996) (using Butler's performance model to analyze sexual orientation and gender identity); Katherine M. Franke, *What's Wrong with Sexual Harassment?* 49 STAN. L. REV. 691, 771 (1997) (using Butler's performance model to analyze gender identity); *see also* Judith Butler, *Burning Acts: Injurious Speech,* 3 U. CHI. L. SCH. ROUNDTABLE 199, 199–204 (1996) (using the performance model to analyze hate speech).

68. *Ozawa,* 260 U.S. at 189.

69. *Id.* at 198.

70. *Thind,* 261 U.S. at 206.

71. *Ozawa,* 260 U.S. at 198 (quoting Davidson v. New Orleans, 96 U.S. 97, 104 (1877)).

72. *See* John H. Wigmore, *American Naturalization and the Japanese,* 28 AM. L. REV. 818 (1894).

73. *Id.* at 827.

74. *Id.*

75. THOMAS PYNCHON, THE CRYING OF LOT 49, 24 (1966).

76. NOEL IGNATIEV, HOW THE IRISH BECAME WHITE 2 (1995).

77. *Id.* at 96.

78. *See* MICHEL FOUCAULT, DISCIPLINE AND PUNISH: THE BIRTH OF THE PRISON (Alan Sheridan trans., Vintage Books 2d ed. 1995) (1978).

79. *See, e.g.,* Samras v. United States, 125 F.2d 879 (9th Cir. 1942) (finding that Asian Indians are not white); De La Ysla v. United States, 77 F.2d 988 (9th Cir. 1935) (finding that Filipinos are not white); United States v. Gokhale, 26 F.2d 360 (2d Cir. 1928) (per curiam) (finding, in a case involving an Asian Indian, that "Hindus" are not white); United States v. Javier, 22 F.2d 879 (D.C. Cir. 1927) (finding that Filipinos are not white); *In re* Cruz, 23 F. Supp. 774 (E.D.N.Y. 1938) (finding that people of three-quarters Native American and one-quarter African blood do not qualify as being of African descent for the purposes of the naturalization statute); *In re* Fisher, 21 F.2d 1007 (N.D. Cal. 1927) (finding that people who are three-quarters Chinese and one-quarter Portuguese are not white); United States v. Mozumdar, 296 F. 173 (S.D. Cal. 1923) (finding, in a case involving an Asian Indian, that "Hindus" are not white); Sato v. Hall, 217 P. 520 (Cal. 1923) (finding that Japanese are not white); De Cano v. State, 110 P.2d 627 (Wash. 1941) (en banc) (finding that Filipinos are not white).

80. Only one litigant in a reported racial-prerequisite case petitioned to be declared black by law for naturalization eligibility.

81. 171 F. 294 (S.D.N.Y. 1909), *aff'd sub nom.* United States v. Balsara, 180 F. 694 (2d Cir. 1910).

82. *Balsara,* 171 F. at 295.

83. 15 F.2d 285 (9th Cir. 1926).

84. *See id.* at 285.

85. 101 F.2d 7 (2d Cir. 1939).

86. *See id.* at 7.

87. *Id.* at 8 (citing *Thind,* 261 U.S. at 214). Admittedly, the *Thind* Court does go on to declare that "there is much in the origin and historic development of the statute to suggest that no Asiatic whatever was included" (*Thind,* 261 U.S. at 214), though it does so in dicta.

88. *Wadia,* 101 F.2d at 9 (citing *Ozawa,* 260 U.S. at 198).

89. 174 F. 834, 835 (C.C.D. Mass. 1909).

90. *Id.* at 835.

91. *Id.* at 837.

92. *Id.* at 838.

93. *Id.* at 837–39.

94. *Id.* at 845.

95. *Id.* at 840.

96. *Id.* at 841. As the court wrote, "They have dealt in business with Greeks, Slavs, and Hebrews, as well as with Turks, they have sought a modern education at Robert College and other American schools in the East, and they have pursued by immigration the civilization of Great Britain and of the United States."

97. 6 F.2d 919 (D. Or. 1925).

98. *Id.*

99. Thus, like the juries on race trials in the antebellum South (*see* Gross, *supra*, at 117, 156–76), judges turned to a performative test for whiteness.

100. *See Cartozian,* 6 F.2d at 920.

101. *See* Trucios-Gaynes, *supra,* at 406.

102. *Cartozian,* 6 F.2d at 920.

103. *Cartozian,* 6 F.2d at 920.

104. *Thind,* 261 U.S. at 215.

105. *Cartozian,* 6 F.2d at 921.

106. Ironically, the court was drawing on expert evidence and the behavior of the aristocracy to determine what common people on the street knew of racial divides.

107. *Cartozian,* 6 F.2d at 921.

108. *See id.* at 921–22.

109. *Id.* at 922.

110. With thanks to SOUL COUGHING, *Is Chicago, Is Not Chicago,* on RUBY VROOM (WEA/Warner Bros. 1994).

111. 211 F. 486 (D.S.C. 1914), *aff'd on reh'g sub nom. In re* Dow, 213 F. 355 (D.S.C. 1914), *rev'd sub nom.* Dow v. United States, 226 F. 145 (4th Cir. 1915).

112. 48 F. Supp. 843 (E.D. Mich. 1942).

113. *See, e.g., Wadia,* 101 F.2d at 7 (denying white status to an individual of Parsee descent); *In re* Din, 27 F.2d 568 (N.D. Cal. 1928) (denying white status to an individual of Afghani descent).

114. 174 F. 735 (C.C.N.D. Ga. 1909).

115. 176 F. 465, 467 (C.C.D. Mass. 1910).

116. 179 F. 1002, 1003 (D. Or. 1910).

117. 226 F. 145, 147–48 (4th Cir. 1915).

118. 180 F. at 694, affirming *In re* Balsara, 171 F. 171 294 (C.C.N.Y. 1909).

119. *Ex parte* Dow, 211 F. 486 (D.S.C. 1914).

120. *Ex parte* Dow, 211 F. at 488.

121. *Id.* at 488 (emphasis added).

122. *In re* Dow, 213 F. at 365.

123. *Id.* at 364.

124. *Balsara*, 180 F. at 696.

125. *See Dow*, 226 F. at 145.

126. *Id.*

127. *In re Dow*, 213 F. at 366.

128. *Id.*

129. *Id.* at 367.

130. *Id.* at 365.

131. *Id.* at 364.

132. 48 F. Supp. 843 (E.D. Mich. 1942).

133. 54 F. Supp. 941 (D. Mass. 1944).

134. *See Hassan*, 48 F. Supp. at 845.

135. *Id.*

136. *Id.* at 846.

137. *See Mohriez*, 54 F. Supp. at 942.

138. *Id.* (citations omitted).

139. *See id.*

140. *Id.* at 943.

141. *See* Trucios-Gaynes, *supra*, at 374.

142. *See, e.g.*, Sale v. Haitian Ctrs. Council, 509 U.S. 155, 201 (1993); Kleindienst v. Mandel, 408 U.S. 753, 766 (1972).

143. By making judicial opinions read like Tristan Tzara's *Dadaist Manifesto—see* Tristan Tzara, *Dadaist Manifesto*, in Seven Dada Manifestos and Lampisteries (Barbara Wright trans., Calder 1977) (1919)—such racial-determination games ultimately undermine the credibility of the rule of law and the alleged reliance of jurisprudence on rationality and logic.

144. Immigration (Dillingham) Comm'n, Dictionary of Races or Peoples, S. Doc. No. 61-662, vol. 5 (3d Sess. 1911) [hereinafter Immigration Comm'n, Dictionary of Races or Peoples].

145. Jacobson, *supra*, at 79 (quoting Immigration Comm'n, Dictionary of Races or Peoples).

146. *Dow*, 226 F. at 146–47 (quoting Immigration Comm'n, Dictionary of Races or Peoples).

147. Alien Property Initiative Act (Alien Land Law) of 1920, 1 Cal. Gen. Laws, Act 261 (Deering 1944 & Supp. 1949).

148. *See* Morrison v. California, 291 U.S. 82 (1934); Cockrill v. California, 268 U.S. 258 (1925); Webb v. O'Brien, 263 U.S. 313 (1923); Porterfield v. Webb, 263 U.S. 225 (1923); Terrace v. Thompson, 263 U.S. 197 (1923).

149. Cheryl I. Harris, *Whiteness as Property*, 106 Harv. L. Rev. 1707 (1993).

150. *See* Robert L. Hayman, Jr., & Nancy Levit, *Un-Natural Things: Constructions of Race, Gender, and Disability*, in Crossroads, Directions, and a New

CRITICAL RACE THEORY 159 (Francisco Valdes et al. eds., 2002); MICHAEL OMI & HOWARD WINANT, RACIAL FORMATION IN THE UNITED STATES (2d ed. 1994).

151. Immigration and Nationality Act of 1952, ch. 2, § 311, 66 Stat. 163, 239 (codified as amended at 8 U.S.C. § 1422 (1994)).

152. *See* Trucios-Gaynes, *supra*, at 399.

153. *See* Gabriel J. Chin, *The Civil Rights Revolution Comes to Immigration Law: A New Look at the Immigration and Nationality Act of 1965*, 75 N.C. L. REV. 273, 298 (1996).

154. U.S. COMM'N ON IMMIGRATION REFORM, BECOMING AN AMERICAN: IMMIGRATION AND IMMIGRANT POLICY 26 (1997).

155. SAMUEL P. HUNTINGTON, WHO ARE WE? THE CHALLENGES TO AMERICA'S NATIONAL IDENTITY (2005).

156. George Martinez, *Immigration and the Meaning of United States Citizenship, Whiteness and Assimilation*, 46 WASHBURN L. J. 335, 339 (2007).

157. Patrick Jonsson, *Backlash Emerges against Latino Culture*, CHRISTIAN SCIENCE MONITOR, July 19, 2006, at 3.

158. *Id.*

159. *See, e.g.*, Rene Galindo & Jami Vigil, *Language Restrictionism Revisited: The Case against Colorado's 2000 Anti-Bilingual Education Initiative*, 7 HARV. LATINO L. REV. 27 (2004).

160. *Id.; see* Garcia v. Gloor, 618 F.2d 264 (5th Cir. 1980) (concluding that English-only rules are not per se discriminatory); Garcia v. Spun Steak Co., 998 F.2d 1480 (9th Cir. 1993) (same).

161. Christopher David Ruiz Cameron, *How the García Cousins Lost Their Accents: Understanding the Language of Title VII Decisions Approving Speak English Only Rules as the Product of Racial Dualism, Latino Invisibility and Legal Indeterminacy*, 85 CAL. L. REV. 1347, 1351 (1997).

162. This initiative was ultimately blocked by the Colorado Supreme Court from appearing on the ballot. *See, e.g.*, Galindo & Vigil, *supra*.

163. It is critical to note that white performance is not the only form of racial dramaturgy. Where nonwhite groups dominate, performance of nonwhiteness can be a condition for nonwhite privilege. For example, Italian American teenagers in the inner city frequently perform nonwhiteness to facilitate their assimilation with other urban youth.

NOTES TO CHAPTER 3

1. Clayton R. Koppes, *Captain Mahan, General Gordon, and the Origins of the Term "Middle East,"* 12 MIDDLE EASTERN STUDIES 95, 95–96 (1976).

2. Alfred T. Mahan, *The Persian Gulf and International Relations*, in RETROSPECT AND PROSPECT 209, 237, 244–45 (1903).

3. José Rabasa, Inventing America: Spanish Historiography and the Formation of Eurocentrism 186, 385 (1993).

4. Sedat Laciner, *Is There a Place Called "the Middle East"?* Journal of Turkish Weekly Opinion, June 2, 2006, available online at http://www.turkishweekly.net/comments.php?id=2117#.

5. Fiore v. O'Connell, 66 N.Y.S.2d 173, 175 (N.Y. Sup. Ct. 1946).

6. Larsen v. Comm'r of Internal Revenue, 23 T.C. 599, 601 (Tax Court 1955).

7. Miller v. United States, 140 F. Supp. 789, 790, 792 (Ct. Cl. 1956).

8. Waldron v. British Petroleum Co., 149 F. Supp. 830, 836 (S.D.N.Y. 1957); United States v. Standard Oil Co. of California, 155 F. Supp. 121, 127 (S.D.N.Y. 1957).

9. Michael Omi & Howard Winant, Racial Formation in the United States 55 (1994).

10. Richard Delgado, *Two Ways to Think about Race: Reflections on the Id, the Ego, an Other Reformist Theories of Equal Protection*, 89 Geo. L.J. 2279, 2283 (2001) (footnote omitted).

11. Richard Delgado & Jean Stefancic, *Images of the Outsider in American Law and Culture: Can Free Expression Remedy Systemic Social Ills?* 77 Cornell L. Rev. 1258, 1262–63 (1992).

12. *Id.*

13. Delgado, *supra*, at 2285.

14. *Id.* at 2283.

15. Delgado & Stefancic, *supra*, at 1271–72.

16. Delgado, *supra*, at 2285–86.

17. Of course, these romantic images have often served less than salutary ends, providing, as Edward Said has argued, implicit justification for colonial and imperial ambitions by the West toward the Middle East. *See* Edward Said, Orientalism (1978).

18. James C. Scott, Seeing like the State (1998); James C. Scott, John Tehranian & Jeremy Mathias, *The Creation of Legal Identities Proper to the State: The Case of Surnames*, 44 Comparative Studies in History and Society 4 (2000).

19. *See, e.g.*, Samuel P. Huntington, The Clash of Civilizations and the Remaking of World Order (1998).

20. *See* Karen Engle, *Constructing Good Aliens and Good Citizens: Legitimizing the War on Terror(ism)*, 75 U. Colo. L. Rev. 59, 75 (2004) (discussing the stereotyping of Middle Eastern individuals as religious extremists and terrorists incapable of assimilation in the United States).

21. Louise Cainkar, *The History of Arab Immigration to the U.S.: An Introduction for High School Students*, in Arab American Encyclopedia (2000), available online at http://www.adc.org/education/AAImmigration.htm (accessed Sept. 12, 2006).

22. LUCIUS HOPKINS MILLER, A STUDY OF THE SYRIAN POPULATION OF GREATER NEW YORK 5 (1904).

23. *Id.* at 22.

24. *Id.* at 25.

25. Joyce Howard Price, *Census Courts 1.2 Million Arabs in U.S.: Most of Them Are Christian*, WASHINGTON TIMES, Dec. 4, 2003, at A1.

26. Engle, *supra*, at 74.

27. Victor Romero, *Race, Immigration and the Department of Homeland Security*, 19 ST. JOHN'S J. LEGAL COMMENT. 51, 55 (2004).

28. *Id.* at 52.

29. *See* Nancy Murray, *Profiled: Arabs, Muslims, and the Post-9/11 Hunt for the "Enemy Within,"* in CIVIL RIGHTS IN PERIL: THE TARGETING OF ARABS AND MUSLIMS 27, 44 (Elaine C. Hagopian ed., 2004).

30. LUCIUS HOPKINS MILLER, A STUDY OF THE SYRIAN POPULATION OF GREATER NEW YORK 41 (1904).

31. *Id.* at 45.

32. *Id.*

33. Charles R. Lawrence III, *The Id, the Ego, and Equal Protection: Reckoning with Unconscious Racism*, 39 STAN. L. REV. 317 (1987).

34. *See, e.g.*, Washington v. Davis, 426 U.S. 229 (1976).

35. Lawrence, *supra*, at 322–23.

36. Such a tack might be acceptable if we truly lived in a race-blind society in which racial perceptions were unimportant and all individuals were dissolved into a single catch-all "human" category. The "selective" aspect of the racialization process, however, belies the notion of race blindness.

37. Scott J. Simon, *Arabs in Hollywood: An Undeserved Image*, LATENT IMAGE (1996), available online at http://pages.emerson.edu/organizations/fas/latent_image/issues/1996-04/arabs.htm.

38. *See* Narmeen El-Farra, *Arabs and the Media*, 1 JOURNAL OF MEDIA PSYCHOLOGY (1996), available online at http://www.calstatela.edu/faculty/sfischo/Arabs.html.

39. *Alice: Florence of Arabia* (CBS television broadcast, Feb. 19, 1978).

40. JACK G. SHAHEEN, THE TV ARAB 64–66(1984). *See also* JACK G. SHAHEEN, REEL BAD ARABS: HOW HOLLYWOOD VILIFIES A PEOPLE (2003).

41. Jay Mohr (friend of Nomar Garciaparra), commentary on the *Jim Rome Show* radio program (sometime around 2001).

42. *See* Kenji Yoshino, *Covering*, 111 YALE L.J. 769, 772–73 (examining three forms of assimilation—conversion, passing, and covering—and how assimilation can be an effect of discrimination, in addition to being an evasion of it).

43. *See* ERVING GOFFMAN, STIGMA: NOTES ON THE MANAGEMENT OF SPOILED IDENTITY 12–13 (1963).

44. *Id.* at 102.

45. Yoshino, *supra*, at 772.

46. *Id.* at 773, 776. Yoshino defines *conversion* as the alteration of one's identity. *Id.*

47. *Id.* at 777, 781. Yoshino defines *passing* as the hiding, rather than alteration, of one's underlying identity. *Id.* at 772.

48. *Id.* at 772 (emphasis omitted).

49. *Id.* at 926.

50. *Id.*

51. There are certainly exceptions to this generalization, but I think it is fair to say that a determined individual of Middle Eastern descent would have a much easier time passing him- or herself off as a member of a different ethnic or racial group, or engaging in the act of covering, than an individual of African or East Asian descent. It should be noted that many Latinos, because of their inextricably mixed heritage, also "enjoy" the option of passing—for better or worse.

52. *See, e.g.,* Lorraine Ali, *Laughter's New Profile*, NEWSWEEK, Apr. 22, 2002, at 61 (quoting a line from a routine performed by an Iranian American comedian: "Since September 11, when people ask me about my ethnicity I look them straight in the eye and say, 'I'm Italian.' . . . We're all named Tony now.").

53. Sunita Patel, *Performative Aspects of Race: "Arab, Muslim, and South Asian" Racial Formation after September 11*, 10 ASIAN PAC. AM. L.J. 61, 83–84 (2005) (describing many of the covering activities undertaken by individuals of Middle Eastern descent in the wake of 9/11).

54. *See, e.g.,* Muneer I. Ahmad, *A Rage Shared by Law: Post–September 11 Racial Violence as Crimes of Passion*, 92 CAL. L. REV. 1259, 1278–79 (2004); NEW YORKER, Nov. 5, 2001 (depicting on the cover a Sikh taxi driver whose cab is covered with American flags).

55. Patel, *supra*, at 84.

56. KENJI YOSHINO, COVERING: THE HIDDEN ASSAULT ON OUR CIVIL RIGHTS 125 (2006).

57. Geary Act of 1892, ch. 60, § 6, 27 Stat. 25 (1892) (repealed) (emphasis added).

58. Gelareh Asayesh, *I Grew Up Thinking I Was White, in* MY SISTER, GUARD YOUR VEIL; MY BROTHER, GUARD YOUR EYES: UNCENSORED IRANIAN VOICES 12, 17 (Lila Azam Zanganeh ed., 2006).

59. *Clueless* (Paramount Pictures 1995).

60. *See* Devon Carbado & Mitu Gulati, *The Law and Economics of Critical Race Theory*, 112 YALE L.J. 1757, 1771–73 (2003) (book review).

61. *Id.* at 1772.

62. *See* 2 READINGS IN EUROPEAN HISTORY 303–12 (James H. Robinson ed., 1904–1906), available online at http://www.fordham.edu/halsall/mod/petergreat.html.

63. Declares Borat, "We support your war of terror. George W. Bush will drink the blood of every man, woman and child in Iraq." David Marchese &

Willa Paskin, *What's Real in "Borat"?* SALON.COM, Nov. 10, 2006, http://www. salon.com/ent/feature/2006/11/10/guide_to_borat/.

64. *Borat: Cultural Learnings of America for Make Benefit Glorious Nation of Kazakhstan* (Twentieth Century Fox 2006).

65. UCLA Office for Faculty Diversity, *Non-Ladder Academic Recruitment and Appointment Compliance Form*, available online at http://faculty.diversity.ucla. edu/03recruit/committee/stk/docs/NonLadderComplianceForm.dot (faculty diversity recruitment form).

66. *See* Sonya Geis, *Iran Native Becomes Mayor of Beverly Hills*, WASHINGTON POST, Apr. 1, 2007, at A3.

67. Prior to that, I would like to think that my uncle, Mansour Kia, was in the running for the title of highest ranking Iranian American elected official. He served as the mayor of the town of Stanton, Iowa (population: 714) at the turn of the century.

68. *In re* Cruz, 23 F. Supp. 774–75 (E.D.N.Y. 1938).

69. By the early 1900s, several Southern states had adopted this "one-drop" rule. *See* Luther Wright, Jr., *Who's Black, Who's White, and Who Cares? Reconceptualizing the United States's Definition of Race and Racial Classifications*, 48 VAND. L. REV. 513, 524 (1995) (documenting the progression of states toward the one-drop rule); PETER WALLENSTEIN, TELL THE COURT I LOVE MY WIFE 142 (2002) (noting that Georgia, Virginia, Alabama, and Oklahoma all had laws defining as black anyone with any drop of African ancestry); Plessy v. Ferguson, 163 U.S. 537 (1896) (assuming that the petitioner, who possessed only one-eighth African blood, was black for the purposes of segregation laws). *But see In re* Cruz, 23 F. Supp. at 775 (finding one-quarter African blood insufficient to gain someone recognition of African descent for naturalization purposes).

70. *See, e.g.*, Rice v. Cayetano, 528 U.S. 495, 507–09 (2000); Stuart Minor Benjamin, *Equal Protection and the Special Relationship: The Case of Native Hawaiians*, 106 YALE L.J. 537, 540, 554 (1996) (citing the Hawaiian Homes Commission Act § 203, which sets aside two hundred thousand acres of land for native Hawaiians to rent at a rate of one dollar per year; the Admission Act, which sets aside public lands for the "betterment of the conditions of Native Hawaiians"; and a 1978 Hawaii state constitutional amendment, which sets aside public funds for "educational programs, grants, low-interest loans, and housing assistance" for the "benefit of Native Hawaiians").

71. *See* Alex Salkever, *Lure of the Lei: Hawaii's Resurgent Cultural Appeal*, CHRISTIAN SCIENCE MONITOR, Oct. 23, 2002, at 2, available online at http:// www.csmonitor.com/2002/1023/p02s02-ussc.html (documenting the rise of Hawaiian chic); *cf.* Suein Hwang, *Long Dismissed, Hawaii Pidgin Finds a Place in Classroom*, WALL ST. J., Aug. 1, 2005, at A1 (documenting the recent embrace of Hawaiian Pidgin English by intellectual circles).

72. *Haole* literally means "foreigner" in Hawaiian and is a colloquial term in

the Hawaiian Islands for white people. Depending on its tone and context, it is considered innocuous (usually when used as an adjective, as in, "He was with two *haole* guys") or an insult (usually when used as a noun, as in, "Hey, *haole*"). *See* the film *North Shore* (Universal Pictures 1987).

73. *See* PUNAHOU SCHOOL, THE OAHUAN (1991–2000) (yearbook).

74. *See* Elizabeth M. Grieco, *Census 2000 Brief: The Native Hawaiian and Other Pacific Islander Population: 2000,* Dec. 2001, at 5, available online at http://www.census.gov/prod/2001pubs/c2kbr01-14.pdf. Of course, direct comparisons between the 1990 and 2000 statistics from the census must be tempered with the understanding that the 2000 census made it easier for individuals to identify themselves with multiple racial designations.

75. This trend is, of course, not limited to recent immigrant groups but has a long history. See, for example, the history of Irish, Greek, Italian, and Slavic assimilation in the United States. *See* NOEL IGNATIEV, HOW THE IRISH BECAME WHITE 2–3 (1995).

76. *See* Worldwide Persian Outreach, *The Persian Diaspora,* FARSINET, http://www.farsinet.com/pwo/diaspora.html (accessed Nov. 21, 2006). Another, more conservative, estimate suggests that the Iranian American population totaled approximately 540,000 by 2003. *See* Iranian Studies Group at MIT, *Factsheet on the Iranian-American Community* (2003), http://isg-mit.org/projects-storage/census/Factsheet.pdf.

77. Iranian Studies Group at MIT, *supra.*

78. *See* Laleh Khalili, *Forgiving Salm and Tur,* IRANIAN.COM, Sept. 29, 1998, http://www.iranian.com/LalehKhalili/Sept98/Race/index.html.

79. Mostofi v. INS, No. 94-70627, 1996 WL 183740, at *1 (9th Cir. Apr. 16, 1996).

80. *Ex parte* Dow, 211 F. 486, 490 (E.D.S.C. 1914), *aff'd on reh'g, In re* Dow, 213 F. 355 (E.D.S.C. 1914), *rev'd,* Dow v. United States, 226 F. 145 (4th Cir. 1915).

81. *In re* Dow, 213 F. 355 (E.D.S.C. 1914).

82. *Id.* at 356.

83. Asayesh, *supra,* at 14.

84. *See* Mark Perry, *Perceptions of Race in the Arab World* 11-12 (2004) (unpublished paper), available online at http://inhouse.lau.edu.lb/bima/papers/Perry.pdf.

85. DANIEL G. BATES & AMAL RASSAM, PEOPLES AND CULTURES OF THE MIDDLE EAST 96 (2d ed., 2001) (1983).

86. RODOLFO ACUÑA, ANYTHING BUT MEXICAN 1–2 (1996); *see also* JOHN R. CHÁVEZ, THE CHICAGO IMAGE OF THE SOUTHWEST 116 (1984).

87. ACUÑA, *supra,* at 8.

88. Hernandez v. Texas, 347 U.S. 475 (1954).

89. Gustavo Garcia, *An Informal Report to the People,* in A COTTON PICKER FINDS JUSTICE! THE SAGA OF THE HERNANDEZ CASE (1954).

90. Neil Foley, *Becoming Hispanic: Mexican Americans and the Faustian Pact*

with Whiteness, in REFLEXIONES 1997: NEW DIRECTIONS IN MEXICAN AMERICAN STUDIES 53, 53 (Neil Foley ed., 1997); Neil Foley, *Over the Rainbow:* Hernandez v. Texas, Brown v. Board of Education, *and Black v. Brown*, 25 CHICANO-LATINO L. REV. 139, 140 (2005) ("Mexican American commitment to a Caucasian racial identity in the 1930s through the 1950s complicated, and in some ways compromised, what at first appeared to be a promising start to interracial cooperation.")

91. Foley, *Becoming Hispanic, supra.*

92. Lawrence, *supra*, at 322.

93. *Id.* at 388.

NOTES TO CHAPTER 4

1. *See, e.g.*, Richard Delgado & Jean Stefancic, *Images of the Outsider in American Law and Culture: Can Free Expression Remedy Systemic Social Ills?* 77 CORNELL L. REV. 1258 (1992) (documenting the social construction of racial stereotypes, particularly through entertainment and pop-culture media).

2. The Hays Code was a production code, in effect from 1930 through 1967, that delineated what constituted morally acceptable content for motion pictures produced by the studios.

3. The intersection of race and love on the big screen demonstrates how media both reflects and perpetuates antiegalitarian norms. Consider the fact that it was not until 1968 that American network television broadcast the first interracial kiss. The kiss, featured on the science-fiction series *Star Trek*, generated a storm of controversy by showing Caucasian Captain James T. Kirk locking lips with African American Lieutenant Uhura. *See Star Trek: Plato's Stepchildren* (CBS television broadcast, Nov. 22, 1968). Notably, the show's writers couched the scene in the context of coercion and a dreamlike sequence in order to dampen the audience's shock. As the storyline of the episode goes, powerful telekinetic forces had gained control over the show's characters and dictated their "illicit" actions. Nevertheless, protests ensued against the series. Even to this day, the mainstream media shy away from depictions of interracial relationships for fear of offending audiences. See generally Glenn Lovell, *Interracial Romances: In Hollywood, Love Is Still a Mostly Segregated Thing*, ATLANTA J. CONST., Sept. 16, 1994, at P11. Witness the big-screen version of *The Pelican Brief*, which starred Julia Roberts and Denzel Washington. Almost any blockbuster featuring two major Hollywood sex symbols would inevitably involve a romance. Like *Romeo Must Die*, however, the movie version of *The Pelican Brief* carefully eschewed any hint of romance, even though the book on which it was based called for it. Similarly, until recently, virtually all television dating shows matched individuals only with members of their own race. Or take the massive public furor caused in February 1993 when Pulitzer Prize–winning novelist Art Spiegelman called for a reconciliation between the Jewish and African American communities in New

York by depicting a Hasidic man kissing an African American woman on the cover of the Valentine's Day issue of the *New Yorker. See Racial Theme of New Yorker Cover Sparks Furor*, L.A. TIMES, Feb. 9, 1993, at 12. Spiegelman meant the cover as a Valentine's Day card to New York City. As he later recalled, "It was amusing that in a week in which 90 percent of the other magazines on the stands had all these S&M covers, because that seems to be very dominant in our culture right now, what got people most upset weren't whips and chains, but two people kissing." Arthur J. Maginda, *Out of the "Maus" Trap?* BALTIMORE JEWISH TIMES, Jan. 20, 1995, at 43. The continual reinforcement of the traditional social opprobrium against interracial relationships is but one small way in which the movie industry has failed minority groups.

4. It should be noted, however, that in recent years African Americans have made significant strides in this area.

5. Keith Aoki, *Is Chan Still Missing? An Essay about the Film* Snow Falling on Cedars *and Representation of Asian Americans in U.S. Films*, 30 UCLA ASIAN PACIFIC AMERICAN LAW JOURNAL 7, 48 (2001).

6. *The Last King of Scotland* (DNA Films 2006).

7. *Blood Diamond* (Warner Bros. Pictures 2006).

8. *See, e.g., The Slanted Screen* (Asian American Media Mafia 2006) (featuring interview with Justin Lin recounting his insistence on Asian American casting decisions in *Better Luck Tomorrow* and *The Fast and Furious: Tokyo Drift*).

9. Edward Guthmann, *From Stereotypes to a Nuanced View*, SAN FRANCISCO CHRONICLE, Sept. 16, 2001, Datebook 49.

10. *See, e.g., Better Luck Tomorrow* (Paramount Pictures 2002); *Harold and Kumar Go to White Castle* (New Line Cinema 2004).

11. *See, e.g., Don't Be a Menace to South Central While Drinking Your Juice in the Hood* (Ivory Way Productions 1996).

12. It should be pointed out, however, that the deconstruction of Middle Eastern stereotypes has begun. The recent Axis of Comedy Tour is a key example. Mainstream Hollywood, however, has not yet altered its product.

13. *See* JACK G. SHAHEEN, REEL BAD ARABS: HOW HOLLYWOOD VILIFIES A PEOPLE (2001).

14. See, for example, the Ben Kingsley vehicle *House of Sand and Fog* (Dreamworks 2003) and Sally Field's movie *Not without My Daughter* (Pathé Entertainment 1991).

15. SHAHEEN, *supra*, at 15 (emphasis added).

16. American-Arab Anti-Discrimination Committee, *Protest of Racist Film "Rules of Engagement" Scheduled for Washington DC*, press release, Apr. 18, 2000, available online at http://www.adc.org/action/2000/18april2000.htm.

17. *See, e.g.,* Paul Clinton, *Review: An Unengaging "Rules,"* CNN.COM, Apr. 7, 2000, http://archives.cnn.com/2000/SHOWBIZ/Movies/04/07/rules.engagement/index.html; Kenneth Turan, *"Engagement" Fails to Step Up in the Face of Tough Questions,* L.A. TIMES, Apr. 7, 2000, available online at http://www.

calendarlive.com/movies/reviews/cl-movie000406-67,0,1228900.story; Lisa Schwarzbaum, *Colonel of Truth*, EW.COM, Apr. 14, 2000, http://www.ew.com/ew/article/0,,275900,00.html; Richard Corliss, *Review: Rules of Engagement*, TIME, Apr. 17, 2000, at 84,; David Sterritt, *The Monitor Movie Guide: Rules of Engagement*, CHRISTIAN SCIENCE MONITOR, Apr. 7, 2000, at 14.

18. Mark Freeman, review of *Rules of Engagement*, SENSES OF CINEMA, Aug. 2006, available online at http://www.sensesofcinema.com/contents/00/9/rules.html.

19. *See, e.g.*, Tony Medley, review of *Letters from Iwo Jima*, TONY MEDLEY WEBSITE, Dec. 13, 2006, http://www.tonymedley.com/2006/Letters_From_Iwo_Jima.htm; Chris Tookey, *Letters That Re-write History*, DAILY MAIL, Feb. 2007, available online at http://www.dailymail.co.uk/pages/live/articles/showbiz/reviews.html?in_article_id=437989&in_page_id=1924.

20. *See* Del James, *The Rolling Stone Interview—Axl Rose, Part I*, ROLLING STONE, Aug. 10, 1989.

21. *One in a Million (Guns N' Roses song)*, WIKIPEDIA, http://en.wikipedia.org/w/index.php?title=One_in_a_Million_%28Guns_N%27_Roses_song%29&oldid=157529659 (accessed Sep. 13, 2007).

22. Laurence Michalak, *Cruel and Unusual: Negative Images of Arabs in Popular Culture*, American-Arab Anti-Discrimination Committee Research Institute Issue Paper No. 15 (1988); Laurence Michalak, *The Arab in American Cinema: From Bad to Worse, or Getting Better?* 42 SOCIAL STUDIES REVIEW: J. OF THE CAL. COUNCIL FOR SOC. STUD. (2002).

23. David Prochaska, *"Disappearing" Iraqis*, 5 SWORDS AND PLOUGHSHARES 13 (1991), available online at http://www.acdis.uiuc.edu/Research/S&Ps/1991-Sp/S&P_V-3/disappearing_iraqis.html.

24. *See, e.g.*, *Anthony Caruso (I)*, INTERNET MOVIE DATABASE, http://www.imdb.com/name/nm0142273/ (accessed Sept. 13, 2007) (Character actor Anthony Caruso, an Italian American who appeared in more than two hundred Hollywood movies during his lifetime, often played Indian, Arab, Persian, Latino, and Native American characters).

25. See, for example, Zena Marshall's portrayal of the Chinese Miss Taro in Ian Fleming's *Dr. No.*

26. Of course, controversy still remains. The casting of Jennifer Lopez, a Cuban American, in the role of Selena in the eponymous movie upset many Mexican Americans. Moreover, casting of mostly Chinese actors in *Memoirs of a Geisha* received criticism from numerous individuals of Japanese descent. The very fact that there was a dialogue over the issue, however, shows how far we have come on the subject of minority representation in Hollywood.

27. Of course, like many projects, *300* was actually filmed outside the Thirty Mile Zone. It was shot in Montreal.

28. *Beverly Hills 90210: April Is the Cruelest Month* (Fox television broadcast, Apr. 11, 1991).

29. Renee Montagne, *Living in Tehrangeles: L.A.'s Iranian Community*, MORN-ING EDITION (National Public Radio broadcast, June 8, 2006), available online at http://www.npr.org/templates/story/story.php?storyId=5459468; *see also* Diane Wedner, *Neighborly Advice; Beverly Hills Close Up, It Looks Different Now*, L.A. TIMES, Jan. 8, 2006, at K2. Overall, the *Washington Post* estimates that approximately a quarter of Beverly Hills thirty-five thousand residents are Iranian. *See* Sonya Geis, *Iran Native Becomes Mayor of Beverly Hills*, WASHINGTON POST, Apr. 1, 2007, at A3.

30. BENDER, GREASERS AND GRINGOS 84, 181 (2003).

31. Interestingly, despite Hollywood's ostensible liberalism on social issues, sexual minorities do not count as a protected group.

32. See SAG's standard Low Budget Agreement (http://www.sagindie.org/docs/sag-lowbudget-2005wm.pdf) and Modified Low Budget Agreement (http://www.sagindie.org/docs/sag-modifiedlowbudget-2005wm.pdf).

33. Screen Actors Guild, *Casting Data Report*, SAG WEBSITE, http://www.sag.org/files/documents/CastingDataReport.pdf.

34. Susan M. Akram & Kevin R. Johnson, *Race, Civil Rights, and Immigration Law after September 11, 2001: The Targeting of Arabs and Muslims*, 58 N.Y.U. ANN. SURV. AM. L. 295, 310 (2002).

35. Kelli Skye Fadroski, *Setting the Terror Level to Funny*, SQUEEZEOC.COM, Mar. 23, 2007, http://www.squeezeoc.com/squeezeoc/goingout/article_1629277.php.

36. Quoted in Brian Whitaker, *The "Towel-Heads" Take on Hollywood*, GUARDIAN INTERNATIONAL, Aug. 11, 2000, available online at http://www.guardian.co.uk/international/story/0,3604,355880,00.html.

37. EDWARD SAID, ORIENTALISM 285 (1978); Ronald Stockton, *Ethnic Archetypes and the Arab Image*, in THE DEVELOPMENT OF ARAB-AMERICAN IDENTITY 138 (Ernest McCarus ed., 1994); Sarah Gualtieri, *Strange Fruit? Syrian Immigrants, Extralegal Violence and Racial Formation in the Jim Crow South*, 26 ARAB STUD. Q. 63 (2004).

38. Stockton, *supra*, at 138.

39. *Id.*

40. Magritte implores us to scrutinize our casual relationship with the environment and to question our most tacit assumptions about reality and representation on several levels. First, his painting emphasizes the inextricable disconnect between representation (the painting of a pipe) and reality (a pipe). Second, the painting deconstructs the fundamental disjuncture among different forms of representation, including visual depiction and linguistic discourse. *See* MICHEL FOUCAULT, THIS IS NOT A PIPE 27 (1983). Observes Michel Foucault in an essay about Magritte's work, the word "this" in *La Trahison des Images* could refer to the sentence, or language, itself: "this is not a pipe . . . but rather a text that simulates a pipe; a drawing of a pipe that simulates a drawing of a pipe; a pipe (drawn other than as a drawing) that is a simulacrum

of a pipe (drawn after a pipe that itself would be other than a drawing)." *Id.* at 49. All told, as Foucault argues, the painting ruptures the implicit link between resemblance and discourse, representation and object. And so must we.

41. *But see Iran—Without My Daughter* (Journeyman Pictures 2003) (a documentary about Dr. Mahmoody's side of the story wherein he denies many of the claims that Betty made about him).

42. See, for example, the fallout from the Don Imus incident involving epithets hurled against the women's basketball team at Rutgers University.

43. *See, e.g.,* Chris Hicks, review of *Not Without My Daughter*, DESERETNEWS. COM, Jan. 11, 1991, http://deseretnews.com/movies/view/1,1257,1336,00.html.

44. BENDER, *supra*, at 181. See also *Seinfeld: The Puerto Rican Day* (NBC television broadcast, May 7, 1998).

45. See, for example, the works of cultivation theorists, as summarized in Daniel Chandler, *Cultivation Theory*, MEDIA AND COMMUNICATIONS STUDIES WEBSITE, http://www.aber.ac.uk/media/Documents/short/cultiv.html.

46. MICHAEL OMI & HOWARD WINANT, RACIAL FORMATION IN THE UNITED STATES: FROM THE 1960S TO THE 1980S 56 (1986).

47. *Id.* at 60.

48. SAID, *supra*, at 26.

49. Andrea Elliott, *Reported Hate Crimes against Muslims Rise in U.S.*, INT'L HERALD TRIB., May 13, 2005, at 2.

50. John Ashcroft, *Attorney General Prepared Remarks on the National Security Entry-Exit Registration System*, June 6, 2002, available online at http://www. usdoj.gov/archive/ag/speeches/2002/060502agpreparedremarks.htm.

51. David Cole, *The Priority of Morality: The Emergency Constitution's Blind Spot*, 113 YALE L.J. 1753, at 1753 (estimating that over five thousand Middle Easterners had been detained after 9/11); David Rosenzweig, *3 Groups Sue Over Arrests of Arab Men*, L.A. TIMES, Dec. 25, 2002, § 2, at 3.

52. Heidee Stoller, Tahlia Townsend, Rashad Hussain & Marcia Yablon, Developments in Law and Policy, *The Costs of Post-9/11 National Security Strategy*, 22 YALE L. & POL'Y REV. 197, 200–22 (2004).

53. U.S. Equal Employment Opportunity Commission, *Questions and Answers about the Workplace Rights of Muslims, Arabs, South Asians, and Sikhs under the Equal Employment Opportunity Laws*, May 14, 2002, available online at http:// www.eeoc.gov/facts/backlash-employee.html (accessed Nov. 25, 2006).

54. George Gerbner et al., *Living with Television: The Dynamics of the Cultivation Process*, in PERSPECTIVES ON MEDIA EFFECTS 17–18 (J. Bryant & D. Zillman eds., 1986).

55. George Gerbner & L. Gross, *Living with Television: The Violence Profile*, 26 JOURNAL OF COMMUNICATION 172, 176 (1976).

56. Saenz v. Roe, 526 U.S. 489 (1999) (finding that the Constitution guarantees a fundamental right to interstate travel).

57. 29 U.S.C. § 44902(b), originally 29 U.S.C. § 1111.

58. 14 C.F.R. 91.3 and 49 C.F.R. 1544.2 15(c).

59. O'Carroll v. American Airlines, Inc., 863 F.2d 11, 12 (5th Cir. 1989).

60. Brown v. Board of Education of Topeka, 347 U.S. 483 (1954).

61. Oversight Hearing on Passenger Screening and Airline Authority to Deny Boarding Before the S. Appropriations Subcomm. on Transportation, Treasury, General Government, and Related Agencies, Comm. on Appropriations, 108th Cong. 2 (2004) (statement of Michael A. Smerconish, Esq.).

62. Complaint in Chowdhury v. Northwest Airlines (N.D. Cal. June 4, 2004), available online at news.findlaw.com/hdocs/docs/aclu/chwdhrynwa60402cmp.pdf.

63. *Id.*

64. Arshad Chowdhury, *Statement on Racial Profiling*, ACLU WEBSITE, http://www.aclu.org/racialjustice/racialprofiling/chowdhury_statement.pdf.

65. Oversight Hearing on Passenger Screening and Airline Authority to Deny Boarding Before the S. Appropriations Subcomm. on Transportation, Treasury, General Government, and Related Agencies, Comm. on Appropriations, 108th Cong. 2 (2004) (statement of Christy E. Lopez, Esq.).

66. *Id.*

67. Quoted in Elizabeth Schulte, *Flying While Arab*, SOCIALIST WORKER, Oct. 19, 2001, at 5, available online at http://www.socialistworker.org/2001/380/380_05_FlyingWhileArab.shtml.

68. Quoted in Sharon Cohen, *Complaints Rise from People with Middle Eastern Names or Appearances, Who Are Told They Can't Fly*, ASSOCIATED PRESS ONLINE, Sept. 25, 2001.

69. FRANZ FANON, THE FACT OF BLACKNESS, BLACK SKIN, WHITE MASKS (1952) (Charles Lame Markmann trans., 1968).

70. KENJI YOSHINO, COVERING: THE HIDDEN ASSAULT ON OUR CIVIL RIGHTS 120 (2006).

71. FRANK WU, YELLOW: RACE IN AMERICA BEYOND BLACK AND WHITE (2002).

72. Quoted in ERIC K. YAMAMOTO ET AL., RACE, RIGHTS, AND REPARATION: LAW AND THE JAPANESE AMERICAN INTERNMENT 474 (2001).

73. Harvey Gee, *From Bakke to Grutter and Beyond: Asian-Americans and Diversity in America*, 9 TEX. J. ON CIV. LIB. & CIV. RIGHTS 129 (2004).

74. *Id.* at 139.

75. *Id.* at 140.

76. *Id.*

77. Adarand Constructors, Inc. v. Pena, 115 S.Ct. 209, 2119 (1995) (Scalia, J., concurring).

78. ALVIN F. POUISSANT & AMY ALEXANDER, LAY MY BURDEN DOWN:

Unraveling Suicide and the Mental Health Crisis among African-Americans (2001).

79. *Id.* at 47.

NOTES TO CHAPTER 5

1. I do not mean to suggest that the lot of all minority groups, save Middle Easterners, has improved since the civil rights movement. For example, the war on terrorism has had a profound collateral effect on Latinos. Some Latinos have suffered because they may look Middle Eastern. More significantly, the concern over border security precipitated by the events of 9/11 has led to increased scrutiny over immigration policies and examinations of ethnic assimilability. The resulting immigration debate has occasionally degenerated into outright xenophobia and racism that has targeted Latinos, especially Mexican Americans.

2. *See, e.g.,* Grutter v. Bollinger, 539 U.S. 306, 353 (2004) (Thomas, J., concurring in part and dissenting in part).

3. Jeff Pearlman, *At Full Blast,* Sports Illustrated, Dec. 27, 1999, at 62 (alteration in original).

4. *Id.*

5. Richard Morin, *A Distorted Image of Minorities: Poll Suggests That What Whites Think They See May Affect Beliefs,* Washington Post, Oct. 8, 1995, at A1 (poll conducted by the *Washington Post,* the Kaiser Family Foundation, and Harvard University).

6. Hernandez v. New York, 500 U.S. 352 (1991).

7. Ariela Gross, *"The Caucasian Cloak": Mexican Americans and the Politics of Whiteness in the 20th Century Southwest,* 95 Georgetown L.J. 337 (2006).

8. *Grutter,* 539 U.S. at 343.

9. *Cf.* Cheryl I. Harris, *Whiteness as Property,* 106 Harv. L. Rev. 1707, 1766–69 (1993) (arguing that the trope of colorblindness advocated by opponents of affirmative action is a doctrinal mode of protecting the property interest in whiteness by limiting remediation for past subjugation and therefore enshrining and institutionalizing centuries of white privilege); Neil Gotanda, *A Critique of "Our Constitution Is Color-Blind,"* 44 Stan. L. Rev. 1, 2 (1991) (arguing that colorblindness is a form of race subordination in that it denies the historical context of white domination and black subordination).

10. *See* Stephen Magagnini, *Many Blacks, Whites Find Race Issue Can Be a Minefield,* Sacramento Bee, Feb. 23, 1999, at A1; Michael A. Fletcher & Dan Balz, *Americans on Race Relations,* Washington Post, June 12, 1997, at A16 (noting, inter alia, a 1997 Gallup poll that found that 76 percent of whites feel that African Americans are now treated the same as whites in their communities);

Jill Darling Richardson, *Poll Analysis: U.S. Nowhere Near Eliminating Racism, but Race-Based Affirmative Action Not the Answer*, L.A. Times, Feb. 6, 2003, at 16, available online at http://www.latimes.com/news/nationworld/timespoll/la-na-poll6feb06-481pa3an,1,3273569.story?coll=la-news-times_poll-nation.

11. Ala. Const. art. IV, § 102. See also *Alabama Repeals Century-Old Ban on Interracial Marriages*, CNN.com, Nov. 8, 2000, http://archives.cnn.com/2000/ ALLPOLITICS/stories/11/07/alabama.interracial/.

12. Loving v. The Commonwealth of Virginia, 388 U.S. 1 (1967).

13. Arab American Institute, *AAI/Zogby Poll on Arab American Experiences and Identity Shows Increase in Discrimination among Young Arab Americans*, July 16, 2007, available online at http://www.aaiusa.org/page/-/Polls/r-2007%20AA%20 Identity%20poll%20-%20FINAL.pdf.

14. *The Politics of National Security: Macho Moms and Deadbeat Dads*, Economist, Mar. 11, 2006, at 25.

15. *See* David Brooks, Op-Ed, *Kicking Arabs in the Teeth*, N.Y. Times, Feb. 23, 2006, at A27 ("This Dubai port deal has unleashed a kind of collective mania we haven't seen in decades. First seized by the radio hatemonger Michael Savage, it's been embraced by reactionaries of left and right, exploited by Empire State panderers, and enabled by a bipartisan horde of politicians who don't have the guts to stand in front of a xenophobic tsunami.").

16. *The Politics of National Security, supra*, at 25; *DP World Seeks U.S. Buyer for Ports*, CNN.com, Mar. 15, 2006, http://www.cnn.com/2006/POLITICS/03/15/ post.sale/index.html.

17. *The Politics of National Security, supra*, at 25.

18. *Id.* On March 8, a Republican-dominated House panel voted 62–2 to block the port deal, despite threats of a presidential veto. *Id.*

19. *Inside the Politics of the Dubai Ports Controversy*, All Things Considered (National Public Radio broadcast, Mar. 9, 2006).

20. *See Bush Says He Will Veto Any Bill to Stop UAE Port Deal*, FOXNews. com, Feb. 22, 2006, http://www.foxnews.com/story/0,2933,185479,00.html.

21. My dad's admission to Sigma Phi Epsilon was not without controversy, however. The national Sigma Phi Epsilon chapter opposed my dad's admission because of his heritage. But the local chapter stood firm and opted to break with the national group if it insisted on denying my dad membership.

22. Although Leti Volpp argues that the events of 9/11 racialized individuals appearing to be Middle Eastern, Arab, or Muslim (*see* Leti Volpp, *The Citizen and the Terrorist*, 49 UCLA L. Rev. 1575, 1575–76 (2002)), Kevin Johnson notes that the racialization of Middle Easterners predates the 9/11 terrorist attacks. Kevin R. Johnson, *The End of "Civil Rights" as We Know It? Immigration and Civil Rights in the New Millennium*, 49 UCLA L. Rev. 1481, 1488–89 (2002).

23. The related "Operation Boulder" targeted Arabs in the United States for

special investigation and discouraged their political activities, especially on is-sues related to the Middle East. *See* Susan M. Akram & Kevin R. Johnson, *Race and Civil Rights Pre–September 11, 2001: The Targeting of Arabs and Muslims*, in CIVIL RIGHTS IN PERIL: THE TARGETING OF ARABS AND MUSLIMS 9, 18 (Elaine C. Hagopian ed., 2004).

24. *See id.* at 17–19; Nabeel Abraham, *Anti-Arab Racism and Violence in the United States*, in THE DEVELOPMENT OF ARAB-AMERICAN IDENTITY 155, 199 (Ernest McCarus ed., 1994); Susan M. Akram & Kevin R. Johnson, *Race, Civil Rights, and Immigration Law after September 11, 2001: The Targeting of Arabs and Muslims*, 58 N.Y.U. ANN. SURV. AM. L. 295, 314, 314 n.107 (2002).

25. Tayyari v. New Mexico State Univ., 495 F. Supp. 1365, 1374 (D.N.M. 1980) (citing Shabani v. Simmons, No. EC80-160-LS-P (N.D. Miss. July 3, 1980)).

26. *Id.* at 1374 n.9.

27. *Id.*

28. On May 9, 1980, the regents of New Mexico State University passed a motion stating that "any student whose home government holds, or permits the holding of U.S. citizens hostage will be denied admission or readmission to New Mexico State University commencing with the Fall 1980 semester unless the American hostages are returned unharmed by July 15, 1980." *Id.* at 1367–68.

29. *Id.* at 1371–75; *see also* Karl Manheim, *State Immigration Laws and Federal Supremacy*, 22 HASTINGS CONST. L.Q. 939, 989–90 (1995).

30. *See, e.g.,* Narjenji v. Civiletti, 617 F.2d 745 (D.C. Cir. 1979).

31. Michael Paulsen, *U.S. Attitudes toward Arabs Souring, According to Poll,* BOSTON GLOBE, Sept. 29, 2001, at A5.

32. *Id.*

33. David Prochaska, *"Disappearing" Iraqis,* 5 SWORDS AND PLOUGHSHARES (1991), available online at http://www.acdis.uiuc.edu/Research/S&Ps/1991-Sp/S&P_V-3/disappearing_iraqis.html).

34. Quoted in *id.*

35. *Id.*

36. Kevin R. Johnson, *Race and Immigration Law and Enforcement: A Response to* Is There a Plenary Power Doctrine? 14 GEO. IMMIGR. L.J. 289, 300 (2000).

37. Kareem Shora & Timothy Edgar, *After 9/11, an Assault on Civil Liberties,* TRIAL, Oct. 2003, at 56.

38. U.S. Equal Employment Opportunity Commission, *Questions and Answers about the Workplace Rights of Muslims, Arabs, South Asians, and Sikhs under the Equal Employment Opportunity Laws,* May 14, 2002, available online at http://www.eeoc.gov/facts/backlash-employee.html (accessed Nov. 25, 2006).

39. LexisNexis search of "Federal and States Cases, Combined" database, March 1, 2008.

40. *Id.*

41. S.B. 60, 2005–2006 Sess. (Cal. 2005) (excluding persons with identity documents issued by "a state sponsor of terrorism" from proposed immigrant driver licensing scheme).

42. David Cole, *Enemy Aliens*, 54 STAN. L. REV. 953, 974 (2002); *see also Attorney General Seeks End to Racial Profiling*, N.Y. TIMES, Mar. 2, 2001, at A20; Shora & Edgar, *supra*, at 60.

43. Cole, *Enemy Aliens*, *supra*, at 974 (citing Gallup Poll, *Do You Approve or Disapprove of the Use of "Racial Profiling" by Police?* Dec. 9, 1999, available at WESTLAW, USGALLUP.120999 R6 009).

44. *Id.*

45. Gallup Poll, *The Impact of the Attacks on America*, Oct. 8, 2001, available online at http://www.galluppoll.com/content/?ci=4972&pg=1 (finding that a third of Americans favor several "more severe measures") (subscription required).

46. *See, e.g.,* Peter H. Schuck, *A Case for Profiling*, AM. LAW., Jan. 2002, at 59; Stuart Taylor, Jr., *The Case for Using Racial Profiling at Airports*, 38 NAT'L J. 2877 (2001); Charles Krauthammer, *The Case for Profiling*, TIME, Mar. 18, 2002, at 104; James Q. Wilson & Heather R. Higgins, *Profiles in Courage*, WALL ST. J., Jan. 10, 2002, at A12.

47. *Apology from Congressman*, N.Y. TIMES, Sept. 21, 2001, at A16.

48. *See Nightline* (ABC television broadcast, Oct. 10, 2001).

49. Ann Scales, *Polls Say Blacks Tend to Favor Checks*, BOSTON GLOBE, Sept. 30, 2001, at A16.

50. *See* NOEL IGNATIEV, HOW THE IRISH BECAME WHITE (1995).

51. Volpp, *supra*, at 1584.

52. Susan Akram & Maritza Karmely, *Immigration and Constitutional Consequences of Post-9/11 Policies Involving Arabs and Muslims in the United States: Is Alienage a Distinction without a Difference?* 38 U.C. DAVIS L. REV. 609, 629 (2005).

53. Akram & Johnson, *Race, Civil Rights, and Immigration Law after September 11, 2001*, *supra*, at 342.

54. Akram & Karmely, *supra*, at 630.

55. *Id.* at 631.

56. John Ashcroft, *Attorney General Prepared Remarks on the National Security Entry-Exit Registration System*, June 6, 2002, available online at http://www.usdoj.gov/archive/ag/speeches/2002/060502agpreparedremarks.htm.

57. *See* Nancy Murray, *Profiled: Arabs, Muslims, and the Post-9/11 Hunt for the "Enemy Within,"* in CIVIL RIGHTS IN PERIL: THE TARGETING OF ARABS AND MUSLIMS 27, 44 (Elaine C. Hagopian ed., 2004).

58. *See* George W. Bush, *Remarks by the President on the Michigan Affirmative Action Cases*, WHITEHOUSE.GOV, Jan. 15, 2003, http://www.whitehouse.gov/news/releases/2003/01/20030115-7.html.

59. One notable exception is, of course, Osama bin Laden, who grew up in a wealthy Saudi Arabian family.

60. Dan Ouimette, U.S. Navy Captain, *America* WAKE UP!, speech before the Pensacola Civilian Club, Feb. 19, 2003.

61. *See* Mary Abowd, *Arab-Americans Suffer Hatred after Bombing*, CHI. SUN-TIMES, May 13, 1995, at 14; Kate Fitzgerald, *Sadness, Shock at Portrayal of Arabs*, ADVERTISING AGE, Apr. 24, 1995, at 4.

62. *Id.*

63. Volpp, *supra*, at 1585.

64. *Id.*

65. STEVEN BENDER, GREASERS AND GRINGOS 207–08 (2003).

66. Michael Lup, *For Exercise in New York Futility, Push Button*, N.Y. TIMES, Feb. 27, 2004, at A1.

67. DAVID COLE, ENEMY ALIENS: DOUBLE STANDARDS AND CONSTITUTIONAL FREEDOMS IN THE WAR ON TERRORISM (2004).

68. *UCLA Student Tasered by Police in Library*, YOUTUBE.COM, Nov. 15, 2006, http://youtube.com/watch?v=5g7zlJx9u2E.

69. Sara Taylor, *Community Responds to Taser Use in Powell*, DAILY BRUIN, Nov. 16, 2006, available online at http://www.dailybruin.com/news/articles. asp?id=38960.

70. Posting of Robert Masters to LAist.com, http://www.laist.com/archives/2006/11/17/ucla_students_demonstrate_against_ucpd_taser_use.php (posting 104, Dec. 6, 2006, 12:00 p.m. PST).

71. Pierre Thomas, *Federal Agents Raid Suspected Terror Cell in Miami*, ABC-NEWS.COM, June 22, 2006, http://abcnews.go.com/US/story?id=2109053.

72. Dale Russakoff & Dan Eggen, *Six Charged in Plot to Attack Fort Dix; "Jihadists" Said to Have No Ties to Al-Qaeda*, WASHINGTON POST, May 9, 2007, at A1.

73. Chris Michaud, *RPT-Update 6: Four Charged in Plot to Blow Up New York Airport*, REUTERS, June 2, 2007.

74. Posting 105 to *UCLA Student Tasered by Police in Library*, YOUTUBE.COM, Nov. 15, 2006, http://youtube.com/watch?v=5g7zlJx9u2E.

75. *The Strange Case of Cyrus Kar*, BBC NEWS WEBSITE, July 7, 2005, http://news.bbc.co.uk/2/hi/middle_east/4659175.stm.

76. Albert W. Alschuler, *Racial Profiling and the Constitution*, 2002 U. CHI. LEGAL F. 163, 168 n.24 (2002).

77. United States v. Montero-Camargo, 208 F.3d 1122, 1130 (9th Cir. 2000).

78. Akram & Karmely, *supra*, at 669. *See also* Kevin R. Johnson, *Racial Profiling after September 11: The Department of Justice's 2003 Guidelines*, 50 LOY. L. REV. 67 (2004).

79. Craig v. Boren, 429 U.S. 190 (1976).

80. *Id.* at 191.

81. *Id.* at 202.

82. Cole, *Enemy Aliens, supra,* at 976.

83. It should also be noted that drunk driving actually causes far more deaths in an average year than terrorism does.

84. Adam Liptak, *In Terror Cases, Administration Sets Own Rules,* N.Y. TIMES, Nov. 27, 2005, at 1.

85. COLE, ENEMY ALIENS, *supra,* at 3.

86. Hamdi v. Rumsfeld, 542 U.S. 507 (2004).

87. Duncan Campbell, *From Hot Tub to Hot Water,* GUARDIAN, July 16, 2002, available online at http://www.guardian.co.uk/bush/story/0,7369,756219,00.html.

88. *See, e.g.,* Mathews v. Diaz, 426 U.S. 67, 79–80 (1976) ("In the exercise of its broad power over naturalization and immigration, Congress regularly makes rules that would be unacceptable if applied to citizens."); Galvan v. Press, 347 U.S. 522, 530 (1954) (discussing Congress's broad plenary power over immigration); Chae Chan Ping v. United States, 130 U.S. 581 (1889) (holding that immigration decisions by the political branches are "conclusive upon the judiciary" without the need for substantial constitutional scrutiny); Chy Lung v. Freeman, 92 U.S. 275 (1875).

89. *See* Victor Romero, *Race, Immigration and the Department of Homeland Security,* 19 ST. JOHN'S J. LEGAL COMMENT. 51, 52 (2004).

90. Chae Chan Ping v. United States, 130 U.S. 581 (1889) (upholding the constitutionality of racial restrictions on immigration). *See also* Yamataya v. Fisher, 189 U.S. 86, 97 (1903) ("That Congress may exclude aliens of a particular race from the United States . . . [is a] principle . . . firmly established by the decisions of this court").

91. *Ping,* 130 U.S. at 609.

92. *Id.* at 595–96.

93. Deenesh Sohoni, *Unsuitable Suitors: Anti-Miscegenation Laws, Naturalizations Laws, and the Construction of Asian Identifies,* 41 L. & SOC'Y REV. 587 (2007).

94. The Supreme Court upheld the constitutionality of the Alien Land Laws in *Frick v. Webb,* 263 U.S. 326 (1923), despite the fact that the case was heard during the height of the *Lochner* era, which fetishized the freedom of contract, economic substantive due process rights, and a laissez-faire ideology. *See* Keith Aoki, *No Right to Own? The Early Twentieth-Century "Alien Lands Laws" as a Prelude to Internment,* 40 B.C. L. REV. 37, 65 (1998).

95. Aoki, *supra,* at 67–68.

96. *Id.* at 44.

97. Quoted in *id.* at 68.

98. *Id.*

99. Cole, *Enemy Aliens, supra,* at 989–90.

100. *Id.* at 990 (citing Brief of Japanese American Citizens League, Amicus Curiae at 198, Korematsu v. United States, 323 U.S. 214 (1944) (No. 22), *reprinted in* 42 Landmark Briefs and Arguments of the Supreme Court of the United States: Constitutional Law 309–530 (Phillip B. Kurland & Gerhard Casper eds., 1975)).

101. *See* Korematsu v. United States, 323 U.S. 214 (1944); Hirabayashi v. United States, 320 U.S. 81 (1943); Yasui v. United States, 320 U.S. 115 (1943).

102. Kevin R. Johnson, *The Forgotten "Repatriation" of Persons of Mexican Ancestry and Lessons for the "War on Terror,"* 26 Pace L. Rev. 1, 5 (2006).

103. Francisco E. Balderrama & Raymond Rodriguez, Decade of Betrayal: Mexican Repatriation in the 1930s 21–22 (1995).

104. Leo Grebler, Mexican Immigration to the United States: The Record and Its Implications 26 (1965) (quoted in Kevin R. Johnson, *The Forgotten "Repatriation" of Persons of Mexican Ancestry and Lessons for the "War on Terror,"* 26 Pace L. Rev. 1, 5 (2006)).

105. Akram & Karmely, *supra.*

106. United States v. Brignoni-Ponce, 422 U.S. 873 (1975).

107. *Id.* at 886–87.

108. Turkmen v. Ashcroft, No. 02-2307, 2006 WL 1662663, at *13 (E.D.N.Y. June 14, 2006).

109. Quoted in Nina Bernstein, *Judge Rules That U.S. Has Broad Powers to Detain Noncitizens Indefinitely,* N.Y. Times, June 15, 2006, at B1.

110. *Turkmen,* 2006 WL at *4.

111. *Id.* at *6.

112. *Id.*

113. *Id.* at *7.

114. *Id.*

115. *Id.* at *8.

116. *Id.* at *8–10.

117. *Id.* at *10–11.

118. *Id.* at *13.

119. *Id.* at *14.

120. *Id.* at *13.

121. *Id.* at *1.

122. *Id.* at *42

123. *Id.* at *43.

124. 59 Mass. 198 (5 Cush.).

125. *Id.* at 206.

126. *Id.*

127. *Id.* at 208.

128. *Id.* at 209.

129. *Turkmen,* at *42.

130. McClesky v. Kemp, 481 U.S. 279 (1987).

131. Reno v. American-Arab Anti-Discrimination Committee, 525 U.S. 471, 490–91 (1999).

132. *See, e.g.,* Planned Parenthood v. Casey, 505 U.S. 833 (1992); Roe v. Wade, 410 U.S. 113 (1973).

133. Justices Scalia and Thomas, for example, have steadfastly maintained that the Constitution virtually dictates absolute race-blindness. *See Grutter,* 539 U.S. at 306 (Scalia, J., concurring in part and dissenting in part) (declaring that race-conscious admissions policies in state education institutions are unconstitutional); *id.* at 378 (Thomas, J., concurring in part and dissenting in part) (quoting Justice Harlan's dissent to Plessy v. Ferguson, 163 U.S. 537, 559 (1896), that "[o]ur constitution is color-blind, and neither knows nor tolerates classes among citizens.").

134. In many ways, it should be noted, the *Turkmen* ruling was not remarkable. This was not the opinion of a rogue federal judge. Instead, the logic was quite reasonable when one considers the existing precedent from the Supreme Court on the issue.

135. Brown v. Board of Education of Topeka, 347 U.S. 483, 495 (1954).

136. El-Masri v. Tenet, 437 F. Supp. 2d 530, 532 n.1 (E.D. Va. 2006).

137. *Id.* at 536.

138. El-Masri v. United States, 479 F.3d 296 (4th Cir. 2007), cert. denied, 2007 WL 1646914 (U.S. Oct. 9, 2007).

139. United States v. Reynolds, 345 U.S. 1, 10 (1953).

140. *Id.* at 11.

141. *El-Masri,* 479 F.3d at 311 ("suggestions that the court ought to have received all the state secrets evidence in camera and under seal, provided his counsel access to it pursuant to a nondisclosure agreement (after arranging for necessary security clearances), and then conducted an in camera trial. We need not dwell long on el-Masri's proposal in this regard, for it is expressly foreclosed by *Reynolds,* the Supreme Court decision that controls this entire field of inquiry. *Reynolds* plainly held that when 'the occasion for the privilege is appropriate, . . . the court should not jeopardize the security which the privilege is meant to protect by insisting upon an examination of the evidence, even by the judge alone, in chambers.' 345 U.S. at 10.").

142. *Turkmen,* at *30.

143. Opening Brief of Petitioner, Al Salami v. Ashcroft, No. 02-70260, 2002 WL 32290573, at *12 (July 26, 2002).

144. *Id.* at *14.

145. *Id.* at *3.

146. *Id.* at *17.

147. This is not to suggest that immigrants who are not of Middle Eastern descent do not suffer under the present immigration system, which is rife with abuse and unchecked exertions of power. As the particular target group at this

point in history, however, individuals of Middle Eastern descent are especially susceptible to the dangerous consequences.

148. Al-Khazraji v. Saint Francis College, 784 F.2d 505, 506 (3d Cir. 1986).

149. Act of Apr. 9, 1866, ch. 31, § 1, 14 Stat. 27 (reenacted as Act of May 31, 1870, ch. 114, § 16, 16 Stat. 140, 144) (codified as amended at 42 U.S.C. §§ 1981, 1982 (1994)).

150. 42 U.S.C. § 1981.

151. 427 U.S. 160 (1976).

152. *See id.* at 168, 174–75.

153. *Al-Khazraji,* 784 F.2d at 514.

154. *Id.* at 509.

155. *Id.* at 514–18. As the Third Circuit concluded, "We are unwilling to assert that Arabs cannot be the victims of racial prejudice." *Al-Khazraji,* 784 F.2d at 517.

156. Saint Francis College v. Al-Khazraji, 481 U.S. 604 (1987). As the Court held, "a distinctive physiognomy is not essential to qualify for § 1981 protection. If respondent on remand can prove that he was subjected to intentional discrimination based on the fact that he was born an Arab, rather than solely on the place or nation of his origin, or his religion, he will have made out a case under § 1981." *Id.* at 605.

157. Sandhu v. Lockheed Missiles & Space Co., 26 Cal. App. 4th 846, 849 (Ct. App. 1994).

158. *Id.*

159. *Id.* at 850 (quoting Judge Peter G. Stone's unpublished opinion for the Superior Court of Santa Clara County No. 718352).

160. 261 U.S. 204 (1923).

161. *Id.* at 206.

162. 606 F. Supp. 1504 (D. Md. 1985), *aff'd,* 785 F.2d 523 (4th Cir. 1986), *rev'd,* 481 U.S. 615 (1987).

163. 42 U.S.C. § 1982 (1994).

164. *See Shaare Tefila Congregation v. Cobb,* 785 F.2d 523, at 526 (4th Cir. 1986).

165. *Id.; see also Shaare Tefila Congregation,* 606 F. Supp. at 1508–09.

166. *Shaare Tefila Congregation,* 785 F.2d at 527.

167. *Id.* at 528 (Wilkinson, J., concurring in part and dissenting in part).

168. *See* Joseph Avanzato, Note, *Section 1982 and Discrimination against Jews: Shaare Tefila Congregation v. Cobb,* 37 Am. U. L. Rev. 225 (1987) (arguing that the Fourth Circuit decided the case incorrectly and that the Supreme Court's reversal of the lower court failed to provide guidance for future § 1982 cases).

169. *Shaare Tefila Congregation,* 481 U.S. at 617 (quoting *Saint Francis College,* 481 U.S. at 613).

170. On a related note, questions abound on the definition of *Jewish. See, e.g.,* Meryl Hyman, "Who Is a Jew?" (1998); Jack Wertheimer, A People Divided: Judaism in Contemporary America 173–80 (1993); Nancy Caren

Richmond, Comment, *Israel's Law of Return: Analysis of Its Evolution and Present Application*, 12 DICK. J. INT'L L. 95 (1993).

171. Avanzato, *supra*, at 255.

172. This assertion directly contradicts the thesis of Donald Braman's article *Of Race and Immutability*, 46 UCLA L. REV. 1375 (1999), which argues that the Supreme Court has consistently, at least since *Ozawa* and *Thind*, moved toward a view of racial status as the product of social and political institutions, and not of biology. First, if this were the case, it would be difficult to rationalize the results of *Al-Khazraji* in the district court and the court of appeals. Second, Braman's article almost entirely ignores the Supreme Court's opinion in *Shaare Tefila Congregation*, even though it was issued in conjunction with *Al-Khazraji*, a case that Braman discusses extensively. *See id.* at 1442–45.

173. *See* Plessy v. Ferguson, 163 U.S. 537, 541, 550 (1896) (upholding as reasonable the classification of an individual of "one-eighth African blood" as black).

174. *In re* Cruz, 23 F. Supp. 774 (E.D.N.Y. 1938).

175. *See* Luther Wright, Jr., *Who's Black, Who's White, and Who Cares? Reconceptualizing the United States's Definition of Race and Racial Classifications*, 48 VAND. L. REV. 513, 524 (1995); PETER WALLENSTEIN, TELL THE COURT I LOVE MY WIFE 142 (2002) (noting that Georgia, Virginia, Alabama, and Oklahoma all had laws defining as black anyone with any drop of African ancestry).

176. Ariela Gross, *"The Caucasian Cloak": Mexican Americans and the Politics of Whiteness in the 20th Century Southwest*, 95 GEORGETOWN L.J. 337, 370 (2006).

177. Ariela Gross, *"The Caucasian Cloak": Mexican Americans and the Politics of Whiteness in the 20th Century Southwest*, USC Legal Students Research Paper No. 06-20, available online at http://ssrn.com/abstract=934574, at 10.

178. Azimi v. Jordan's Meats, Inc., 456 F.3d 228 (1st Cir. 2006).

179. *Id.* at 232.

180. *Id.*

181. *Id.*

182. *Id.* at 233.

183. *Id.*

184. *Id.*

185. Brief for Abdul Azimi as Amici Curiae Supporting Appellant, Azimi v. Jordan's Meats, Inc., 456 F.3d 228 (1st Cir. 2006) (No. 05-2602) (ACLU Urges Appeals Court Action on Behalf of Muslim Man Harassed by Coworkers).

186. *Azimi,* 456 F.3d at 237–38.

187. Adam Liptak, *Impressions of Terrorism, Drawn from Court Files*, N.Y. TIMES, Feb. 19, 2008.

188. 127 S.Ct. 2738, 2768 (2007).

189. Cerqueira v. American Airlines, Inc., __ F.3d __, 2008 WL 104105, at *15 (1st Cir. 2008).

190. Lisa W. Foderaro, *Judge's Offhand Terrorism Remarks Anger Arab-American*, N.Y. TIMES, May 22, 2003, at B1.

191. Robert Morlino, *"Our Enemies among Us!" The Portrayal of Arab and Muslim Americans in Post-9/11 American Media*, in CIVIL RIGHTS IN PERIL: THE TARGETING OF ARABS AND MUSLIMS 71, 72 (Elaine C. Hagopian ed., 2004).

192. Vanessa Blum, *Putting Islam on the Stand*, LEGAL TIMES, July 8, 2005, available online at http://www.law.com/jsp/article.jsp?id=1120727114514.

193 *Id.*

194. Johnson, *The Forgotten "Repatriation," supra*, at 25.

195. Kevin R. Johnson & Bernard Trujillo, *Immigration Reform, National Security after September 11, and the Future of North American Integration*, 91 MINN. L. REV. 1369, 1399 (2007).

196. *Id.*

197. Kevin R. Johnson, *September 11 and Mexican Immigrants*, 52 DEPAUL L. REV. 849 (2003).

NOTES TO CHAPTER 6

1. *See* American-Arab Anti-Discrimination Committee, *ADC Presses CBP on Census Data*, press release, Aug. 13, 2004, available online at http://adc.org/index.php?id=2303. *See also* Susan Akram & Maritza Karmely, *Immigration and Constitutional Consequences of Post-9/11 Policies Involving Arabs and Muslims in the United States: Is Alienage a Distinction without a Difference?* 38 U.C. DAVIS L. REV. 609 (2005).

2. ADC, *supra.*

3. *Id.*

4. Dave Orrick, *Police Recording "Race" of Drivers but Some Groups Worry New Law Will Create Inaccurate Data*, CHI. DAILY HERALD, Jan. 2, 2004, at 1.

5. Jennifer Golz, *New Study Examines Racial Profiling*, COLUMBIA CHRON. (COLUMBIA COLLEGE), Jan. 12, 2004, available online at http://www.pbs.org/weta/washingtonweek/voices/200401/0112profiling.html.

6. Orrick, *supra.*

7. *Id.* (omission in original).

8. *See, e.g.*, Ronald Weitzer & Steven Tuch, *Racially Biased Policing: Determinants of Citizen Perceptions*, 83 SOC. FORCES 1009 (2005) (survey conducted December 2002); Wash. Post, Kaiser Family Found. & Harvard Univ., *Race and Ethnicity in 2001: Attitudes, Perceptions, and Experiences*, available online at http://www.kff.org/kaiserpolls/upload/Race-and-Ethnicity-in-2001-Attitudes-Perceptions-and-Experiences-Toplines-Survey.pdf (survey conducted March 2001). For an overview of these studies, see Amnesty Int'l USA, *Threat and Humiliation: Racial Profiling, Domestic Security, and Human Rights in the United States* (2004), available online at http://www.amnestyusa.org/racial_profiling/report/rp_report.pdf.

9. Matthew R. Durose, Erica L. Smith & Patrick A. Langan, *Bureau of Justice Statistics Special Report: Contacts between the Police and Public, 2005* (U.S. Department of Justice Office of Justice Programs) (2007), available online at http://www.ojp.usdoj.gov/bjs/pub/pdf/cpp05.pdf.

10. Statement by Arab American Institute Deputy Director Helen Samhan to the House Subcommittee on Census, Statistics and Postal Personnel, June 30, 1993; Sarah Gualtieri, *Strange Fruit? Syrian Immigrants, Extralegal Violence and Racial Formation in the Jim Crow South*, 24 ARAB STUD. Q. 63 (2004).

11. Office of Management and Budget, *Revisions to the Standards for the Classification of Federal Data on Race and Ethnicity*, 52 Fed. Reg. 58,872 (Oct. 30, 1997).

12. Office of Management and Budget, *Recommendations from the Interagency Committee for the Review of the Racial and Ethnic Standards to the Office of Management and Budget Concerning Changes to the Standards for the Classification of Federal Data on Race and Ethnicity*, 62 Fed. Reg. 36,874 (July 9, 1997).

13. *Id.*

14. Derived from Jessica S. Barnes & Claudette E. Bennett, *Census 2000 Brief: The Asian Population: 2000*, Feb. 2002, available online at http://www.census.gov/prod/2002pubs/c2kbr01-16.pdf.

15. Derived from G. Patricia de la Cruz & Angela Brittingham, *Census 2000 Brief: The Arab Population: 2000*, Dec. 2003, available online at http://www.census.gov/prod/2003pubs/c2kbr-23.pdf; and Angela Brittingham & G. Patricia de la Cruz, *Census 2000 Brief: Ancestry: 2000*, June 2004, available online at http://www.census.gov/prod/2004pubs/c2kbr-35.pdf. The 2000 census counts a minimum of 1,189,731 Arab Americans, 338,266 Iranian Americans, and 117,575 Turkish Americans living in the United States.

16. Ariela Gross, *"The Caucasian Cloak": Mexican Americans and the Politics of Whiteness in the 20th Century Southwest*, 95 GEORGETOWN L.J. 337, 389 (2006).

17. See Susan Khosy, *Category Crisis: South Asian Americans and Questions of Race and Ethnicity*, 7 DIASPORA 285, 285–320 (1998); Vinay Harpalani, *Formal, Material, and Symbolic Modes of Racialization: Examining South Asian Americans' Access to "Whiteness"* (2007) (unpublished manuscript on file with author).

18. Harpalani, *supra*, at 20.

19. *See* U.S. Census Bureau, *2005 American Community Survey: Selected Population Profile in the United States, Population Group: Asian Indian Alone or in Any Combination* (2005), available online at http://factfinder.census.gov/home/saff/main.html?_lang=en (follow Data Set [American Community Survey], Geography, Population Groups, Asian Indian alone or in any combination).

20. Gualtieri, *supra*.

21. *Id.*

22. *See* U.S. Bureau of the Census, *16th Census of the United States: 1940*,

Population (Florida), Vol. 2, at 33 (Washington, DC: Government Printing Office, 1943).

23. 4 SYRIAN WORLD 53 (Sept. 1929).

24. Sarah Gualtieri, *Becoming "White": Race, Religion and the Foundations of Syrian/Lebanese Ethnicity in the United States,* 20 J. OF AMERICAN ETHNIC HISTORY 29 (Oct. 2001).

25. Meenoo Chahbazi, *Can Iranians File Suit for Racial Discrimination? Demystifying the Paradox between Federal Agency and Court Categorizations of Iranian and Middle Eastern Race,* 2 IRANIAN-AMERICAN BAR ASSOCIATION REVIEW 32 (Spring 2006).

26. *Id.* at 36.

27. University of California at Los Angeles, *Academic Recruitment-Selection Date and Compliance Form,* available online at http://www.apo.ucla.edu/forms/aaform.pdf.

28. *See* Grutter v. Bollinger, 539 U.S. 306, 330 (2004).

29. 438 U.S. 265 (1978).

30. *Grutter,* 539 U.S. at 324 (quoting *Bakke,* 438 U.S. at 313) (internal quotation marks omitted).

31. *Cf.* Richard Delgado, *The Imperial Scholar: Reflections on a Review of Civil Rights Literature,* 132 U. PA. L. REV. 561 & n.1 (1984) (providing specific counts of "Black," "Hispanic," and "Native American" law professors using existing publicly available data).

32. John A. Sebert, *From the Consultant,* SYLLABUS: A.B.A. SEC. LEGAL EDUC. AND ADMISSIONS TO BAR 4 (Feb. 2005).

33. *Id.* at 5.

34. Nancy McCarthy, *Changing the Color of the California Bench,* CALIFORNIA BAR JOURNAL 1 (Apr. 2007).

35. Delgado, *The Imperial Scholar, supra,* at 563; *see also* Richard Delgado, *The Imperial Scholar Revisited: How to Marginalize Outsider Writing, Ten Years Later,* 140 U. PA. L. REV. 1349 (1992).

36. Delgado, *The Imperial Scholar, supra,* at 566–73.

37. Derrick A. Bell, *Who's Afraid of Critical Race Theory?* 1995 U. ILL. L. REV. 893, 898 n.16 (1995) (noting that Derrick Bell, Richard Delgado, Charles Lawrence, Mari Matsuda, and Patricia Williams are usually considered the founding members of critical race theory).

38. *See, e.g.,* Devon W. Carbado, *Race to the Bottom,* 49 UCLA L. REV. 1283, 1305–12 (2002) (insightfully discussing the perils of the "Black/White paradigm" but never once addressing the impact of the divide on individuals of Middle Eastern descent, though extensively contemplating the effect of the paradigm on Asian Americans, Latinos, and Native Americans).

39. Sumi Cho & Robert Westley, *Critical Race Coalitions: Key Movements That Performed the Theory,* 33 U.C. DAVIS L. REV. 1377 (2000).

40. *Id.* at 1421–22.

41. Devon Carbado & Mitu Gulati, *What Exactly Is Racial Diversity?*, 91 CAL. L. REV. 1149, 1163 (2003) (book review).

42. *Cf.* Robert S. Chang, *Toward an Asian American Legal Scholarship: Critical Race Theory, Post-Structuralism, and Narrative Space*, 81 CAL. L. REV. 1241, 1245–46 (1993) (noting an increase in the number of Asian Americans in the legal academy and a corresponding increase in Asian American legal scholarship).

43. Carbado & Gulati, *supra*, at 1150.

44. *Id.* at 1151.

45. In this way, the Middle Eastern population is quite similar to the Asian American population. *Cf.* Chang, *supra*, at 1249–50 (arguing that "the exclusion of Asian Americans from the political and legal processes has led to an impoverished notion of politics and law that furthers the oppression of Asian Americans").

46. 1 ALEXIS DE TOCQUEVILLE, DEMOCRACY IN AMERICA 355 (Francis Bowen ed., Henry Reeve trans., Univ. Press 4th ed. 1864) (1835).

47. Carbado & Gulati, *supra*, at 1154.

48. *Number of Muslim (Most Recent) by Country*, NATIONMASTER.COM, http://www.nationmaster.com/red/graph/rel_isl_num_of_mus-religion-islam-number-of-muslim&b_printable=1 (accessed May 30, 2007).

49. Michael Aushenker, *Praying for Justice*, JEWISH J. OF GREATER L.A., Apr. 14, 2000.

50. Houman Sarshar, *Preface* to ESTHER'S CHILDREN: A PORTRAIT OF IRANIAN JEWS ix, x (Houman Sarshar ed., 2002).

51. Under the leadership of King Trdat III, Armenia became the first Christian nation in 301 AD. *See* Michael Bobelian, *Vartke's List*, LEGAL AFFAIRS 38 (March/April 2006).

52. *But see* Daniel A. Farber & Suzanna Sherry, *Telling Stories Out of School: An Essay on Legal Narratives*, 45 STAN. L. REV. 807, 809–19 (1993) (questioning the assumption of a "voice of color"); Randall L. Kennedy, *Racial Critiques of Legal Academia*, 102 HARV. L. REV. 1745, 1787–810 (1989) (challenging the idea that scholars of color have unique standing in, or contribute a unique voice to, race-related scholarship).

53. Carbado & Gulati, *supra*, at 1157.

54. For example, the development of critical race theory itself stemmed from the presence and activism of students of color on several major law-school campuses. *See* Carbado & Gulati, *supra*, at 1163 (arguing that "[t]he development of Critical Race Theory . . . is directly linked to the presence and activism of students of color at Harvard Law School and Boalt Hall, among other institutions"); CRITICAL RACE THEORY: THE KEY WRITINGS THAT FORMED THE MOVEMENT xiv, xix (Kimberlé Crenshaw et al. eds., 1995); MARI J. MATSUDA, WHERE IS YOUR

BODY? AND OTHER ESSAYS ON RACE, GENDER, AND THE LAW 50 (1996); Cho & Westley, *supra,* at 1378–79, 1404.

55. Delgado, *The Imperial Scholar, supra,* at 573.

56. *Id.* at 572.

57. *Id.*

58. Jerome M. Culp, Jr., *Toward a Black Legal Scholarship: Race and Original Understandings,* 1991 DUKE L.J. 39, 40–41 (1991) (citation omitted).

59. Chang, *supra,* at 1245–46.

60. *Id.* at 1246 n.8.

61. *Id.* at 1249 (referring to the development of an Asian American legal scholarship).

62. Gelareh Asayesh, *I Grew Up Thinking I Was White,* in MY SISTER, GUARD YOUR VEIL; MY BROTHER, GUARD YOUR EYES: UNCENSORED IRANIAN VOICES 12, 15 (Lila Azam Zanganeh, ed. 2006).

63. Chang, *supra,* at 1246 n.7 (citation omitted).

64. Kenji Yoshino, *Covering,* 111 YALE L.J. 769, 933 (2002).

65. University of California Board of Regents Res. SP-1 (1995, rescinded 2001), available online at http://www.universityofcalifornia.edu/news/compreview/sp1.pdf (forbidding the consideration of race, ethnicity, and sex in admissions decisions in the University of California system).

66. CAL. CONST. art. I, § 31 (eliminating all affirmative-action programs in public employment, public education, and public contracting in the State of California).

67. *See, e.g.,* ANDREA GUERRERO, SILENCE AT BOALT HALL: THE DISMANTLING OF AFFIRMATIVE ACTION 105–09, 171 (2002).

68. *See* Carbado & Gulati, *supra,* at 1153.

69. *Id.*

70. Angela P. Harris, *Race and Essentialism in Feminist Legal Theory,* 42 STAN. L. REV. 581, 610–12 (1990) (arguing that we must not rationalize all racial or gender experiences as unique because doing so eliminates the ability to generalize and coalesce interests strategically).

71. Chris Iijima, *The Era of We-Construction: Reclaiming the Politics of Asian Pacific American Identity and Reflections on the Critique of the Black/White Paradigm,* 29 COLUM. HUMAN RIGHTS L. REV. 47, 49, 54 (1997).

72. Carbado, *supra,* at 1295; *see also* Anthony Paul Farley, *All Flesh Shall See It Together,* 19 CHICANO-LATINO L. REV. 163, 167 (1998) ("Blacks, like Latinos/as or Asian Pacific Americans, are neither an 'ethnicity' nor a 'race.' We too may opt to consider ourselves an amalgamation of national origins—a 'conflation' of national origins. We, especially, have been forcibly thematized as an amalgamation of national origins.").

73. Chang, *supra,* at 1321–22.

74. *Id.* at 1321 (citation omitted).

NOTES TO THE CONCLUSION

1. Summary File 4, 2000 U.S. Census; Ali Mostashari & Ali Khodamhosseini, *An Overview of Socioeconomic Characteristics of the Iranian-American Community Based on the 2000 U.S. Census* (Iranian Studies Group at MIT), available online at http://isg-mit.org/projects-storage/census/Socioeconomic_Iran_American_Census2000_Final.pdf. Iranian American per capita income was estimated at $30,143, Turkish American per capita income was estimated at $27,554, and Arab American per capita income was estimated $24,061, compared to a figure of $21,587 for the general population.

2. *Id.*

3. *Id.*

Index

Aaliyah, 91

ABA Journal, 97

ABC News, 122

Abortion-clinic bombings, 127

Absconder Apprehension Initiative (Operation Absconder), 125, 139. *See also* Department of Justice, U.S.

Acuña, Rodolfo, 87

Adachi, Jeff, 91

The Adventures of Tom Sawyer, 35

Aegean Sea, 66

Affirmative action, 37–38, 64, 82, 114–15, 125, 149, 169, 174–75, 181, 225n66

Afghan. *See* Racial/ethnic categories, Afghan

Afghanistan, 66, 132, 134, 150. *See also* Racial/ethnic categories, and Afghanistan

Afrasiabi, Peter, ix, 155

Africa, 16, 24, 56, 66–67, 91. *See also* Racial/ethnic categories, and Africa

African American. *See* Racial/ethnic categories, African American

Agassi, Andre, 74

Aghdashloo, Shohreh, 92–93

Airlines (air travel), 106–9, 118, 127, 130

Akram, Susan, 101, 125, 133, 139

Alabama, 23, 25, 117, 118–19, 160, 203n69, 220n175. *See also* Court of Appeals, Alabama

Aladdin, 75

Alaskan Native. *See* Racial/ethnic categories, Alaskan Native

Albania, 150

Albanian. *See* Racial/ethnic categories, Albanian

Alexander, Amy, 113

Al-Fayed, Dodi, 74

Alice, 75–76

Alien, 15, 39, 43–45, 101, 139–40, 144, 186n5, 186n10, 216n90; enemy alien, 7, 65, 70, 138, 184. *See also* Illegal alien

Alien Land Law, 16, 137, 186n10, 216n94; California Alien Land Law, 186n10; Washington Alien Land Law, 186n10

Alien Torts Statute, 150

Al-Khazraji v. Saint Francis College, 157–58, 171, 219–20

Allen, Theodore, 19, 45

Allied Forces, 122

al-Masri, Khalid, 150

Alpine. *See* Racial/ethnic categories, Alpine

Al-Qaeda, 130, 134–35, 150, 163

Al Salami, Salah Abbod Saleh, 151–56

Alshafri, Jehad, 107, 109

Al-Timimi, Ali, 162–63

American. *See* Racial/ethnic categories, American

American Airlines, 107–8, 130

American-Arab Anti-Discrimination Committee, 93, 123, 168

About the Author

JOHN TEHRANIAN is Professor of Law at Chapman University, School of Law. He has previously served as Professor of Law at the University of Utah, S.J. Quinney College of Law, and as Visiting Professor of Law at Loyola Law School. A graduate of Harvard University and Yale Law School, he is the author of numerous works on race, civil rights, and constitutional law. A frequent commentator on legal issues for the broadcast and print media, he is also a noted entertainment and intellectual-property litigator based in Southern California.